SLAUGHTER OF THE INNOCENTS

COERCIVE BIRTH CONTROL IN CHINA

John S. Aird

THE AEI PRESS

Publisher for the American Enterprise Institute

Washington, D.C.

John S. Aird is former senior research specialist on China at the U.S. Bureau of the Census. Dr. Aird is the author of *Population Estimates for the Provinces of the People's Republic of China* and other monographs, of reports for the U.S. Joint Economic Committee, and of articles in the *China Quarterly* and other journals and books.

Distributed by arrangement with

National Book Network
4720 Boston Way
Lanham, Md. 20706

3 Henrietta Street
London WC2E 8LU England

Library of Congress Cataloging-in-Publication Data

Aird, John S. (John Shields), 1919–
    Slaughter of the innocents : coercive birth control in China /
John Aird.
      p. cm.
    Includes bibliographical references.
    ISBN 0-8447-3703-8 (alk. paper).

    1. Birth control—Government policy—China. 2. Family size—
Government policy—China. 3. China—Population policy. I. Title.
HQ766.5.C6A48   1990
363.9'6'0951—dc20

R0127072078
SSCCa

89-77305
CIP

1 3 5 7 9 10 8 6 4 2

AEI Studies 498

The AEI Press
Publisher for the American Enterprise Institute
1150 17th Street, N.W., Washington, D.C. 20036

Printed in the United States of America

Contents

Preface

Among the sayings of Mao Zedong still quoted in the People's Republic of China is one advising that before beginning any undertaking one ought to "start from reality," meaning that a good foundation in fact is essential to its success. It was one of the most pragmatic and sensible of all Mao's aphorisms. If he had followed his own advice, China might have been spared some of his disastrous policy mistakes, including collectivization, the Great Leap Forward, and the Great Proletarian Cultural Revolution, which were inspired not by "reality" but by ideology.

China's compulsory family planning program, begun by Mao and continued vigorously by his successors, Jiang Qing, Hua Guofeng, and Deng Xiaoping, is another great misadventure that is founded on ideology rather than reality. In this case, however, it was not Mao's adaptation of Marxism-Leninism but Western neo-Malthusianism that provided the impetus. The attitude of Marxism-Leninism toward population was essentially optimistic. Population growth would never cause difficulties for a socialist country, Engels once wrote, but if it ever did, a socialist country could easily solve them. That optimism flourished from the founding of the People's Republic of China in 1949 until the census of 1953, succumbed to pessimism during the next four years, was revived briefly at the start of the Great Leap Forward in 1958, then withered away. By the 1960s, all that remained of it was the conviction that the State would solve all problems.

The confidence of China's leaders that they could make compulsory family planning work seemed to be justified when the birth rate declined rapidly during the 1970s, an accomplishment in which they still take pride. Their achievement won them the admiration of most of the international family planning community, who praised the Chinese program and commended it as an example for other countries. As often happens with humanitarians and idealists dedicated to a single purpose, means became less important than ends and success was hailed without much concern about how it was won.

Like the intellectuals of the 1930s who admired the apparent efficiency of Stalin, Hitler, and Mussolini, family planning advocates saw their population control objectives being attained more speedily in China than in developing countries with less centralized governments, and they were inclined to ignore or excuse the cost in human rights and other human values. This is a further demonstration, if any were needed, that power corrupts, even secondhand and at a distance.

Among foreign family planners, the "corrupting" influence has undermined both their principles and their integrity. Although they profess to believe in reproductive freedom as a human right and insist that they support only voluntary family planning, many rushed to embrace the Chinese family planning program, identified its objectives with their own, and helped disseminate the deliberately deceptive Chinese claims that the program is voluntary. Some demographers, public health specialists, and others have also engaged in misrepresentations of the Chinese program. The deception has had a measure of success, but history has a way of exposing large-scale fraud sooner or later. In the last analysis ethical compromises made in the name of an ethical cause often discredit both the cause and those who serve it.

There is an element of bitter irony in this case, because *voluntary* family planning *is* a humanitarian cause with a major and direct bearing on human rights. The principle of reproductive freedom cannot be brought to full realization without it. But no such justification can be found for *coercive* family planning. Although rapid population growth may in some situations adversely affect human welfare, the relationship between population and welfare is complex and the effect of one on the other cannot be determined with enough certainty to justify violating human rights to reduce birth rates. Lack of concern about violations of human rights in the Chinese program is a sign that the international family planning movement has crossed the line from humanitarianism into zealotry. It needs desperately to be called back before it does itself further damage.

If political changes in the People's Republic of China render compulsory family planning unenforceable within the next few years, foreign family planning advocates may forget the program's coercive past or pretend it never happened. The fact remains, however, that the claim by foreign family planners to respect the right of couples to determine freely the size of their families and the choice of contraceptive methods was put to its first test in China in the 1980s and failed. They sided with a brutally repressive regime against its people because it implemented their agenda. There is as yet no sign that they have learned anything sobering from this experience.

The account of recent developments in family planning in China given in this volume is based mainly on Chinese sources, particularly those that show what policies, instructions, exhortations, and models the central authorities transmit to the provincial and lower levels and those that indicate how the central directives are being carried out. Limited credence has been accorded to what Chinese spokesmen say to foreign audiences about their family planning program, which often differs from what they tell their own people. The documents, directives, and exhortations transmitted from the central authorities through domestic channels constitute the real family planning policy. As with other policies in China, local implementation has at times been less severe than the central authorities wanted, but local deviations do not redeem central intent. However much compliance may vary over time or from one place to another, if the policy calls for or leads to coercion, it is a coercive policy.

Tracing the development of family planning policies in China requires a careful examination of all the relevant source materials available. I am deeply indebted to Florence Yuan, of the China Branch of the Census Bureau's Center for International Research, who selected and translated hundreds of Chinese texts not translated elsewhere. Her long experience in following developments in population and population policy in China, her astuteness in recognizing significant items, and her thorough familiarity with Chinese family planning terminology have been invaluable in choosing texts to translate and in providing an accurate rendering. Andrea Miles of the China Branch was indefatigable in locating and copying materials from Chinese publications in English and from the U.S. government translation services.

For critical comments and suggestions on the draft version of this text, I am particularly indebted to my colleague Judith Banister, chief of the China Branch, and one of the few China population specialists who have consistently dealt forthrightly with the coercion issue. I have also received detailed and very helpful comments from Nick Eberstadt and Beth Blackshire of the American Enterprise Institute for Public Policy Research, and from Professor William Peterson of Ohio State University. Responsibility for what is said or left unsaid in the final text remains exclusively my own.

1
The Coercion Controversy

China's birth control program has earned a worldwide reputation as the most draconian since King Herod's slaughter of the innocents. Because of the program's coercive tactics, the U.S. Agency for International Development (AID) has suspended its contributions to the United Nations Population Fund (UNFPA),[1] which has been supporting the Chinese program since 1980. In the past several years, however, some foreign defenders of China's family planning program have been arguing in newspaper and magazine articles and letters to the press that the Chinese government significantly modified program requirements and curbed harsh enforcement measures after the coerciveness reached its all-time peak in 1983.[2] They imply that the program is no longer coercive, hence U.S. funding for the UNFPA can now be resumed.

This conclusion is contradicted by evidence from the Chinese media, which shows that what the central authorities sought in the spring of 1984 was only a slight easing of family planning requirements and avoidance of only the more overtly coercive measures. Family planning targets were still to be met on schedule, and sterilization for couples with two or more children, abortion for unauthorized pregnancies, and the absolute prohibition of third and higher order births were to continue. Compliance with central directives *did* falter seriously for several years as the local authorities carried the relaxation far beyond what the central authorities intended; but from the end of 1985 onward central demands escalated again, and in 1989 they became more peremptory, reckless, and shrill than at any other time since 1983. The Chinese program remains highly coercive.

The issue has implications not only for U.S. funding of the UNFPA but also for human rights in China and for the credibility of claims by the UNFPA and other international organizations cooperating with the Chinese program that they support only voluntary family planning. Some demographers have joined family planning advocates in the defense of the Chinese program, denying, ignoring, or excusing its coercive aspects at the risk of their own credibility as

1

social scientists and humanitarians. Moreover, the coercion issue prompts a re-examination of the "population crisis" belief, the relationship between population growth and human welfare in general, and the place of human rights in population policy.

Human Rights in China

From the founding of the People's Republic of China (PRC) in October 1949, its leaders have seldom allowed human rights to stand in the way of their policies and programs. In the early 1950s the land reform program and the campaign against "counter-revolutionaries" (people suspected of opposing the new regime) reportedly resulted in the summary execution of one to three million persons, and some estimates run much higher.[3] Agriculture was forcibly collectivized in the mid-1950s without regard to the wishes of the peasants, whose newly acquired land was confiscated in violation of promises made to them during land reform. In the "hundred flowers" movement of 1956–57 China's intellectuals were invited to criticize the government, threatened when they hesitated, then persecuted as "rightists" when they finally complied.

Violence against individuals was officially encouraged during the so-called Great Proletarian Cultural Revolution of 1966–69, as Mao Zedong, who had lost power within the top echelons of the Party after his Great Leap Forward policies failed, struggled to regain full control of the government. Even high-ranking Party leaders were among the victims.

Violations of human rights in China have continued since the Cultural Revolution but, except for the birth control program, on a lesser scale. In a 1983 campaign against "bourgeois liberalization," an estimated 100,000 people were arrested and some 5,000 executed according to foreign reports.[4] Dissidents are still imprisoned for long periods without trial. In 1985 and 1986–87 student demands for greater freedom of the press and more democracy were rebuffed with mass arrests. The violent suppression of Tibetan nationalist uprisings in 1987 and 1989 showed the ruthlessness of which the Chinese leaders were still capable.[5] But it was the brutal slaughter of student protesters in Tiananmen Square on June 4, 1989, that revealed more clearly than any previous outrage how little regard the present leadership has for human rights.[6]

The ostensible legal basis for the Party's frequent abrogations of both human rights and constitutional rights is Article I of the PRC Constitution as revised in 1982, which says that "The People's Republic of China is a socialist state of the people's democratic dictatorship

2

led by the working class and based on the alliance of workers and peasants."[7] Under the "dictatorship" principle, the Party leaders affirm their right to use dictatorial methods in imposing unpopular policies on the grounds that whatever the Party does represents the will of the people, hence those who dissent are "counter-revolutionaries" who must be forcibly suppressed. In the middle 1970s the principle was invoked to justify compulsory family planning measures, and all opposition was attributed to "class enemies," who were to be subjected to "class struggle" and defeated.[8]

Although Chinese spokesmen have sometimes criticized alleged human rights violations in other countries, the Chinese authorities have consistently maintained that criticism of their own record is an intolerable encroachment on Chinese sovereignty,[9] and the same argument has been used in rejecting any criticism of China's family planning tactics.[10] Recently one Chinese writer argued that human rights in family planning were a foreign luxury that China could not afford.[11]

On the whole, until June 1989, foreign criticisms of human rights violations in China, in family planning or any other sphere, were remarkably few. In February 1989, a leading Chinese dissident, physicist Fang Lizhi, charged that U.S. foreign policy did not hold China to the same human rights standards it applied to other countries,[12] and the same charge could be levelled at many other countries which have accorded China special indulgence. Deng Xiaoping reportedly said that foreigners cared only about China's stability, not about its human rights record;[13] he could have cited the enthusiastic support of foreign family planning advocates for China's family planning program as a case in point.

Value Conflicts

Family planning advocates may be reluctant to criticize the Chinese program in part because it involves conflicting values if not conflicts of interest for many of them. The value conflicts for family planning organizations are immediate and direct. All such organizations at least nominally disapprove of coercive methods in family planning work. The UNFPA charter affirms and UNFPA leaders maintain that they oppose coercion in family planning as a matter of principle.[14] The World Population Plan of Action adopted by the 1974 World Population Conference in Bucharest recognized "the basic human right of all couples and individuals to decide freely and responsibly the number and spacing of their children"[15] and the 1984 conference in Mexico City reaffirmed the principle and added that parents should

3

be allowed to fulfill their responsibilities "freely and without coercion."[16] The Chinese government maintains that its program is in accord with the "Plan of Action" endorsed by both conferences, and, despite abundant contrary evidence, family planning advocates generally accept the claim.

The coerciveness of the Chinese program is potentially embarrassing to family planning advocates, and if the program had proven ineffective, they might have hesitated to become involved with it. But the Chinese program is, without doubt, the most successful state-sponsored family planning effort in a developing country, if success is defined exclusively in terms of reductions in birth and population growth rates. A desire to be identified with that success may have been a major reason why the UNFPA began to provide assistance to the program in 1980, although reports of coercion had already appeared in the press and in scholarly publications.[17]

From the middle 1970s onward, declining fertility in China, with its one billion people, also brought down the world average birth and natural increase rates, giving encouragement to family planners everywhere. The Chinese success was welcomed and applauded without apparent concern for the methods by which it had been achieved. Indeed, some family planning advocates began to cite the Chinese program as a model for other countries, not recognizing, or at any rate not acknowledging, that compulsory family planning measures cannot be carried out in countries where popular acceptance is prerequisite not only for the success of social policies but for the viability of the government itself.[18]

Defenders of the Chinese program often represent it as voluntary and attribute its results to such factors as effective propaganda, effective delivery of services, a clear definition of goals, and a firm government commitment to the cause.[19] They seldom allude explicitly to the program's coercive measures, although they sometimes characterize it suggestively as "highly organized," "aggressive," "determined," or "rigorous."[20] Ignoring the coercive aspects of the program or veiling them in euphemisms avoids raising the issue of coercion versus reproductive freedom, but it also shows which of the conflicting values family planners invest with the higher priority. If they had been more deeply committed to voluntary family planning, the reports of coercion in the Chinese program might have given them pause. Before endorsing the program they might have tried to ascertain whether China's population problems were so acute that coercive family planning measures would be less injurious to human welfare in China than the consequences of uncontrolled population growth, a conclusion that could not have been reached without a systematic,

4

thorough, and objective analysis of all relevant circumstances. They might also have questioned whether the problems could not be ameliorated by other means that did less violence to human rights, such as changes in economic, political, and social policies. Even if the analysis indicated that compulsory family planning measures offered the only practical solution, family planners who cared about human rights would have sought assurances that no more coercion was used than was absolutely necessary. This would have required a determination as to how much fertility reduction was needed and how quickly it must be attained to avoid serious overpopulation. If family planning advocates gave these matters serious thought, there is little indication of it in the public record.[21]

Once the UNFPA and other family planning organizations had established links with the Chinese program, evidence of its coerciveness posed a serious dilemma for them. To withdraw their support would have outraged the Chinese authorities and drawn attention to their own ineptitude in blundering into the relationship in the first place, but to continue their ties while acknowledging that the Chinese program was coercive would have demonstrated that their public posture of approving only voluntary family planning was insincere. Presumably the course of minimal damage was to ignore the evidence on coercion, avoid the subject insofar as possible, and maintain their contacts with Chinese family planning agencies.[22]

This is the course that the UNFPA and other advocacy organizations with ties to China have been following. In 1983, when coercion in the Chinese program reached its all-time peak, a UN committee on which the late Raphael Salas, then Executive Director of the UNFPA, served as advisor gave the first two UN population awards to Qian Xinzhong, the Minister-in-Charge of the State Family Planning Commission (SFPC) who directed the implementation of the coercive measures, and Prime Minister Indira Gandhi of India, whose government had been toppled in part because of its support for a compulsory sterilization campaign in 1975–77.[23]

Presenting the awards in September 1983, UN Secretary-General Javier Perez de Cuellar expressed "deep appreciation" for the way in which the Chinese and Indian governments had "marshalled the resources necessary to implement population policies on a massive scale."[24] Later in that same year, the Members' Assembly of the International Planned Parenthood Federation (IPPF) decided not to endorse a strong human rights report prepared by a special "working group" at its direction, some of whose recommendations conflicted with IPPF policies, and welcomed the Chinese Family Planning Association (CFPA) to full membership.[25]

5

Three articles by *Washington Post* Beijing correspondent Michael Weisskopf early in January 1985[26] brought the coerciveness of the Chinese program to the attention of the U.S. Congress and the Agency for International Development, which took steps to withhold part of its 1985 contribution to the UNFPA. The UNFPA responded in February with a "briefing note" to AID in which it asserted that the Chinese government "advocates" but does not require observance of the one-child limit, that couples who wish to have a second or third child may do so, and that the Chinese government had made it clear that coercion in family planning was not permitted[27]—allegations that were palpably false, as even a casual examination of Chinese domestic sources would have shown.

In May 1988 the International Council on Population Program Management, meeting in Beijing, gave the SFPC its 1988 population award.[28] In January 1989 the UNFPA concluded an agreement for its third five-year, multimillion-dollar program of assistance for China's "population activities," including family planning.[29] In April Dr. Aprodicio Laquian, the UNFPA deputy in Beijing, told a Chinese reporter that U.S. charges of coercion in the Chinese program were "groundless."[30] In May Nafis Sadik, the current Executive Director of the UNFPA, said in a speech in the Cannon House Office Building in Washington that the Chinese program was "totally voluntary."[31] Statements such as these, which show a reckless disregard for the truth, can only damage the UNFPA's credibility.

Other value conflicts arise from the fact that to justify the program's extreme measures the Chinese authorities have adopted the "population crisis" idea widely used by family planners elsewhere to lend urgency to their cause. Until the late 1970s, the Chinese leaders dismissed the idea contemptuously. In Bucharest in 1974, China joined other third world governments in charging that the notion of a crisis had been devised by Western countries as an excuse for not providing economic assistance to developing countries. The PRC spokesman insisted that imperialism was the cause of third world poverty and that population growth was no impediment to economic development.[32] But by the time of the Mexico City conference in 1984, the crisis idea had become part of the received wisdom in intellectual and political circles in most of the third world, including China, which has since maintained that population growth threatens national economic development and even the national food supply.[33]

Outside China, the crisis idea has not gone unchallenged. Since the late 1970s, increasingly divergent views have emerged in academic circles over the actual relationship between population growth and economic development. Many demographers and economists still adhere to the crisis view, and some who reject it believe that population growth may nevertheless have deleterious effects on economic development and other aspects of human welfare. Others maintain that the relationship is complex and not yet well understood and that there is therefore no basis either for complacency or for alarm. A few have argued that population growth has been more of a stimulus than a deterrent to economic development and to social progress in general.[34]

The results of the most systematic recent study of the question were made public in April 1986, when the National Academy of Sciences issued a summary report by its Working Group on Population Growth and Economic Development. The study examined some widely held opinions about the effects of lower population growth rates on availability of resources, environmental pollution, income, education, health, and employment and tested them against recent world experience. It concluded that lower rates of population growth would be "beneficial to economic development for most developing countries" but that the amount of benefit was likely to be modest. Although the working group felt that state-sponsored family planning programs could be justified as a human right and might improve the lives of people in the developing countries, they questioned the justification for programs that impose "drastic financial or legal restrictions on childbearing."[35] They found no empirical support for the idea that population growth constituted an imminent crisis.

The findings and methods of the report came immediately under attack as "revisionist" by adherents of the crisis view, and further debate on the basic issues will undoubtedly continue.[36] But the debate is not likely to alter the conclusion that, as one member of the working group put it, much of the "doomsday rhetoric" about population problems is "simple minded and incorrect," and those family planning advocates who resort to it risk damage to their credibility and their cause "if and when the balloon bursts."[37]

Because the crisis idea has a superficial plausibility and is highly dramatic, it is easy to popularize. It ascribes many of the world's ills—including poverty, hunger, health problems, housing shortages, transportation problems, illiteracy, lack of education, unemployment, overcrowding, resource depletion, soil erosion, and environmental degradation—to a single factor, prescribes a single remedy, and invests the combination with a sense of great certitude. The simplicity and convenience of diagnosis and prescription appeal to humanitarians eager to dedicate their efforts and resources to an all-encompassing global cause. It is the sort of cause that inspires zeal. For governments in developing countries, the population crisis idea has the added virtue of putting the blame for socioeconomic problems on the reproductive habits of the people rather than on defective political leadership or misconceived policies.

Acceptance of the crisis idea is presumably the reason why quite a few demographers have been willing to consider the use of coercion in family planning at least as a necessary evil. Of the members of the Population Association of America responding to a 1978 survey, 34 percent subscribed to a statement that "coercive birth control programs should be initiated in at least some countries immediately," and 56 percent endorsed the opinion that "if world population continues to grow at its present rate, coercive birth control will have to be initiated within the next fifty years."[38] Those who held these views would presumably not have been inclined to condemn China's resort to increasingly coercive measures, nor would the Chinese action have prompted them to re-examine the underlying rationale. Nevertheless, few demographers have ventured to express openly their approval of coercion in the Chinese program.[39]

Some have argued that the exercise of reproductive freedom by individual couples may, in some situations, result in population growth rates that are incompatible with the collective welfare. This argument suggests that in such cases the government might reasonably decide that parental rights were being exercised "irresponsibly" and curtail reproductive freedom for the greater good. This is what the Chinese authorities did in adding to their Constitution in 1982 a stipulation that family planning is a citizen's duty and in ordering the adoption of provincial and local laws to make compliance mandatory. But if compulsory measures are opposed by a majority of the population, they can be implemented only by authoritarian regimes with strong enforcement systems. If they are opposed by a minority, they can be implemented only by disregarding minority rights. Those who justify such measures in effect advocate the curtailment of democratic and human rights to attain demographic goals,[40] apparently unaware that under those circumstances the rights of demographers might be curtailed also. Thus coercive family planning poses value conflicts in the political sphere, including encroachments on academic freedom.

In supporting the Chinese program, foreign family planning advocates have sided with an authoritarian government against its people, a precarious position given present political conditions in China. The prestige of the Party and its leaders, including Deng Xiaoping, has declined markedly in recent years, and disillusionment and discontent have become widespread, especially among the urban population. The brutal suppression of the student protest movement of April-June 1989 greatly accelerated this trend, discrediting the regime both in China and throughout the world. As its power wanes, so will its ability to enforce unpopular policies. If popular demands for more democracy, freedom, and human rights ultimately triumph, coercive birth control in China will probably be abandoned, and it may be strongly repudiated. Foreign family planning advocates who identified themselves with the program in spite of its coercive methods may then be repudiated in China along with their cause.

Conflicts of Interest

In addition to value conflicts, the Chinese program involves some direct conflicts of interest both for family planners and for demographers. In the past two decades, as a result of the population crisis belief, some international aid funds have been redirected from economic, health, and other programs into family planning programs and demographic research on the premise that money spent for other purposes would be wasted if population growth consumed all the gains. Even funds for child health programs were reportedly reduced on the premise that saving children's lives would only worsen population problems.[41] Thus family planners and at least some demographers have a financial stake in promoting the crisis idea.

Some family planning advocacy organizations and demographic research institutions have a direct interest in the resumption of U.S. funding for the UNFPA because the UNFPA has been funding their activities. Two recipients of UNFPA funds, the Population Institute and the Population Council, filed suit unsuccessfully to prevent the cut-off of U.S. funds to the UNFPA in 1985. The affidavit of the representative of the Population Council stated that he had "formed the opinion" that the Chinese family planning program was not coercive.[42] Spokesmen for the Population Institute have frequently expressed the same opinion. A number of other such organizations have also lobbied for the restoration of U.S. funds for the UNFPA and have ignored or denied the coercive aspects of the Chinese program. When money talks, family planners and demographers are no less attentive than other mortals.

Demographers interested in research on the population of China face another conflict of interest. Acceptance of the crisis idea by China's leaders in the late 1970s led to a revival of demography in China, to a new interest in taking censuses and surveys, and to a desire for contacts, technical advice, training, and assistance from foreign demographers. The Chinese 1982 census and the 1982 fertility

9

survey provided the world with a vast quantity of high quality demographic data, with the result that, almost overnight, China was no longer the world's greatest demographic enigma but had become demographically one of the best understood of the developing countries. Foreign demographers have been eager to gain access to China's demographic data and to engage in joint research undertakings with Chinese colleagues.

But China's demographic investigations have as one of their stated objectives the aim of helping to make the family planning program more effective. This was part of the justification for the 1982 investigations and is said to be the main objective of the 1988 fertility survey and the forthcoming 1990 census.[43] Indeed, since the early 1980s the officially designated role of demography in China has been to provide a "scientific" justification for national population policies and propaganda in support of the family planning program.[44] Not all Chinese demographers have accepted this assignment. It is reported that many have opposed the extremes in family planning policy, an issue that has been hotly debated at times in off-the-record meetings in China. A few have vetured to dissent in public and pointed out the dangers of a rapidly aging population in the future because of the one-child policy,[45] but others have argued against the easing of restrictions on the one-child limit.[46]

In any case, foreign demographers and research institutions that provide technical assistance to China in conducting demographic research may be contributing to the effectiveness of the coercive family planning measures. Their involvement is not as direct as that of the UNFPA, which has aided the Chinese government in producing IUDs with a lower spontaneous expulsion rate than those designed in China, thus adding to the coerciveness of compulsory IUD insertion,[47] or that of other foreign agencies that have helped the Chinese acquire and develop new contraceptive and abortifacient technologies that are more amenable to compulsory applications than are traditional methods.[48] But the use of modern demographic survey techniques has certainly helped the Chinese authorities to identify population subgroups and localities that have been successful in resisting family planning demands and units that have falsified demographic data to conceal their noncompliance. This information enables the government to apply its coercive efforts more efficiently.[49]

Another conflict of interest occurs when demographers avoid mention of coercive family planning practices in China for fear of offending the Chinese authorities and risking their access to Chinese population data, their contacts with Chinese demographers, and their participation in joint research projects with Chinese colleagues and institutions. Some foreign demographers deplore the excesses of the Chinese program in private conversation but are careful not to repeat their objections in print or in public meetings where Chinese are present. Some claim that they can exert a moderating influence on Chinese population policies if they maintain good relations with the Chinese authorities.[50] After a decade of opportunity, however, not much moderation has occurred for which they can claim credit.[51] Meanwhile, their reticence has served their professional and personal interests better than it has the interests of an informed public.[52]

Even more offensive from an ethical standpoint is the behavior of foreign population specialists who know that the Chinese program is coercive but describe it in their publications as voluntary. By repeating the false Chinese cover story, they practice deception on their own people to ingratiate themselves with the Chinese authorities. Judith Banister, who cites two instances, argues that

> journalists and scholars who research, write about, and speak about the demography of China have a moral and ethical obligation not to gloss over the compulsory and coercive qualities in China's family planning program, so that their audiences can reach an informed judgment.[53]

All too often, this obligation is not fulfilled.

In sum, the issue of coercion in the Chinese family planning program tests the sincerity of family planning advocates, demographers, and others who claim to respect the principle of reproductive freedom. Many fail the test. When they echo the official denials about coercion, pretend that the facts are still in doubt,[54] or argue that moderation of the program has made the matter moot, they do not do justice to the evidence. In April 1984 the *Wall Street Journal* editorialized that "by now the evidence about coercive birth control in China is overwhelming."[55] In 1989 it is even more so.

The Evidence on Coercion

The evidence does not lend itself to casual perusal. The published record is fragmentary, sometimes contradictory, and not very accessible except to China scholars. Some major family planning policy documents have not been released, nor have many of the follow-up instructions given at national family planning meetings and in telephone conferences with provincial officials, which explain how policies are to be interpreted and implemented.[56] The meaning of the documents that are published or quoted is frequently obscured by the use of euphemisms and apparently innocuous abstractions that

11

presumably convey specific messages to family planning officials and cadres.

In some cases, the intent can be inferred from the context. The expression "remedial measures" is a standard Chinese euphemism for mandatory abortions, as is obvious from the fact that the "remedies" are prescribed regularly for women who get pregnant without official permission.[57] In other cases, the meaning is only apparent when a number of contexts are examined. Injunctions to local leaders to "grasp firmly" or "get a good grasp of" family planning work usually mean to tighten control and prevent noncompliance, as is apparent in such contexts as "We must get a good grasp of family planning and strictly control population growth."[58] "Technical services" is a euphemism for birth control surgeries—IUD insertions, sterilizations, and abortions—as is apparent in many contexts.[59]

Seemingly innocent expressions may disguise sinister intent, as when "propaganda" is used to refer not just to publicity but to compulsory sterilization, IUD insertion, and abortion, and "persuasion" denotes not only oral argument but official harassment, threats, and heavy fines.[60] Official policy says that the state "advocates" that each couple have only one child, and Chinese spokesmen sometimes assure foreigners that advocating is not the same as requiring, but in fact, as one Chinese source indicates, the Chinese expression translated "advocate" (*tichang*) actually encompasses "ideological mobilization, economic measures, and rewards and punishments," and implies that these are to be "supplemented with administrative measures."[61] The phrase "administrative measures" is itself a euphemism, standing for unspecified applications of bureaucratic power at the grassroots level.[62] In such cases the purpose of the obscure language is obviously deception. Because of such obscurities, understanding what is implicit in policy statements often requires a careful study of the official idiom. Even then, the meaning of some significant expressions remains elusive.

Despite euphemisms and some deliberate misrepresentations, Chinese sources are often quite candid about family planning policies and measures for implementation, particularly in communications intended for domestic audiences. The most authoritative are the national health and family planning journals, which summarize policy documents, directives, and speeches by family planning leaders, specify priorities and concrete measures, and cite for emulation the methods and tactics used successfully in particular localities. Among national newspapers, the *People's Daily*, organ of the Party Central Committee, speaks with the greatest authority but guardedly since it is widely translated and quoted abroad. Provincial newspapers and

radio broadcasts often indicate how central policies are to be interpreted and implemented and sometimes reveal aspects of central
policies not otherwise disclosed, hence they are an important supplement to the national journals.

Chinese publications in English and other foreign languages,
which are specifically designed to influence foreign public opinion,
are generally less reliable than domestic sources. English language
dispatches issued by Xinhua, the official Chinese news agency, are
authoritative, but they often omit mention of family planning tactics
strongly advocated in the domestic media that do not accord with
official claims that the program is voluntary. The Beijing English
newspaper *China Daily* and propaganda journals for foreigners, such
as *Beijing Review* and *China Reconstructs*, also tend to censor their
accounts, but they sometimes contain information and commentary
not found in other sources. Their omissions indicate aspects of the
program that the Chinese authorities want foreigners to overlook.

In private conversations with foreign reporters, journalists, demographers, and other visitors, Chinese officials, administrators, and
scholars often provide information not elsewhere available, particularly about differences of opinion among Chinese family planners
and demographers and proceedings at meetings and conferences that
are not fully reported, as most are not, in the Chinese media. Such
contacts can, however, be used manipulatively by Chinese informants, who may try to save face for themselves or their country by
obscuring the harsher realities of China's family planning program.
Moreover, these informants know that they invite serious risk if they
reveal matters the government wants concealed that may later be
quoted with attribution in a foreign publication.

Foreigners who wish to retain their Chinese contacts and ingratiate themselves with the Chinese authorities may also manipulate
the information available to them through private contacts in China.
Some foreign visitors have been known to withhold information from
Chinese sources which they thought would reflect adversely on
China or support a view of Chinese programs and policies less
sympathetic than their own. The least trustworthy of the foreign
sources are reports by visitors who go to China, sometimes as guests
of the State Family Planning Commission, with the evident intent to
find good things to say about the family planning program.[63] Their
embellishments sometimes exceed those of the Chinese propaganda
journals. Such reports should not be accepted without corroborating
evidence from more reliable sources.

The least reliable Chinese sources on the family planning program are presentations by Chinese officials to foreign audiences,

particularly those given to UN agencies and other international bodies, and interviews with foreign journalists. In such circumstances even high Chinese officials sometimes engage in apparently deliberate deception. For example, in 1983, when abortion of all unauthorized pregnancies was mandated by the central authorities, Qian Xinzhong, head of the State Family Planning Commission, who was responsible for implementing the policy, told an Indian visitor that "We don't advocate abortions, let alone force people to accept this method."[64] In July 1984, on a visit to the United States before the Mexico City international population conference, Wang Wei, successor to Qian as head of the SFPC, said at a press briefing that in China abortion was "permitted on condition that it is voluntary and safe technical measures are taken." He also said that the one-child policy was just a "recommendation" and that the policy had "gained the masses' support." All three statements were false, as Wang was in a position to know.[65]

In an interview with the editor of a foreign family planning journal toward the end of 1988, the current head of the SFPC, Peng Peiyun, said she was in favor of allowing more exceptions to the one-child limit,[66] but in a February 1989 article in a domestic journal she said that the purpose of the policy of allowing rural families with one daughter to have a second child was to tighten, not loosen, the one-child limit.[67] In an interview with the *Washington Post* Beijing correspondent in March 1989, Peng said, "We encourage couples to have one child, but it is not a must."[68] But in her February article she had insisted that "the various localities must strictly implement the policy and allow no variations or exceptions,"[69] and a Xinhua-English dispatch quoted a warning by Peng that "legal punishments will be meted out to . . . family planning offenders."[70] To represent these demands as "encouragement" is dishonest.

Apparently as part of an ideological facade, the domestic media sometimes put forward official statements that most Chinese would recognise from personal experience as untrue. Among these are the recurrent assertions that the Chinese masses support the family planning program and that the program combines state guidance with the "voluntarism" of the masses. Both assertions are contradicted by the evidence of Chinese public opinion polls, by the fact that birth rates soar the moment the pressure is eased, and by the admission that family planning work is an "arduous task" because of continuing popular resistance. The contradiction is explicit in a 1988 statement by Peng to the Sixth National Women's Congress:

> The implementation of family planning must be based on
> the principle of combining state guidance with the willing-

ness of the masses. We should realize that there is still a gap between China's current family planning policy and the wishes of the masses on childbirth . . . Propaganda and education must be put in first place to enable the foundation of family planning to be laid in voluntary action on the part of the masses.[71]

Obviously, the "principle" cannot become a reality as long as the masses, despite two decades of "propaganda and education," continue to oppose the program. Yet Chinese spokesmen have frequently cited the "principle" as though it were a statement of fact.[72]

Even with a relatively complete collection of the most reliable sources, tracing family planning developments in China is not easy. Policies change without any change in what are ostensibly the governing documents. Some of the key documents contain contradictory instructions about priorities and tactics—so contradictory in fact that Chinese family planning workers are occasionally confused by them. The actual direction of central policy at any given time often depends upon which of the conflicting elements is being emphasized, and at times this can be inferred only by sifting through hundreds of national and provincial news items to detect changes in style, theme, or intensity.

Over the years, the central authorities themselves have at times seemed uncertain as to what direction family planning policy should take. They have allowed family planners and demographers inside China to debate different approaches and the opposing positions have occasionally surfaced in the Chinese media. In such periods, provincial and lower level family planning leaders, with or without central authorization, have pursued different policies. At other times central policies have been relatively firm and only centrally sanctioned variations have been permitted.[73] Except for China's largest minority, the Zhuangs, minorities in China have until recently been granted more lenient treatment, as have inhabitants of remote areas and people who live on boats on China's coastal and inland waterways, but some of these latitudes are now being withdrawn.[74] The central authorities are striving mightily to "unify thinking" throughout the country, to "stabilize the policies," and to hold all but the smaller ethnic minorities to uniform standards of compliance.[75] Divergent views still appear in print, but the current official line is quite clear.[76]

Although the public record on China's family planning policies is incomplete and in some respects ambiguous, the quantity of evidence on coercion that has accumulated since the late 1970s is enormous and the conclusion to which it points is unmistakable. On the question of whether the program is coercive by central design

15

and intent, the evidence is definitive. Since the early 1970s and especially since 1979, despite intermittent variations in intensity, coercion has been an integral element in the Chinese family planning program.

Definitions of "Coercion"

Chinese claims to the contrary are partly misrepresentation and partly due to their use of an extremely narrow definition of coercion, which is never spelled out. When they disavow coercion, the Chinese authorities seem to refer only to overt physical coercion and the use of administrative commands without accompanying propaganda.[77] The authorities concede that local cadres occasionally resort to this kind of coercion in violation of central instructions. They insist that these infractions are punished as soon as they are detected,[78] but no specific case has yet been reported in the media. Significantly, none of the provincial family planning laws published thus far prohibits or penalizes the use of coercive tactics. In domestic communications, periodic condemnations of "coercion and commandism" alternate with demands for the fulfillment of population and family planning targets and quotas. When family planning demands are being escalated, warnings against coercion are infrequent.

Within its narrow range, the Chinese operating definition of coercion in the family planning sphere has expanded and contracted, depending upon whether demands were being eased or intensified. Some tactics rejected as coercive in one year have been encouraged in the next. For example, during an anticoercion campaign in 1978, so-called "planned parenthood pacts with the masses," mandatory signed commitments to practice family planning or pay heavy penalties, were called coercive, as was the denial of food and drinking water to noncompliant families. The next year, however, "planned parenthood pacts" were again authorized,[79] and more recently some places have cut off drinking water and electricity to noncompliant families without any demur from higher authorities.[80]

Physical force has never been advocated explicitly in a published directive, but at times its use has been applauded as "meticulous ideological work,"[81] or encouraged by central injunctions not to rely on propaganda alone but to take "action" and show "practical results."[82] When the authorities want to encourage the use of physical force, they sometimes give oral assurances that cadres will not be held accountable for whatever means they use and instruct the police not to accept complaints about coercive treatment by the cadres.[83]

Some tactics that are clearly coercive have never been disapproved by the central authorities. Among these are the mass "mobilizations" for sterilization and abortion, from which women often flee from their homes and go into hiding because once caught up in a "mobilization" they have little chance of refusing what the cadres demand. Another is requiring women pregnant without permission to attend "study classes" where they are pressured and threatened by the presiding cadres and not allowed to return to their families until they consent to an abortion. Still another is the so-called "heart-to-heart talks" with cadres who repeatedly visit the homes of women who refuse IUD insertion, sterilization, or abortion until they and their families break under the strain and comply. Then there are penalties that threaten family subsistence: heavy fines for noncompliant families, sometimes amounting to more than their annual earnings; loss of employment for urban families; and revocation of land contracts for rural families. Finally, there are the collective punishments and rewards designed to induce the entire workforce of a factory or the whole population of a rural political unit to denounce, harass, and ostracize families who resist the policies. Tactics such as these that compel people to submit to family planning demands against their will *are* coercive, whatever the Chinese authorities or their foreign apologists say.[84]

Even under a totalitarian system, control is not absolute. From the early 1970s onward, the Chinese media have cited abundant evidence of popular resistance in which local cadres and officials have frequently joined. Some women have escaped compulsory sterilization and abortion measures by abandoning their home villages and taking refuge with relatives or friends in other places until the itinerant surgical teams have left their area and the "mobilizations" for birth control surgery have passed. With the recent loosening of controls over migration, more and more couples pregnant without authorization leave their home communities so that they can give birth without government interference.[85] Rural migrants into major urban centers known as "floating population" are also taking advantage of their anomalous status to have children in violation of family planning regulations.[86]

Sometimes central policies adopted for other purposes have weakened the control of local authorities over pregnant women. A January 1989 newpaper article complained that in recent years family planning work had been "pounded three times," first by the revision of the marriage law in 1980, second by the institution of the "responsibility system" in agriculture in 1981, and third by expanding the categories of couples eligible to have a second child in 1984.[87] All three measures made family planning more difficult to enforce.

The marriage law revisions were meant to solve social problems created by delaying marriage but precipitated a sudden rise in marriage rates by allowing young people to marry earlier.[88] The "responsibility system" virtually dismantled the collectivization of agriculture in a highly successful effort to increase peasant incentives for production. Since it permitted peasants to farm as individual families on land contracted out to them by the local government, selling a part of their crops back to the government and disposing of the surplus as they saw fit, the rural cadres found it more difficult to maintain surveillance over pregnancies.

Although the 1984 policy change allowed only a small increase in exceptions to the one-child rule, increasing the proportion of one-child couples eligible to have a second child from about 5 to about 10 percent and later to about 20 percent, it was widely taken as a signal that the one-child limit had been abolished. The same thing seems to have happened as a result of the decision in 1988 to let some rural couples with only one daughter have a second child. It has proven difficult to confine the authorizations to the specified categories. Frequent small changes in family planning requirements have compromised the effectiveness of the program by confusing both the cadres and the people.[89]

Moreover, the policy of encouraging peasants to become wealthy through their own efforts, advanced in the middle 1980s made it possible for the more successful rural families to pay stiff fines for family planning violations without suffering much economic deprivation. The increase in corruption among Chinese officials at all levels in the past several years, widely reported in the Chinese media, has also enabled some couples to escape the restrictions by bribing the cadres responsible for their enforcement. An attempt is now being made to replace the older control systems with a new "family planning management system," but it is still too early to know how effective it will be.[90]

As a result of these and other problems, the compliance with population policy at the grass-roots level has varied considerably over time. In presentations to foreigners, Chinese spokesmen have sometimes cited the extensive noncompliance as proof that the program is not really coercive, even while domestic communications showed that the authorities were doing their best to stamp it out.[91] Foreign apologists have sometimes used the same argument, implying that failure of execution was proof of benign intent.[92] But regardless of how effective implementation may be at any given time, the objectives of the policy and the tactics used to attain them leave no doubt that the policies are meant to compel observance by those who cannot be persuaded to conform voluntarily. The Chinese family planning program is profoundly and intentionally coercive.

To understand the vital role that coercion has played in the program and to put the coercive measures of the past several years in perspective, it is necessary to trace the evolution of the program since the 1950s, and especially during the years from 1979 through 1983, when its coerciveness reached an all-time peak under orders from the Chinese Communist Party Central Committee and the State Council.

2
Birth Control in China, 1949–1983

The People's Republic of China was a late convert to the belief that population growth needed to be controlled. When the new government was established in 1949, Mao Zedong asserted confidently that population growth would never cause problems for China because the productivity of the masses after revolution would be almost unlimited. Birth control was denounced as "anti-humanitarian" and as a way of "killing off the Chinese people without shedding blood."[1] Imports of contraceptives were banned. A large population was said to be an asset for national economic development. In Mao's own words,

It is a very good thing that China has a big population. Even if China's population multiplies many times, she is fully capable of finding a solution; the solution is production . . .

Of all things in the world, people are the most precious. Under the leadership of the Communist Party, as long as there are people, every kind of miracle can be performed . . . We believe that revolution can change everything and that before long there will arise a new China with a big population and a great wealth of products, where life will be abundant and culture will flourish. All pessimistic views are utterly groundless.[2]

The First Campaign

But by the spring of 1953, even though official spokesmen continued to denounce the idea that overpopulation contributed to the poverty of the Chinese masses, persistent food shortages had already convinced some of the Chinese leaders that a large population was not an unqualified blessing. In April 1953 a *People's Daily* editorial said that increasing demands for grain would be hard to meet "in our country with such a large population" and warned that the food problem would remain an urgent one for many years to come.[3] In July the Party's Director of Rural Work, Deng Zihui, acknowledged that the 1952 grain crop was insufficient to meet the needs of the increasing population.[4] When the first census of the PRC, taken in 1953–54, counted a population total about 100 million larger than the official figure used previously, the Party reacted with shock. While still insisting that a large population was a "good thing," census official Bai Jianhua conceded that "in an economically underdeveloped country, a rapid increase in population may cause difficulties in living."[5] Meanwhile, in August 1953, before any census results had been reported, the State Council had instructed the Ministry of Health to assist the Chinese masses in practicing birth control.[6] In July 1954 the Health Ministry presented its proposals to the government for review.[7]

The first public call for birth control was delivered at the National People's Congress on September 18, 1954, not by a government or Party leader but by a non-Communist intellectual, Shao Lizi, who had been an advocate of birth control before 1949. Shao reiterated Mao's argument that a large population was a good thing but, citing recurrent natural calamities and the slow pace of economic development in China, he added that "in an environment beset with difficulties, it appears that there should be a limit set." He called on the state to give the people "practical guidance" in birth control. Significantly, his speech was printed in full the same day in the *People's Daily*.[8]

At the end of December 1954, two months after the final census results had been published, Liu Shaoqi, Mao's second in command, convened a symposium in Beijing to discuss "the problem of birth control" at which he affirmed that the Party was in favor of birth control, that China had all the people it needed, but that propaganda should be carried out only by word of mouth and not in rural areas.[9] These steps were tentative and seemed to lack a sense of urgency. By 1955, however, Mao was apparently convinced that a large population was a liability.[10] In 1956 he became concerned about shortages of grain to feed the growing population,[11] and advised that "all areas with high population densities should publicize and promote birth control."[12] In 1957 he reportedly warned that uncontrolled population growth could lead to the "extinction" of the Chinese people and that the human race was procreating "in a state of total anarchy" and "must control itself to achieve a planned increase."[13] As Mao's anxieties rose, birth control efforts intensified. In August 1956 the Ministry of Public Health issued a directive requiring local health agencies to promote birth control actively, and thereafter a major propaganda campaign was waged.[14]

Although the authorities maintained that birth control was a response to "the universal demand of the masses,"[15] the only evidence cited in support of this claim was a few letters written to a

21

women's magazine by women cadres, and they may have been solicited.[16] Shao Lizi conceded that "only a small number of people . . . desire to practice birth control at the moment."[17]

In fact, the program encountered strong popular resistance, especially in the rural areas, whereupon the authorities angrily denounced the "feudal mentality," "outworn and erroneous thinking," "suspicions and doubts," and "stupid ideas" of the masses.[18] They said that the "conservative tendency" among the people was a "social problem" that "must be solved by . . . applying the force of society,"[19] that birth control was not a "private affair" but a matter of importance for the national welfare and therefore an "affair of the state,"[20] and that because the "prosperity of the nation" and the "happiness of the people" were involved, "the Party and the Government cannot help interfering" in birth control matters.[21]

The authorities insisted that birth control was "not to be forced on anybody," that it should not be promoted by "pressure and demands," that "acts of compulsion must be avoided," and that coercive tactics "will not be tolerated."[22] Nevertheless they put pressure on the local cadres to achieve immediate results, which induced the cadres to force the masses to conform, as had happened during land reform, collectivization, and other mass campaigns.

In some cities women factory workers were required to write out "birth plans" and pledge that they would not have another child during the next five-year plan period. Those who refused were denounced in wall posters.[23] Such measures reportedly led many people to believe that birth control was "compulsory."[24] Thus the discrepancy between official claims and actual practice in regard to coercion that has been so conspicuous in the family planning campaign of the 1970s and 1980s was already apparent in the 1950s.

In the first campaign, however, coercion did not reach the point where it could effectively overcome popular resistance. One reason was that the authorities continued to maintain the position that birth control was inspired not by fears of population growth but merely by concern for the health and welfare of mothers and children.[25] Another was that sterilization and abortion did not play a major role. At the beginning of the campaign both sterilization and abortion were available only under stringent limitations. In March 1956 the Ministry of Health decided to ease the restrictions somewhat by reducing from six to four the number of healthy surviving children applicants must have to qualify for the surgery,[26] but it still required that a woman be "in poor health, over 30 years of age, busy with her studies, and in financial difficulties" before she could be sterilized.[27]

Abortion was allowed only in cases where the pregnancy was

considered undesirable for medical reasons or where the interval since the last birth was too short and the mother was experiencing difficulties in breastfeeding the previous child. Even so the operation could only be performed at the request of both husband and wife with a certificate from a doctor and the approval of the work unit to which they belonged.[28] Efforts by the authorities to eliminate these restrictions encountered opposition from virtually the entire Chinese medical establishment, including health officials and the Chinese Medical Association.[29] The All-China Women's Federation and even some birth control advocates also opposed the change.[30] Despite the opposition, the Ministry of Public Health, apparently under pressure from the political leadership, took steps to relax restrictions on both sterilization and abortion in March, April, and May 1957.[31] However, many Chinese doctors continued to observe the old rules.

The main reason why the birth control drive made little progress during the first campaign was the lack of an effective field organization for translating the Party's policies into action. Responsibility for setting up local guidance centers and providing contraceptives was left to the public health agencies, whose limited staff were already fully occupied providing basic health services and were reluctant to take on the task of promoting birth control. Although Liu's inhibitions against press propaganda and the promotion of birth control in rural areas were abandoned by 1956 and local units throughout the country were instructed to set up birth control "guidance committees" in 1957, the campaign moved slowly and seemed rather uncoordinated. There is no evidence that a national birth control organization had evolved by the time the Great Leap Forward disrupted the effort in the spring of 1958.

The Great Leap Forward

In 1958 Mao reverted to his earlier idea that China's masses, fired by revolutionary enthusiasm, could produce far more than they consumed. He argued that both in agriculture and in industry "miracles" of production were possible. "The more people," he said, "the more views and suggestions, and the more intense the fervor and the greater the energy." Even the poverty of China's people was a "good thing" because it made them more revolutionary and eager for change.[32] Political awareness could lead to a sudden advance in national economic development on all fronts, Mao asserted, and the advances could be renewed year after year. He called for three years of all-out efforts to produce a "Great Leap Forward" all across the land.

Consistent with Mao's new theory, statisticians were required to forswear objectivity and produce figures that would inspire the masses to greater feats of production. The resulting statistical fabrications seemed to confirm Mao's belief in miracles. Leap figures showed that grain production had more than doubled during 1958, and industrial production figures also registered extreme increases.[33] In the rural areas peasants were encouraged to consume food recklessly, a fallow land program was initiated, some standing crops were left unharvested, and much time was spent in unproductive mass labor projects.

Encouraged by the Leap statistics, Mao and his colleagues reexamined China's economic prospects and decided once again that a large population was an asset instead of a liability. In April 1958 Hu Yaobang, who was then Secretary of the Communist Youth League, told a national conference of youth work representatives that there was "great hope" for the future development of the country, in which China's large population would be a factor of "decisive significance." He ridiculed those "pessimists who seem to believe that a huge population is a catastrophe" (among whom Mao might have been counted a year earlier) and stated the Party leaders' new position as follows:

> We Marxists believe that, for the sake of the health of our people and the welfare of the next generation, planned parenthood should be promoted. However, a large population is a good, not an undesirable thing. A larger population means greater manpower. This is simple logic . . . The force of 600 million liberated people is tens of thousands of times stronger than a nuclear explosion. Such a force is capable of creating wonders which our enemies cannot even imagine. Facts since the Great Leap Forward movement have sufficiently proved this point.[34]

While the general euphoria of the Leap lasted, birth control lost its priority and was neglected. Press coverage and other domestic propaganda efforts lapsed, the production of contraceptives faltered, and public health workers and political administrators turned to other concerns.

The illusions of the Great Leap Forward were soon shattered. At the end of 1959 food shortages were reported in various areas. In the next two years, widespread famine and undernutrition caused an estimated 30 million above-normal deaths in China.[35] Early in 1962, when the famine was over, the promotion of birth control was quietly resumed.[36]

The Second Campaign

Although popular resistance to birth control remained strong during the second campaign, Chinese sources convey the impression that promotional tactics were generally less aggressive than in the first campaign except for efforts to increase the average age of marriage for young people. Press propaganda during the second campaign was comparatively subdued and seemed to be under tighter control than in the first campaign. The authorities reiterated their position that having children was "not altogether a personal matter" because the State had to supply the food, clothing, housing, education, transportation, and employment for the children as they grew up,[37] but there were few statements about the relationship between population growth and economic development and no theoretical treatises on the difference between Marxist and Malthusian reasons for population control, a subject of endless debate during the first campaign.

The main theme of the second campaign was that love and marriage corrupted the revolutionary enthusiasm of youth and that sex and childbearing sapped the physical and emotional strength of both wives and husbands! The alleged deleterious effects ranged from sensational to downright bizarre.[38] It is doubtful whether such propaganda had much effect on traditional values supporting early marriage and childbearing.

There were, however, some improvements in organization. The local birth control "guidance committees" instituted during the first campaign were gradually re-established, this time under the sponsorship of Party and government leaders at all levels, who now took an active part in the work of the committees. The officials were also required to take the lead in practicing birth control as an example to others. According to one spokesman whose opinions were prominently featured in press propaganda, couples should have no more than two children with a three to five year interval between them. A third child might be "considered" if family circumstances permitted, but it was best to have no more than three.[39] It was later reported that Premier Zhou Enlai spoke on the importance of late marriage and birth control "many times at various meetings," but this fact was not revealed at the time in the Chinese media. In 1964 the State Council established a national family planning office to guide the work.[40]

Better organization undoubtedly contributed to the somewhat greater success of the second campaign, along with more effective contraceptive methods. Intrauterine devices were introduced for the first time, and the development of a new suction device for carrying out abortion reportedly made it much safer than the conventional curettage method. Both these methods were probably available only in urban areas. There was also an effort to promote vasectomy during the second campaign on the grounds that it was a much simpler and safer procedure than tubal ligation and that it was unfair that women should have to assume a major share of the burden in sterilizations, but these ideas encountered strong popular resistance.

Many years later the 1982 fertility survey disclosed that fertility levels in urban areas began to fall during the early 1960s but not those in rural areas.[41] When the national vital rates for the 1960s were released during the 1970s, it was apparent that the national birth rate reached a peak in 1963 and did not decline much during the remainder of the decade; the change in urban areas was presumably masked by the continuing high rates among the 80 percent of the population that was rural.

The second campaign was disrupted in 1966 when Mao launched his Great Proletarian Cultural Revolution. Its ostensible purpose was to eliminate influences that Mao believed had corrupted the Chinese Communist Party and turned it away from his revolutionary ideals and purposes, but it was also an attempt by Mao to regain full control of the Party organization by destroying former colleagues who had attempted to limit his powers after the disaster of the Leap Forward.

The Cultural Revolution paralysed the civil control apparatus and substituted a kind of mob rule by "revolutionary" youth groups, who rampaged from city to city taking revenge on Mao's alleged enemies. But the youth groups soon fell to feuding among themselves, fighting pitched battles in the streets with weapons seized from urban arsenals. The turmoil reached such extremes that Mao could bring it under control only with the intervention of the military. When order was finally restored in 1969 the third birth control campaign began.

The Third Campaign

Again Zhou Enlai played a leading, though somewhat secretive, role in family planning work. At an unreported national family planning symposium in 1969 he said that during the Cultural Revolution marriages and births had both increased and that "birth control work must be carried out firmly."[42] In July 1971 the State Council under Zhou's personal direction approved a new official document calling for strengthened leadership over family planning work and set a limit of two children per family instead of the previous three-child limit. In the next three years, reports from all parts of the country indicated a major birth control campaign under way. Official statistics later revealed that IUD insertions in China had risen sharply from 6 million in 1971 to 14 million in 1973. In August 1973 the State Council revived its family planning leadership office, which had apparently expired during the Cultural Revolution, and in December the slogan "late, spacing, and few," the watchword of the third campaign during its first decade, was first put forward at a national birth control conference.[43] In 1975 Mao said that "population must be controlled" and called for the application of "social forces" to see that everyone complied.[44] In that year IUD insertions climbed further to almost 17 million, the highest single year total until the peak coercion year of 1983.

The new campaign required local authorities to "grasp tightly the work of planned parenthood"[45] and made the struggle for birth control part of the "class struggle." Popular opposition was attributed to the "class enemy."[46] Local cadres were told that family planning was essential for "socialist revolution and socialist construction" and that it was also in accord with "the fundamental interests of the masses."[47] Although, as before, the authorities sometimes warned against using coercive tactics,[48] they also demanded results that could not be achieved by a voluntary birth control program. Target birth and natural increase rates were handed down from higher levels.[49] Units that achieved their targets were labelled "progressive"; their leaders were praised and promoted. Other units were criticized as "backward" in planned parenthood and told to "strengthen their leadership."[50]

In response to these efforts, China's natural increase rate as compiled from provincial reports dropped sharply from almost 26 per thousand population in 1970 to 12.6 in 1976.[51] Encouraged by this trend, the then Party chairman, Hua Guofeng, told the Fifth National People's Congress in February 1978 that all areas should strive to lower China's population growth rate to less than ten per thousand within three years,[52] and the national goal immediately became the goal for all the provinces.

The new goal turned out to be a miscalculation. Abuses of power by local officials, reportedly rampant during Mao's last years, had provoked a strong reaction among the people. In the summer of 1978 the Party leaders charged the lower level cadres with resorting to "coercion and commandism" in all aspects of policy implementation, including birth control. Practices that had been encouraged or at least tolerated in prior years were specifically denounced. Many family planning cadres became discouraged and stopped enforcing family planning policies.

Instead of continuing its downward trend, China's natural increase rate levelled off at about 12 per thousand in 1977 and 1978,

27

and it became apparent that the goal of under 10 per thousand by 1980 was unattainable. Moreover, population projections had demonstrated that China's population would continue to grow as long as Chinese women were allowed two children each. Early in 1979 Deng Xiaoping ordered that family planning work be strengthened "vigorously" and said that even a cessation of population growth would not suffice to end China's population problems.[53] The implication was that fertility should be reduced below the replacement level. Therefore, the anti-coercion drive was abandoned and a policy of limiting Han couples to one child was instituted.[54] Initially the policy called on all couples to have "only one child if possible, two at the most, with a period of three or four years between them,"[55] but before many months had passed, the option of having "two at the most" was dropped. A major escalation of birth control demands was under way.

The One-Child Policy

The new limitation was extremely unpopular. It meant that henceforth about half of all rural Chinese families whose first and only child was a daughter would have no one to look after them in old age, since, by Chinese custom, a girl marries into the family of her husband and is no longer responsible for her own parents. Immediately the practice of female infanticide, which had been common in China before 1949 but had been virtually eradicated early in the 1950s, was revived in some areas.[56]

At first the Chinese authorities tended to dismiss the infanticide problem, but beginning in November 1982 the media, obviously reflecting official concerns, issued a cry of alarm. One newspaper warned that if infanticide were not stopped at once a serious imbalance between the sexes would occur and in twenty years' time "a large number of young men will be without spouses."[57] Others described in gruesome detail how the infanticides were being carried out.[58] Statistics on births from various localities showed disproportionate numbers of males. The 1982 census data on births during 1981 indicated 112.45 male births per 100 female for Anhui Province, the highest provincial birth sex ratio in the country; the national average was 108.47. County figures as high as 139 male births per 100 female births, commune figures of up to 175 males per 100 females, and brigade ratios as high as 800 males per 100 females were reported from several areas.[59]

When the foreign press began to repeat what the Chinese media were saying about infanticide and its connection with the one-child policy, Chinese sources began to deny the seriousness of the problem. The Minister-in-Charge of the State Family Planning Commission at that time, Qian Xinzhong, argued that the one-child policy was not the cause of female infanticide in China because the problem had existed long before.[60] Qian ignored the fact that the practice had been in abeyance until the one-child limit was imposed.

After the one-child policy was instituted, several measures denounced as coercive in 1978 were once again approved.[61] Family planning cadres in Sichuan Province, criticized for their coercive practices in 1978, were told that, far from "overdoing things," they had not done enough.[62] Guangdong Province told its cadres that "any policy that is advantageous to planned parenthood must be carried out."[63]

In April 1979 a conference of Party and Government leaders in Beijing recommended that the national population total be limited to less than 1.2 billion in the year 2000. This goal was officially adopted by Hua Guofeng in September 1980.[64] In June 1979 Hua had told the Second Session of the Fifth National People's Congress that "This year we must do everything we can to lower the country's population growth rate to about 10 per thousand" and added that by 1985 the rate should drop to 5 per thousand.[65] Shortly afterward, Vice-Premier Chen Muhua repeated Hua's demand and announced a further goal of getting the natural increase rate down to zero by the year 2000.[66]

Early in 1979, the provincial authorities began to pass laws requiring that all couples practice family planning and imposing severe financial penalties on those who had unauthorized second or higher order births. These laws, obviously instigated by the central authorities, had to be submitted beforehand to the State Family Planning Commission for clearance. They differed only in detail, apparently because they were modelled on a national draft law that was circulated but never formally adopted or made public. By November 1979, twenty-seven of the twenty-nine provincial level units in China had passed such laws.[67]

As family planning demands escalated, official attitudes toward those who dared to resist hardened. In August, Chen Muhua asserted that if the family planning program posed a conflict between the interests of the individual and those of the state, the individual's interests should be subordinated.[68] Tianjin Municipality said that in the last three months of the year the practice of bearing more than one child was to be "stopped in the main" and that beginning with the first quarter of 1980 "nobody should bear more than one child."[69] Guangdong Province announced that beginning in January 1980 "no one in the province is allowed to have a third child."[70] Other provinces adopted similar rules and demanded that their cadres implement them. More emphasis was placed on "remedial measures" (mandatory abortions) for unauthorized pregnancies.[71] Although the central authorities did not publicly withdraw previous admonitions against coercion, their silence on the subject as demands were escalating sent a clear signal to lower levels that results mattered more than methods.

The coercive family planning tactics of 1979 reportedly again "alienated" the people.[72] Therefore a second anti-coercion campaign was initiated in February 1980 and continued until the spring of 1981, this time focussed specifically on family planning. The cadres were warned that coercive measures "can only bring damage and destruction to our work"[73] and told to devote more effort to "meticulous ideological work" and persuasion, improve their "work style," be "fair and reasonable," and avoid methods that were "divorced from the masses."[74] In September 1980, a widely publicized "open letter" from the Party Central Committee, while emphasizing the need to control population growth by enforcing the one-child policy, concluded with an exhortation to "all comrades" to "persuade" the masses to accept the policy and to "urge" the cadres not to resort to coercion.[75]

Once again, some cadres took the warnings against coercion as a signal to ease the pressures on birth control work, which promptly began to lag. Hopeful rumors began to circulate that the one-child policy was about to be abandoned.[76] An upsurge of births was reported in much of the country, due partly to the relaxation of birth control work but even more to two changes in official policy. The first was the passage of the new marriage law in September 1980 that invalidated local administrative restrictions on age at marriage, permitting people to marry three or four years earlier than previously allowed, apparently on the assumption that with family planning strongly enforced, age at marriage no longer mattered.[77] The result was a tidal wave of marriages, followed in due course by a wave of first births.[78]

The second policy change was the institution of the "responsibility system" in agriculture, which virtually dissolved collective farming operations under the communes. Individual peasant families were allowed to farm sections of commune land under contract, remanding an agreed quantity of grain and other products to the collective and selling or consuming the rest at their own discretion. Although the policy was quite successful in arousing the peasants' "enthusiasm for production," it made family planning harder to enforce because the local cadres no longer maintained daily surveillance over women working in the fields. The cadres in many areas again threw up their hands and stopped enforcing the policies.[79]

By the second half of 1981 the central authorities, foreseeing a deluge of births, declared that population growth was "out of control" in many areas. They foresaw a new "baby boom" and a "population explosion" that threatened to "wipe out all the family planning achievements of the 1970s."[80] Concern about coercion had once again been replaced by concern about population growth. In March 1982 the authorities issued a directive calling on local organs to do "still better family planning work" and insisting that they "tackle the new situation and new problems that have cropped up" and make the one-child policy virtually universal. Although the directive insisted that "we should rely primarily on ideological education and encouragement to promote family planning work," it also stated flatly that "no one is allowed to have a third child, no matter what."[81]

This time the response at lower levels was confused. Some localities reinstated methods considered coercive in 1978, which had been abandoned for the second time in 1980, and added "administrative disciplinary measures," forbidden during the 1980 anti-coercion campaign, to the economic penalties allowed under the provincial family planning laws.[82] They issued calls for "rigorous enforcement," "decisive and urgent measures," "inflexible" family planning tactics, and "forcib[ly] implement[ing] various measures," which sounded like invitations to use coercion.[83] In other places, the work virtually ceased, childbearing was allowed to "take its course," and "a state of anarchy" prevailed in family planning work.[84]

By the end of 1982 the central authorities became aware of another threat to population control. The preliminary results of the census of July 1, 1982, showed that the bulge in the Chinese age structure caused by the high birth rates after the famine of 1959–61 would soon reach the ages of marriage and childbearing. The resulting rise in births would threaten the national goal of a population total under 1.2 billion in the year 2000. In November 1982 Qian Xinzhong told a national family planning conference:

> Our country is now facing a new peak in population growth rates . . . Only by maintaining the annual net increase in population at around 10 million for the next 18 years can we achieve the fighting goal of limiting the population to under 1.2 billion by the end of this century.

He added that family planning must be implemented "resolutely" for a long time to come.[85] The conference mapped out plans for a "family planning propaganda month" to begin on January 1, 1983,

31

and continue until after Spring Festival. At the same conference, State Councillor Bo Yibo warned that the next three years would be crucial for family planning in China and added that "necessary measures" must be taken to ensure its success.[86] The "necessary measures" turned out to be the most coercive family planning program the world has ever seen.

The Peak of Coercion: 1983

It was soon made clear that much more than "propaganda" was planned for the new year. On December 6, 1982, a circular issued jointly by the State Family Planning Commission, the Party Central Committee, and several other central ministries and mass organizations announced that the "propaganda month" program would require sterilization of one partner of every couple that had two or more children and the prompt abortion of all unauthorized pregnancies. The circular insisted that "propaganda month activities must be carried out solidly and stress must be put on practical results."[87] On December 19, Qian Xinzhong disclosed that, in additon, "women of childbearing age with one child must be fitted with IUDs."[88]

Meanwhile, the 1983 economic plan for the PRC, approved by the National People's Congress on December 10, 1982, demanded full propaganda mobilization for birth control and the adoption of "necessary measures" to increase the numbers of one-child families, "strictly control" second births, and "firmly put an end" to having more than two children.[89] A *People's Daily* article of December 23 said that the propaganda month drive was "expected to yield practical and solid results."[90] Qian Xinzhong also revealed in a national telephone conference on January 10, 1983, that a "central leadership comrade," presumably Deng Xiaoping, had summarized the lessons from recent family planning experience as: "(1) Rely on political mobilization; (2) rely on the law; and (3) rely on technical measures."[91] The reliance on "technical measures" was immediately incorporated into the instructions issued by the provincial authorities.[92] Even the *China Daily*, despite its accessibility to foreign readers, sounded a patently coercive note:

> Persuasion is preferable to administrative and pecuniary measures, and contraception to abortion. Compliance must be ensured, however, for the population problem in China today is of such a pressing nature that individual whims must be subject to the interests of society as a whole.[93]

When the "propaganda month" was over, Deng indicated that its measures were to continue indefinitely.[94] In June Premier Zhao Ziyang's government work report stated:

We must persistently advocate late marriage and one child per couple, strictly control second births, prevent additional births by all means, earnestly carry out effective birth control measures, and firmly protect infant girls and their mothers.[95]

The significance of "by all means" and "effective . . . measures" was not lost on the central family planning leaders. Qian Xinzhong immediately relayed its message, asserting that Zhao had said the measures must be implemented "resolutely and relentlessly."[96]

With encouragement from Qian Xinzhong and the "central leadership comrade," sterilization presently emerged as the principal "technical measure" under the new program.[97] Couples with two or more children were designated as persons "who should be sterilized," and the provincial authorities estimated their numbers and made plans to complete the surgeries over the next several years.[98] Official statistics subsequently revealed that sterilizations in China increased sharply in 1983 to nearly three times the number in the previous peak year, which was 1979. Of the 20.8 million sterilizations in 1983, almost 80 percent were female.[99]

The advantage of compulsory sterilization over other forms of birth control was obvious: it was permanent. There was no further need to monitor unauthorized pregnancies among sterilized women or to spend long hours "persuading" them to have abortions. Women coerced into being sterilized were coerced forever. But in 1983 the Chinese media had little to say about coercion in family planning.

As the year came to an end, a number of provinces were planning a second "propaganda month" in January 1984 to continue and even to intensify the sterilization drive,[100] but these plans were presently interrupted by another central policy change. In December 1983 Qian Xinzhong, who only three months earlier had been given one of the first two United Nations population awards for his contribution to family planning but had been strongly identified with the coercive measures, was removed without explanation from his post as head of the SFPC.[101] In January 1984 the new head, Wang Wei, signalled a different approach to family planning by asserting that the work must be "based on local conditions" and carried out "reasonably to win the support of the broad masses." He urged the cadres to find ways of doing family planning work effectively while at the same time "building a close relationship between the Party and the people,"[102] an indication that, as before, coercive family planning tactics had alienated the masses and needed to be disavowed.

What followed was a period of confusion both in China and

abroad about what tactics the Chinese authorities wanted local cadres to use in promoting family planning. Some foreign apologists for the program seized upon the apparent relaxation to assert or imply that coercion was no longer being used and that the political problems it posed for the rest of the world were now a thing of the past. That was a gross misreading of the evidence, as the following chapters show.

3
The Confusing Signals of
Party Document No. 7

The change in family planning policy was confirmed at a ten-day conference in Beijing in March 1984. Provincial family planning officials were told that measures must henceforth be "more realistic," fair and reasonable, supported by the masses, and easy for the cadres to carry out, and that the cadres must "improve [their] work style," "refrain from coercion," and "strictly forbid any illegal and disorderly action." While the one-child limit should still be promoted, the conditions under which a few couples were allowed to have a second child should be enlarged a little. But since the still stringent limits on national, provincial, and local population growth based on the target of under 1.2 billion in the year 2000 were not to be exceeded,[1] only a limited number of additional second births could be permitted.

Previously, urban couples could have a second child only if the first was so disabled by a nonhereditary impairment as to be unable to work, or if one spouse had had a child in a previous marriage but the other had not, or if the couple became pregnant after adopting a child because of infertility. In the rural areas a few other situations were added,[2] but altogether only about 5 percent of Chinese couples could qualify for a second child.[3] The new policy enlarged the number to "about 10 percent," a change that was referred to as "opening a small gap," but it also stipulated that before the "small gap" could be opened, the "big gap" of unauthorized births must be closed.[4]

As one Chinese population specialist later observed, the "small opening" was in reality nothing new. The options it added had always been there in actual practice. The new policy was intended to legitimize exceptions already recognized, eliminate the "backlash" that resulted when they were denied, and use the "small opening" as a device to strengthen control over the "large opening" of unauthorized births, and thus "turn a negative factor into a positive factor."[5] Apparently a general relaxation of family planning efforts was not what the policy makers had in mind.

35

Contents of Document No. 7

The new policy was set forth on April 12, 1984, by the Party Central Committee in a statement called "Document No. 7," which for the next two years was said to be the basic policy guiding family planning work. Some of its provisions were quoted or paraphrased in public sources, but the full text has never been published. Evidently it included provisions that the central authorities chose not to reveal.

Those that have been disclosed contain an interesting contradiction: they call for moderation of tactics and yet require attainment of the same targets by essentially the same means as in 1983. From the start the contradiction caused confusion among family planning cadres. For example, the document insisted that family planning work must be "grasped firmly and well." Since the early 1970s, "grasp firmly" had been in frequent use in demands that the cadres make sure that people complied with family planning requirements. In April 1984 they were told, no doubt much to their surprise, that it meant something different:

> A few comrades do not understand what is meant by [the phrase] family planning work must be "grasped firmly" as stated by the Party Central. They thought that "grasped firmly" meant that policy regulations must be carried out strictly . . . The formulation of policies must be based on objective reality. If the policy is too strict and is beyond objective reality, sometimes it may be temporarily effective but often it cannot last long . . .[6]

Previously, injunctions to "do well" in family planning work seemed to mean that the cadres should faithfully follow directives and fulfill their targets. But in 1984 they seemed to imply the avoidance of coercive tactics. Linking the two expressions in one phrase sent conflicting signals to the cadres. Yet the central authorities insisted that the two instructions were perfectly compatible. In July 1984, Wang Wei said:

> Document No. 7 points out that family planning work "must be done with a tight rein and be done well with great effort . . ." Some comrades . . . think that having a tight rein is one matter whereas doing well is another matter. They think that having a tight rein means the fulfillment of targets and doing well means the implementation of policies and solution of work style problems. Some even think having a tight rein and doing well are opposites. How can they be understood in this way?[7]

The answer was, very easily, given the central authorities' penchant for changing the interpretation of key words and phrases in their directives while pretending that the policies had not changed.

The ambiguities in Document No. 7 were not a new feature in China's family planning guidelines. The Party's "open letter" of September 1980 and other central instructions contained similar ambiguities, warning against coercive tactics while insisting on targets that could only be attained by coercive means. These ambiguities seem to serve two useful functions for the central leadership. They permit the leaders to shift emphasis from meeting targets to improving "work style" and back again in response to public reactions without having to admit that previous orders were mistaken or had been changed. They also make it easy for the central authorities to attribute coercion to local misunderstanding of central policy when they wish to avoid responsibility for it. Hence the real meaning of Document No. 7 lay not in the literal interpretation of its provisions but in the changing emphasis placed on them by the central authorities over the next two years.

The First Interpretation—A Slight Easing of Controls

When Document No. 7 was issued, the Chinese authorities made it quite clear that the relaxation of family planning policies was meant to be very limited. They stated explicitly that very few couples were to be allowed a second child, that one child was still the normal prescription, and that "unplanned" (that is, unauthorized) births and "excessive" (third and higher order) births were to be "resolutely" prohibited. The April 1984 article in the national family planning journal cited above explained that

> to understand and implement fully the guidelines of the Party directives means that, based on the extensive promotion of one child per couple, the allowance for a second child in a planned way in rural areas may be widened a little. At the same time, strict control must be applied to unplanned second births and to excessive births . . . under the premise that the population by the end of this century will not exceed the target of 1.2 billion . . .[8]

Many sources made it clear that a general relaxation of family planning requirements was *not* intended. A *People's Daily* article in March 1984 said that "family planning work must not be weakened and relaxed."[9] Other sources warned against "wavering" and said that the work "must not be slackened in the slightest."[10] Many others insisted that targets must still be attained on schedule.[11]

Moreover, although some sources said that people were to be allowed more freedom in the choice of contraceptives, a number of areas were still requiring IUDs for women with one child, sterilization for couples with two or more children, and "remedial measures" for all unauthorized pregnancies,[12] policies that had been enforced rigorously in 1983. Despite numerous warnings against "coercion and commandism" in family planning work[13] (so numerous as to contradict official claims that such incidents were few and isolated), the Party leaders also praised the "achievements" of the extremely coercive 1983 campaign. At the March 1984 conference of provincial family planning directors, Party spokesmen declared that the Party's past policies had been "consistent and entirely correct" and specifically lauded the "great results" of the work done in 1983.[14] This "high appraisal" was said to have "given great encouragement" to those attending the conference.[15]

Despite the warnings that no relaxation of family planning requirements was intended, both the cadres and the people interpreted the new policy as a signal to ease up. Rumors swept the country that all couples were now allowed to have a second child, and the rumors persisted through 1986 in spite of repeated official denials.[16] Late in 1984 Liaoning Province reported:

> After Party Central Committee Document No. 7 was transmitted to the lower levels, some basic level cadres were afraid to reveal the document to the masses. They were worried that the masses would think that the policy was relaxed and make demands that would be contrary to the spirit of the document. This kind of condition in which the masses are delighted and the cadres are worried is quite prevalent.[17]

In Lhasa the popular perception was that "the storm in planned parenthood is over"; the cadres had to make people understand that it was not.[18] The authorities took considerable pains to make clear that the prohibition of coercive tactics and the demands that the cadres improve their work style did not mean that the pressure on family planning was off.

Cadres in other provinces were also confused by the shift in policy. Guizhou Province warned its cadres that they must not let their resolve to implement family planning be shaken by the changes.[19] Heilongjiang's cadres were told that passivity, laxity, inaction, and laissez faire were contrary to "the spirit of the Document" and that "they must never hesitate, watch and wait, and bide their time."[20] In Guangxi the cadres were afraid of making "mistakes" by enforcing policies that might later be abandoned. They noted that the

Cultural Revolution had been repudiated and they wondered whether family planning would be also.[21] Hainan Island detected a mood of "slackening and war-weariness" among its cadres.[22] Zhejiang said that some cadres had "certain doubts and misconceptions" and as a result had "relaxed their leadership" over birth control work, while others were "afraid of difficulty and dare[d] not work in a bold manner."[23]

How far the relaxation in family planning enforcement had actually gone was probably not known to the central authorities during 1984. The evidence would have become available to them only when the family planning statistics for 1984 were compiled by the central Ministry of Health in 1985. The annual Health Ministry yearbooks gave national totals for IUD insertions and removals, vasectomies, tubal ligations, and abortions for each year from 1971 onward with a one-year lag for the latest figures. Thus, the 1985 yearbook, issued in March 1986, included for the first time the statistics for 1984. The figures (see table on next page) indicate that in 1984 IUD insertions dropped back to 66 percent of the number in 1983, sterilizations to about one-third of the 1983 level,[24] and abortions to about 62 percent of the 1983 level.

The Second Interpretation—A Slight Tightening

The relaxation in 1984 was only relative, but it went far beyond what the authorities had intended. By August 1984, even without statistics, they became aware of what was happening and began to demand that the cadres tighten up. Several provincial family planning conferences were held to transmit "recent instructions" from the central authorities that reaffirmed the importance of family planning and "set forth new demands." As a result, Guizhou Province resolved that "from now on . . . resolutely prevent[ing] additional births" would be the focal point of its family planning work, and that all areas must "strengthen [their] resolve" and "mobilize the initiative of the cadres and the masses."[25] Heilongjiang was "emphatically" told that "cadres in charge of family planning work must better achieve the work in line with the demands of the central authorities," and that "Party committees and governments at all levels must strengthen their leadership over family planning work and mobilize and organize the forces of the whole society to achieve it."[26] Hainan Island demanded that its cadres "correct [their] understanding, strengthen leadership, and rapidly whip up a second stage in the planned parenthood drive in September."[27] Guangxi revealed that the new

39

BIRTH CONTROL SURGERIES: 1971–1986

Year	IUD Insertions	IUD Removals	Vasectomies	Tubal Ligations	Abortions
1971	6,172,889	—	1,223,480	1,744,644	3,910,110
1972	9,220,297	853,625	1,715,822	2,087,160	4,813,452
1973	13,949,569	1,126,756	1,933,210	2,955,617	5,110,405
1974	12,579,886	1,352,787	1,445,251	2,275,741	4,984,564
1975	16,743,693	1,702,213	2,652,653	3,280,042	5,084,260
1976	11,626,510	1,812,590	1,495,540	2,707,849	4,742,946
1977	12,974,313	1,941,880	2,616,876	2,776,448	5,229,569
1978	10,962,517	2,087,420	767,542	2,511,413	5,391,204
1979	13,472,392	2,288,670	1,673,947	5,289,518	7,856,587
1980	11,491,871	2,403,408	1,363,508	3,842,006	9,527,644
1981	10,344,537	1,513,376	649,476	1,555,971	8,696,943
1982	14,069,161	2,056,671	1,230,967	3,925,927	12,419,663
1983	17,755,736	5,323,354	4,359,261	16,398,378	14,371,843
1984	11,751,146	4,383,129	1,293,286	5,417,163	8,890,140
1985	9,576,980	2,278,892	575,564	2,283,971	10,931,565
1986	—	—	—	—	11,580,000
1971–85	182,691,497	31,124,771	24,993,383	59,051,848	111,960,987

SOURCE. Figures for 1971–1985: Yearbook Compilation Committee, *Zhongguo weisheng nianjian 1986 (Public Health Yearbook of China, 1986)* (Beijing: Renmin weisheng chubanshe, 1986), p. 475. The 1986 figure, given in the source as 11.58 million, is from Agence France Presse, Beijing, July 8, 1987, FBIS, No. 130, July 8, 1987, p. K1.

instructions from the central authorities included a "demand" that minority nationalities with a population exceeding 10 million meet the same family planning requirements as the Hans, instead of being treated more leniently as under previous policies, and told its cadres that it was "imperative to get a thoroughly good grasp of planned parenthood work . . . and take effective measures."[28] Similar orders to tighten control were issued in other provinces in 1984.[29]

In the fall of 1984 the State Family Planning Commission warned local authorities to control more strictly the allowances for second births under Document No. 7. In July 1984 Wang Wei had said that "opening a small gap" should not be set against "blocking the large gap,"[30] but in September the SFPC noted that "some areas" had "overly relaxed the restrictions on the birth of a second child" and urged the cadres to "follow the regulations strictly."[31] In October an article in the national family planning journal said that "closing the big gap is a prerequisite and an important condition for doing well in opening a small gap."[32]

Meanwhile, on October 10 Wang Wei, in one of his most contradictory public statements, told a national family planning conference that the implementation of Document No. 7 had been "firm and effective" and that the cadres were changing their "work style" and showing more trust in the masses, but he also said that there was "great unevenness" in the work from one place to another. He added that the cadres lacked a "complete understanding" of Document No. 7 and were "ideologically confused" and that the initiative of birth control activists had been "blunted" by "mistakes in our work."[33] At almost the same time, the central family planning journal advised in an editorial that Document No. 7 could not simply be interpreted as saying "there is a relaxation in family planning work" and hence that the work could be slackened, nor should emphasis be placed on "taking charge firmly" without regard for doing a good job.[34]

These equivocal communications seemed to be overridden two weeks later by another article in the same journal citing a report from Guangdong Province which outlined the "essential and crucial points in family planning work" as follows:

1. To strengthen leadership. The crucial point in whether the masses implement birth control or not is whether the leadership has tight control over the matter or not.

2. To carry out the policy and birth control measures firmly, so that every couple of childbearing age will carry out their birth plans according to policy . . .

3. To persist in carrying out the "three combinations," which are (1) to combine education with economic sanctions. . . , (2) to combine carrying out the work on a regular basis with organizing necessary activities. . . , (3) to combine having the entire Party take part in the work with the work of the full-time family planning workers.

[Of] the three points mentioned above . . . the most important one is to strengthen Party and government leadership, otherwise the other two points will come to nothing.[35]

These statements indicate that central policy on family planning hardened during the late summer and fall of 1984.

The Third Interpretation—"Work Style" Reform

In December 1984, central policy shifted again, this time away from control of population growth and back toward improving relations with the masses, hence a softening of the line on family planning. The new signals were given at a national conference on "experimental" family planning work convened by the SFPC in Beijing at which Wang Wei and SFPC Assistant Director Zhou Boping both made important speeches. The full texts are not available, but summaries in the national family planning journal make it clear that family planning cadres were to stress "two services," that is, "to serve the overall situation and to serve the masses." The "overall situation" refers to the need to control population growth for the sake of economic development, but the emphasis this time was on the second expression, which implied avoidance of coercion and efforts to restore relations with the "masses."[36]

What prompted the change is not entirely clear, but it appears that a general drive for Party "rectification" and reform that had affected many other spheres of administration in China since early in the year had finally reached family planning work and taken precedence over concerns about lax implementation. At the conference on experimental work, Wang Wei said that Document No. 7 "shows the road to reform in family planning work" and "clarifies the direction of family planning work in the areas of ideology, policy, system, and work style." Explaining the reform program, he made six points, most of them characteristically vague and equivocal, that on balance seem to point toward moderation.[37]

The first point called for "straightening out the thinking" of family planning leaders, which apparently meant that they were to be conscious of the role of family planning in attaining national economic targets and goals, an idea with hard-line implications. The second point was to make family planning policy "more perfect," which can mean moderating the policy to appease the "masses" or tightening it to assure results; in this instance it seemed to mean the latter. The third point was to reform the family planning "contract system," the system under which families and units are obliged to commit themselves under contract to attain specific family planning targets; the "reform" was aimed at improving relations with the masses and persuading them to comply voluntarily, so this was a soft-line measure. The fourth point was to focus propaganda on solving "ideological problems" and providing technical information, implying more emphasis on persuasion, hence a soft-line measure. The fifth was to improve statistical work for family planning (meaning to get rid of falsification of statistics), a hard-line measure. The sixth was to improve work style and therefore clearly soft line.

The new policy was also conveyed at a two-week national conference on family planning propaganda and education held in Chengdu December 10–26, 1984. According to an article in the national family planning journal,

The conference . . . emphatically pointed out that propaganda work on birth control is meant to serve the masses. Propaganda and service are important tasks of the birth control departments . . . Therefore, in order to do a good job in our birth control propaganda work, we must establish the idea of trusting the masses, relying on the masses, and wholeheartedly serving the people. We must ideologically and emotionally shift our focus to "serving the masses."[38]

An accompanying editorial explained,

In 1985 . . . we must carry out reform in our birth control policies. Our policies must be established on the basis of showing understanding and reason, receiving the support of the masses, and making it easy for the cadres to do their work, as well as on the basis of seeking truth from facts . . .

We must carry out reform in our work style. We must earnestly set straight the relationship between our birth control cadres and the vast ranks of the masses and change from unilaterally asking the masses to do this and that to everywhere thinking on behalf of the masses, looking after the masses, doing everything for the people, and doing everything by relying on the people . . . Population targets transmitted from higher to lower levels must be flexible. Initiative must be given to the lower levels to permit family planning work to adapt to new conditions . . .[39]

The conference was told that the cadres must "truly move from the position of 'controlling the masses' to the position of 'serving the masses.'"[40] At a January mobilization meeting in Beijing, Wang Wei called on leading cadres to continue to have a "firm grasp" of family planning work, but he also advised them not to be "too rigid in delivering sermon[s] to the masses" and told them to become "people the masses can confide in."[41]

Until about March 1985 the new reform called for by the central authorities was echoed in provincial and local family planning dispatches. Shanghai's family planning commission said that propaganda must be used to induce the masses to practice family planning voluntarily.[42] Gansu, while insisting that there be no halt in family planning enforcement, urged that the policies be "gradually perfected" and "work style" improved.[43] Guangxi urged its cadres to "act as the close friends of the masses" and treat them as the "masters" and said that it had succeeded in effectively controlling population while maintaining close ties between the Party and the masses.[44] And Sichuan claimed that after using "a relatively simple work style" that had "created adverse opinions among the masses" in recent years, many cadres were now visiting the people they had abused to "make as many friends as possible" and were exhibiting "an attitude characterized by the heart of a dear mother, the advice of a grandmother, and the love of a sister."[45] But on the whole, the local response to the call for a change in work style seems to have been neither widespread nor strong.

The Fourth Interpretation—Ambiguities and Contradictions

By mid-February 1985 the enthusiasm of the central authorities for moderation and reform seems to have cooled and another shift in family planning policy appeared. In interviews for the Chinese radio network, Wang Wei claimed that great progress had already been made in improving work style since Document No. 7 was issued but said he was equally concerned with implementing family planning requirements and attaining targets.[46] Although at a March family planning conference he again alluded to the need "resolutely" to correct "the extremely bad work style of acting blindly" and "crudely and carelessly issuing orders and commands," his main emphasis was on preventing unauthorized births and fulfilling targets.

Even during the period when "serving the people" was the watchword, national family planning requirements had not been eased. In January 1985 the SFPC still insisted emphatically that "unplanned births must be prohibited."[47] Guizhou told its cadres that they must

> correctly propagate and implement the policy on planned parenthood work and resolutely forbid all births beyond the plan. It is necessary to lay stress on resolutely forbidding multiple births and to firmly grasp it and never slacken it.[48]

The Shaanxi provincial Party newspaper said that, although women who had successfully controlled births by other methods could continue to use them,

> either the husband or the wife of a couple that have two or more children should be sterilized. Ideological education and technical services should be stressed, particularly in areas where families tend to have many children. We should implement thoroughly our policy on sterilization in those areas and resort to remedial measures when dealing with pregnancies that do not comply with planning.[49]

In February the national family planning journal cited for emulation a Zhejiang town that had established a "control system" for temporary residents so that it could "mobilize" them to practice birth control. Under this system, "when unplanned pregnancies are discovered, they must be reported promptly to their units, which will assist in doing ideological and mobilization work."[50]

In March another locality was held up for emulation because of its aggressive punishment of four other problems viewed as "sabotage" of family planning:

> The [Shengqiu County, Henan] people's congress issued the following public notice:
> 1. Those who deliberately attack and take revenge against family planning cadres and destroy their crops and assets will be severely treated according to the seriousness of their cases. They will be investigated and held criminally responsible.
> 2. Those who secretly remove IUDs and issue false documents will be treated as sabotaging family planning.
> 3. Those who insist on having a second or excessive birth must be treated according to the prescribed policies. If they are Party members or cadres, it is proposed that they be given Party and administrative discipline.
> 4. Those who mistreat female babies and their mothers must be given severe punishment according to the seriousness of their cases and be held criminally responsible.[51]

On April 12, 1985, an editorial in the national family planning journal marking the first anniversary of Document No. 7 claimed great progress in making the policy "perfect," improving work style, and bringing about a closer relationship between the party and the masses, while still controlling population growth. It said that the cadres had changed their relationship to couples of childbearing age from one of "control" to one of "service."[52] The writer clearly expected that the reform of family planning tactics was to continue. Local reports asserted that people everywhere were saying that the policy was one which "loves the people," that family planning cadres had become "bosom friends" of the people, that they had altered their methods "from blocking and controlling to serving the masses," and that "the work style of the cadres has obviously changed."[53] During the next several months, the SFPC declared that the policy had won the support of the "broad masses," that family planning compliance was becoming increasingly voluntary, and that complaints about cadre work style received by the commission in 1984 were down 43 percent from 1983.[54] This was the first time the SFPC had revealed that it had received *any* complaints about work style.

While some sources were reporting this happy state of affairs, however, others were expressing concern over the poor performance of units that were "backward" in birth control work, the large numbers of "excessive" births, rising birth rates, the failure to control fertility among the temporary population in the cities, and the falsification of family planning statistics. As the year wore on, the family planning authorities were increasingly preoccupied with overcoming a "slack mood" among the cadres, and getting them to "grasp the work firmly" and meet their targets. In April Hunan's family planning cadres were told:

> We should continue to advocate the plan of one child per couple, and that a second child may be allowed provided that the conditions of the couple concerned meet the requirements and the couple has received approval from the authorities. We should resolutely check families with many children and the practice of having an additional child or children . . . Under no circumstances should the leadership slacken efforts.[55]

Guizhou's cadres were told to "put family planning work high on their agenda and seriously and properly grasp it" and to "fulfill the birth control plan."[56] The lieutenant governor of Sichuan said its cadres must "fulfill completely the various targets of family planning."[57] Hebei told a provincial forum that

> the key objective of the family planning program for 1985 in Hebei Province is to prevent each couple from conceiving and raising two or more than two children as part of a vigorous effort to cut to the minimum the number of counties which have lagged behind in family planning.[58]

In May the government of Guangxi called on its cadres to exhibit "determination" and overcome the "backwardness" of its family planning work and warned that

> units that fail to fulfill their family planning tasks will not be named advanced units. Cadres who fail to fulfill their family planning contract obligations will not be able to receive the full reward . . . Those cadres who are highly efficient and have achieved good results must be given large rewards and promoted.[59]

The Fujian provincial Party secretary told the cadres that they must not slacken efforts in family planning but should strengthen leadership and that they should "take a firm grip" on the work in May and June to assure fulfillment of the year's family planning targets.[60] Tianjin implemented a new form of population plan contract with local units designed to link local population targets with the national target of under 1.2 billion population by the year 2000.[61] The draft economic and social development plan for Shanxi Province said that in 1985 the cadres "should continue to grasp well the work of family planning and control the natural growth rate of the population to within . . . 8.9 per thousand."[62] Ningxia described its provincial plan for 1985 as follows:

> The natural growth rate of the population for 1985 is planned at 1.33 percent, and by the end of the year the population must be within 4.124 million. It is necessary to carry out propaganda and education in family planning and to provide technical services for family planning so as to ensure that the natural growth rate of the population will be kept within the limits of the plan.[63]

By April 1985 the central authorities became increasingly aware of the growing millions of "floating population" in the cities, rural migrants who are allowed to engage in licensed trade, industry, transport, construction, and service activities, who arrange for their own housing and food and are not registered as urban residents and therefore take advantage of their anomalous status to ignore family planning requirements.[64] They began to appear in major cities in the late 1970s, but at that time they tended to stay only for short periods, returning to their permanent residences in the rural areas from which they had come. After Deng Xiaoping's economic reforms in the early 1980s, their numbers increased sharply. Articles in the national family planning journal outlined the problem and solution as follows:

> The regulations on family planning in some places were just not able to touch them, and they remained in "nobody's jurisdiction . . ." We must do everything to eliminate the "nobody's jurisdiction" problem and let family planning work develop a closed circuit . . . Temporary household registration must be required . . . Birth control should be enforced . . . Measures to reward good and punish evil should be implemented.[65]

> After these people enter a city, their original place [of abode] loses control over them and the cities are unable to control them. As time goes by they form a "forgotten corner . . ." If no attention is paid to this "corner" and no practical measures are adopted in time, not only will family planning policy be affected but all the successes attained over the years will relapse for lack of a final effort.[66]

> The numbers of the floating population in and out of the cities and rural areas are increasing . . . [In Shijiazhuang

Municipality] control over these people is the responsibility of the district offices, which visit these people periodically, bring the records up-to-date, and hold meetings to explain the relevant policies and make specific demands on them . . . Some of the offices stipulate that residents, cadres, employees, and workers on leave of absence without any pay must show up in person once a month, undergo an examination each quarter, and be fluoroscoped every six months . . . All newly married couples who are expecting must show their planned birth certificates. Those who are unable to produce a permit will have to undergo birth control measures [abortions].[67]

Women of childbearing age [in Xinjin County, Sichuan] must first obtain approval and a certificate from the family planning cadre of their unit before carrying out the procedure for leaving their place of residence. Collectives which sign contracts for outside work [for contracting labor out] must sign a family planning contract at the same time . . . Women of childbearing age who are away for a long period of time should persist in having a physical examination every three months.[68]

In June the *People's Daily* printed a letter about the "serious problem" of migrant families in Yunnan Province who were "having children without paying attention to family planning":

They are all in the prime of life. Many of them have brought their wives with them. One of their purposes in bringing their wives with them is to give birth to more children . . . Their answers to the question why they have done so are almost the same: "I would never have been permitted to give birth to another child in my home village. Since I am from another locality and my residence is not registered here, nobody will interfere with how many children I am going to have."[69]

The attempt by migrant workers to escape the surveillance of their local family planning cadres in order to have unauthorized children is one of many incidental indications in Chinese sources that, despite protests to the contrary by Chinese officials, especially in pronouncements addressed to foreign audiences, family planning in China is *not* voluntary.

During the summer of 1985 the central and provincial family planning authorities again tried to curb excessive coercion. In July 1985 Shandong issued a general notice charging that some of its cadres had used their powers and positions to ride roughshod over the masses and seek personal gain. A few cadres acted crudely, forced and ordered the masses to do something, and even acted as tyrants in causing some people to die. The problems are especially prominent in the fields of readjusting land, procuring grain, collecting retention funds, planning for new villages, electing members of organs of political power at the grassroots level, and practicing the family planning policy.[70]

In August Jilin Province claimed that it had achieved good results in family planning recently because the cadres

changed from just giving orders and maintaining control to looking at the orders and examining what methods and measures are being used to carry out the orders. In their methods of control they changed from giving the masses a hard time and controlling them to serving the masses. In their birth control measures they changed from relying principally on technical measures [i.e., IUD insertion, sterilization, and abortion] to combining allowances for individual differences with the practice of birth control measures.[71]

In September a general article in the national family planning journal, implicitly admitting that the coercion problem was not over, warned:

We must pay attention to two kinds of errors now made by family planning cadres everywhere. The first error is to believe that policies are improving gradually, that the work is going well, and so there is no reason to make still greater efforts in education and propaganda. The second error is to believe that propaganda and education do not solve problems and that stern measures will do the job. Thus two tendencies have appeared in practical work: One is to yield to the wishes of a certain number of the masses that a general arrangement be made for a second child and not actively do propaganda and explanation work. The second is to carry out frequent rebuking and suppressing, thereby raising tensions in the relationship with the masses . . .
It is . . . important not to believe that if individuals do not change their thinking at once, primitive, harsh measures may be used to force them to submit. Harsh measures are often counterproductive.[72]

In the latter quotation, as in other disavowals of coercion by the central authorities, the concern, obviously, is not about the adverse effects on the victims but about the adverse effects on the program.
But the main preoccupation of the authorities in 1985 was with

the failure of some localities to implement policies, the threat of a new "baby boom," and the need to "strictly control population growth." In April they had been concerned about the "uneven" implementation of the policies and the large number of "backward" units.[73] Shandong Province inspected its "backward" units and found that "above quota" births were "out of control," leadership was negligent, and organization was weak.[74] Guangxi proposed to deny cash awards to backward units.[75]

Later in the year the same problem was discovered in several other areas. Inner Mongolia reported that it had thirteen county level units in which more than 20 percent of the births were second parity or higher, and in one the proportion was almost 40 percent; Gansu said it had twenty-two counties in which the combined rate for births "not covered by the plan" and "excessive" births was over 35 percent and in some counties the figure was over 43 percent; and Zhejiang noted that there were some "weak links" in various places.[76] In December the national family planning journal said that "family planning work in about one-fourth of the areas in the country is still comparatively backward."[77]

Several provinces reported that birth rates were rising and that population was again beginning to increase. In October Guangxi said it had 11,000 more births in the first half of 1985 than in the same period in 1984.[78] Shanxi said that some units had registered an increase in births "beyond the plan" and a rise in the rate of second and higher order births during the first half of 1985:

> This high rate of births was caused mainly by a lack of comprehensive understanding of the Central Committee's policy on improving the family planning program, by overly emphasizing material production and neglecting population proliferation, by failing to come to grips with these two aspects of production in some prefectures and units, by the execution of a liberalization policy by some prefectures, and by the failure of some Party members, cadres, and China Youth League members to carry out the Central Committee's policy calling on each couple to bear only one child, because some of them have even gone so far as to encourage their wives to bear three or four children or more.[79]

In November Hebei said:

> Although we have scored very many achievements in this work since the beginning of this year, we failed to block the big hole in unplanned births. From January to September, unplanned births totaled more than 70,000, and there are

more than 10,000 pregnant women ready to have unplanned births this year. In addition, there are 600,000 people who have not used any contraceptive methods . . .

We should greatly strengthen basic work, conscientiously implement various contraceptive and remedial measures, and resolutely block the big hole in unplanned births.[80]

Liaoning reported, however, that multiple births and births "not covered by the plan" had declined in the province since the previous year. Accordingly, it announced on October 5:

From now on, any couple in which at least one spouse is a peasant and which has only one daughter may ask to have another child. If the couple really has practical difficulties, consideration will be given to allowing them the right to bear a second child in line with the stipulated conditions and with the approval of the department concerned . . . However, none of the couples covered by the aforementioned conditions will be allowed to break the limits for bearing children; still less will they be allowed to have yet more children not covered by plans.[81]

As 1985, the final year of the Sixth Five-Year Plan period, drew to a close, the prospects of fulfilling its population plan looked good, thanks largely to the low rate of population growth in 1983 and 1984 caused by the highly coercive 1983 family planning drive, with its 35 million sterilizations and abortions. In September 1985 an article in the national family planning journal noted that projections based on the year-end 1984 population total and the trend of the first eight months of 1985 indicated that the year-end 1985 figure would be some 10 million less than the planned target of 1,060 million. Family planning work, the writer observed, had gained "new strength" during the Sixth Five-Year Plan period.[82] In October another writer said that the target would "definitely be reached" and added that the emphasis during the Seventh Five-Year Plan period would be on preventing a third birth peak from taking place.[83]

Concern about a third birth peak had been expressed several times by the central authorities in 1984 and 1985. In March 1984 an editorial in the national family planning journal said that

we must clearly see that the task ahead of us is still very difficult . . . The next 10 years will be a birth peak period for the population of China, therefore family planning work cannot be slackened.[84]

In September 1984 Wang Wei also called attention to the forthcoming "baby boom."[85] In July 1985 an article in China's leading demographic

51

journal said that the Seventh Five-Year Plan period would be "crucial" for population growth in China as the cohorts born during the second birth peak reached the childbearing ages and that the task of controlling population growth would become "quite arduous."[86] In October papers presented at a national census conference noted that China's total fertility rate, which had dropped by half in the previous ten years, would swing back in the next ten years to the level at the beginning of the 1980s.[87]

As was to be expected, the provincial authorities echoed these concerns. In September Guangxi told its cadres:

> Practice has shown that if family planning work is neglected, the population will explode; if the work is carried out in a blind and unplanned manner, the relations between cadres and the masses will worsen; and if things are left to drift along in family planning work, it will be difficult to control population growth.[88]

In October Tianjin said that the municipality would soon experience a third baby boom, Shandong conveyed the same message in December, and the warning was repeated by other provinces,[89] all echoing the national line.

The Fifth Interpretation—Firm Control

As fears about the "baby boom" rose, the demand that population growth be controlled became more insistent. The draft Seventh Five-Year Plan, adopted by a national Party conference in September 1985, included the following section on population:

> We must strictly control population growth, expand public health services, and improve people's health. During the plan period, the number of persons entering the marriage and childbirth years will reach a peak. We must place greater emphasis on family planning, carry it out unswervingly, and try to reduce the average annual population growth rate to 12.5 per thousand within five years.[90]

In November Wang Wei, in his usual equivocal fashion, cautioned against "one-sidedness" in carrying out family planning work:

> In order to attain good social efficiency, we must guide family planning work meticulously . . . If we only pay attention to population quotas but neglect the opinions of the masses, it cannot be said that good social efficiency has been achieved. If we only pay attention to the opinions of the masses but fail to carry out mass work and let them carry

on freely causing a loss of control, it cannot be said that good social efficiency has been achieved.

He also repeated some of the ideas from the previous winter that had not been mentioned for many months:

Family planning is related to the interests of the masses. Without the support of the masses and their voluntary action, it is impossible to implement family planning. Family planning cadres at all levels must resolutely have faith in the masses, rely on them, care about them, and serve them wholeheartedly.

But he again made clear that these benign sentiments did not mean that one should defer to the wishes of the masses in regard to having children:

The emphasis in family planning work is not only on meeting a certain population plan quota but also on relieving the masses of the influence of old ideology, on changing their customs, habits, and views on having children. Changing their views on having children is a long process in the construction of socialist spiritual civilization. This demands that we persist in taking firm charge of the construction relentlessly.[91]

Thus the cadres were charged not just with changing the numbers of children born to Chinese couples but also with changing their attitudes toward having children.

In December an article in the national family planning journal almost seemed to take issue with Wang. To consider the needs of the country and the wishes of the people in family planning was "entirely realistic," it argued, but "if we only stressed the wishes of the masses and permitted two children per couple universally, together with some excessive births, our population would reach 1.3 billion by the end of this century and . . . 1.8 billion . . . by 2050." The author concluded:

In addition to a reasonable and fair policy and a realistic population target, we must take firm charge of the work. Without taking firm charge of the work, even with a correct policy and a correct population target, it is difficult to achieve results . . . We must resolutely and strictly control the growth of the population.[92]

Despite Wang's temporizing, firm control was becoming the main theme in family planning policy at the end of 1985.

That message had already been received at the provincial level.

In November and December 1985 numerous local news items on family planning echoed the injunction to "strictly control population growth" and demanded stronger leadership, a firm grasp, thorough implementation of policies, and the "resolute" curbing of "unplanned" and "excessive" births.[93]

Anxiety about the birth peak increased in 1986. In January the authorities announced that, according to the Seventh Five-Year Plan, "family planning must be placed in a more important position" and "population growth must be resolutely and strictly controlled."[94] These demands were repeated in provincial pronouncements.[95] In March a *People's Daily* article called on leaders of the Party and government to "implement the spirit of Document No. 7," which had been reinterpreted to emphasize "effective control over population growth" and the fulfillment of the Seventh Five-Year Plan targets based on the target of "under 1.2 billion" in the year 2000.[96]

Early in 1986 official circles were still ostensibly optimistic about the likelihood of meeting these targets. In February the New China News Agency announced that at the end of 1985 China's population totalled 1,046 million, 14 million less than the target of 1,060 for 1985 in the Sixth Five-Year Plan, according to the State Family Planning Commission, which was confident that the figure could be kept under the 1.2 billion mark by the year 2000.[97] Some provinces reported that they had bettered their own Sixth Five-Year Plan targets for population size, natural increase rates, and numbers of births.[98] Local leaders in China often try to exceed their targets to gain special recognition, awards, and advancement, but their efforts to impress their superiors also increase the pressure on lower levels cadres and on the people.

Although they were aware of the prospective difficulties in reaching future targets, the authorities did not change the provincial population targets that had been based on the 1.2 billion in the year 2000. According to the Seventh Five-Year Plan, the national population was to be kept "within 1,113 million" as of the end of 1990, and the average national growth rate was to be limited to around 12.4 per thousand per year.[99]

Consistent with these figures, some provinces announced new targets for 1986 and 1990 and reaffirmed the old targets for the year 2000. Hunan demanded that the provincial natural increase rate be kept below 9 per thousand during the Seventh Five-Year Plan period.[100] Guizhou told its cadres they must "strive" to control the natural increase rate at under 10 per thousand in 1986, increase the "planned birth rate" to 70 percent, and reduce the percentage of "excessive" births to 15 percent.[101] Shanxi was committed to keeping its natural increase rate below 10.5 per thousand during the Seventh Five-Year Plan period and limiting the population to about 27.6 million by the end of 1990.[102] Qinghai was to keep its population under 4.47 million by 1990.[103] Shanghai said that during the Seventh Five-Year Plan period its natural increase rate "must be controlled at 6.5 per thousand."[104] Sichuan confidently reaffirmed its long-established goal of keeping the population under 120 million by the year 2000.[105]

As the year wore on, however, pessimistic reports continued to come in from some provinces. Anhui noted a slackening of effort and fear of difficulties among family planning cadres in some areas and an upswing in birth rates, unplanned second births, and "excessive" births and added that early marriage and childbearing were a serious problem.[106] A survey in Shaanxi found that "the proportion of early marriages is still high and the number of excessive births is considerable," and a subsequent report said the reason was that the cadres were "afraid of confusion" and were "seeking stability" instead of enforcing policies.[107] Sichuan reported that in some areas the numbers of "unplanned" pregnancies and births had increased compared with 1985 and that the proportion of couples accepting "one-child certificates" had declined.[108] Hunan reported a "rising trend of having an additional child."[109] Guangdong said that there were "many instances" of rural women having second children "in excess of the plan" and that "state cadres, workers, and urban residents, who were not eligible for second births under current policies, were also starting to press for permission to have a second child."[110] Guizhou detected signs of a rise in the birth rate.[111]

Meanwhile, surveys showed that a significant proportion of the population, especially in rural areas, still wanted two or more children. Some of the studies seem to have been designed to show popular support for official policies, but even so the persistence of traditional preferences was evident in the reported results. A Zhejiang study used a "sample" of 1,571 unmarried young people in the ages 15 to 30, of whom only 237 were "ordinary peasants," yet even in this highly urban group 28 percent wanted to have two children.[112] A survey of one-child households in the rural suburbs of Tianjin Municipality found that "about 80 percent" of them hoped to have two children and that some of them had accepted one-child certificates only because they felt they "had no choice but to follow the main trend."[113] A survey in Beijing reportedly showed that "less than one-third of the young people in the city proper want to have two or more children," but another in Sichuan found that 65.9 percent of the Han people wanted two children, 82.9 percent of Sichuan's

Tibetan minority also wanted two, and 75 percent of its Yi minority wanted at least three.[114] In China, where the wishes of the authoritarian government are well known and dissenting opinions might lead to investigation, such surveys probably understate the extent of popular disagreement with official policies. Hence these results showed conclusively that, contrary to frequent Chinese claims, the one-child limit did not reflect the wishes of the people.

Another perennial problem that was becoming more acute was the falsification of data on plan fulfillment by local cadres and officials. The tendency seems to be inherent in the Chinese administrative system and affects all kinds of statistical data. Diatribes against falsification of economic statistics go back to the 1950s. Complaints about falsified family planning data have been recurrent at least since 1980,[115] and the problem reportedly has mushroomed as the pressures on the cadres for attainment of population targets have increased. In 1984 only a few such reports appeared in the Chinese media.[116] In 1985 reported instances became more numerous.[117] In July 1985 an SFPC circular acknowledged that "underreporting and misreporting of statistics is fairly severe in some areas" and that "the main reason is to gain honor by cheating."[118] A report from Liaoning Province in August was more explicit about the reasons:

> Some units, in reporting to superiors on birth rates and rates of natural increase, reported what was pleasing and not what was unpleasing, and the circumstances of deception were rather serious. . . . There are two reasons for this deception: 1) The thinking guiding the affairs of the . . . birth planning committee is not sufficiently correct. In order to compete for top place throughout the province and ensure that they are progressive, they have year after year, when transmitting instructions, raised the quota to where it is not in keeping with reality. 2) A minority of basic level cadres, in order to get money awards, have taken the incorrect approach of "concealing information" and "giving false information."[119]

An article in the national family planning journal in November 1985 added:

> A few leadership persons in the pursuit of a name for themselves do not put effort into their work but instead work on the data which they report to their supervisors. Some of the family planning cadres are afraid that they will be reprimanded if they fail to report the truth to their supervisors, and yet they are [also] afraid that if they report

the truth they will be given "tight shoes" to wear by the local government leadership.[120]

In January 1986 a letter to the same journal said that some local leaders advise their cadres to report fewer births to make things easier at the year-end evaluations.[121] In March another letter writer said that a survey in his area had found a "shocking" number of cases of omission and concealment of births.[122] By the latter part of 1988 the problem was apparently worse, and the authorities at last began to have some idea of its seriousness. In October 1988 the *People's Daily* said that when provincial birth rates obtained in a 1987 national sample survey were compared with the figures given in the regular statistical reports:

> Four [provinces] . . . had a difference of less than 10 percent, three had a difference between 10 and 20 percent, six had a difference between 20 and 30 percent, ten had a difference between 30 and 40 percent, and six had a difference of more than 40 percent.[123]

In December a national journal added that the true national birth rate for 1987 was 2.22 per thousand higher than the reported figure of 21.04 per thousand, implying a national undercount of births of just under ten percent. This does not appear to be compatible with the figures in the quotation if all the differences are in the same direction.[124] About the causes of the undercount, however, there is no disagreement. As the *People's Daily* article puts it:

> The targets set are unreasonable . . . During the process of signing the responsibility contracts from the higher levels to the lower levels, the targets are raised from level to level, making the targets progressively higher and harder to reach. As a result, the leadership at the grassroots levels conceal statistics to evade their responsibility . . . Some local leaders . . . compete in setting targets with no regard for reality. When they fail to reach the targets, they falsify the figures.[125]

Meanwhile, Chinese demographers continued to warn the authorities about the forthcoming birth peak. In February 1986 an eminent demographer pointed out that fertility levels in China were already low and that further declines would therefore be more difficult to achieve.[126] In April three writers in the national family planning journal estimated that within the next eleven years 230 million children would be born if women entering the childbearing ages were assumed to have an average of 1.2 children each. This, they said, would mean that the natural increase rate would rise and the national population total would reach 1.2 billion before the year 2000.[127] In the same month Deng Xiaoping explained to Japanese Prime Minister Fukuda that "strict control over population growth" was in China's best interests and that the country was "striving" to control the population at 1.2 billion by the end of the century.[128] But in May, another article in the national family planning journal pointed to the inertial property of demographic phenomena and raised doubts about whether the goal could be attained.[129] The general mood by late spring 1986 was one of deepening pessimism.

4
Party Document No. 13
and the Crackdown

In response to the growing uncertainty about the effectiveness of local family planning efforts, the prospects for eradicating traditional values about childrearing, and the likelihood of achieving the population targets in the Seventh Five-Year Plan, the central authorities launched a new policy initiative. In May 1986 they adopted and disseminated a new set of guidelines called Party Central Committee Document No. 13, which was said to clarify the provisions of Document No. 7 of April 1984.

Contents of Document No. 13

Like No. 7, this document has not been published, but several descriptions of its contents and a few direct quotations have appeared in print. On June 13, 1986, an article in the national family planning journal called attention to a recent circular by the State Family Planning Commission which "demanded that all areas study and implement Document No. 13 conscientiously." The circular noted that Document 13 "affirms the achievements of family planning work during the Sixth Five-Year Plan period in controlling population, improving work style, building closer relations between the Party and the masses, promoting stability and unity, and socialist construction," which means that the Party leaders do not acknowledge any policy mistakes in the previous five years. Apparently summarizing the message of Document No. 13, the article continues:

> The Party Central Committee in particular points out that during the Seventh Five-Year Plan period, the population will be in the midst of a birth peak. Party committees at all levels must strengthen their leadership to strictly control population growth, must not lower their guard and become negligent, must conscientiously sum up experiences, overcome defects, solve problems, and continuously make their birth control policies better.

The article adds that Central Committee Document No. 13 is "of very great significance in giving guidance,"[1] which serves notice that provincial and local policies must conform to it. An August article quoted from the Document itself: "Policies which are favorable to controlling population growth and which can be accepted by the masses by means of education must be formulated based on reality."[2]

A third article cited several instructions in Document No. 13 on strengthening family planning organizations:

> Document No. 13 points out that "the building of family planning cadre ranks must be truly strengthened," and that "cadres who are resolute in executing the Party's guidelines and policies, who have an upright work style, who know the business, and who are devoted to this work must be promoted. The leadership of family planning work organs at all levels must be consolidated and strengthened . . ." Document No. 13 also points out that "the organizational structure must be strengthened."[3]

In September two other direct quotations from Document No. 13 appeared in the national family planning journal:

> Document No. 13 states that "Party committees and governments at all levels must attach importance to supervising departments of health, civil affairs, planning, finance, medicine, industry, and commerce, labor unions, Communist Youth Leagues, and women's associations and [must] take family planning work as one of their important tasks. They must furnish the necessary manpower, materials, and technical skills to reach the population control targets stipulated in the Seventh Five-Year Plan together with family planning departments." This requires that we take more initiative and perform the services well.[4]

> Document No. 13 states that "those areas and units which are trailing behind must adopt effective measures to catch up in their family planning work."[5]

In December 1986 a provincial source disclosed that Document No. 13 contained six major instructions: (1) to strengthen leadership and control fertility strictly to eliminate birth peaks during the Seventh Five-Year Plan period; (2) to focus family planning efforts on rural areas and especially on units where the work was lagging; (3) to "start from reality and formulate policies that are conducive to controlling population growth and are acceptable to the absolute majority of the masses after education"; (4) to strengthen research, investigation, and statistical analysis; (5) to strengthen family planning organizations and improve the quality of the cadres; and (6) to strengthen coordination between departments in support of family planning work. The emphasis throughout was on results and targets.[6]

Implementing the Guidelines

Immediately after it was issued, the provinces reported that they were studying the document and taking action to implement it. In June 1986, Anhui Province held a meeting of directors of prefectural and municipal family planning commissions for this purpose.[7] At the end of the month, a Guangxi official called for study and implementation of Document No. 13 and said that it "sums up the situation and basic experiences in birth control work during the Sixth Five-Year Plan, points out the existing problems, and also gives views on further improving birth control work during the Seventh Five-Year Plan." He also reaffirmed the "three-no-change" principle that had been mentioned in local dispatches for several years and was apparently repeated either in the SFPC circular or in Document 13 itself: No change in birth control as a basic state policy; no change in the one-child policy; and no change in the goal of 1.2 billion by the year 2000.[8]

From July onward similar announcements were made in Sichuan, Tianjin, Hunan, Hebei, Shaanxi, and Haerbin Municipality,[9] and other provinces announced measures to tighten up their birth control work without ascribing them to Document No. 13. Among the recurrent demands in the local dispatches were the familiar injunctions to "strengthen leadership," "grasp the work firmly," insist on the one-child limit, use IUDs for women with one child, sterilization for couples with two or more children, and abortion for unauthorized pregnancies, and meet the population targets for the Seventh Five-Year Plan period. Here are some examples:

> The meeting demanded that the province get a still better grasp of birth control work, bring population growth control onto the track of economic development, and continue to control the province's population growth. [Anhui][10]

> The provincial family planning conference . . . stressed: We should never ignore family planning work and should firmly grasp it. In the future our province should continue to advocate the one-couple, one-child policy and to strictly control the excessively rapid increase in population. [Jilin][11]

> Place the control of population growth at the forefront and . . . change the backward situation [that exists] in 40 percent of the [local] areas. [Hunan][12]

At the provincial family planning work conference [it was] pointed out that we should continue to strictly control population growth . . . We should thoroughly and deeply grasp basic family planning work . . . We should firmly foster the idea of strictly controlling population growth . . . and strive to make a new change within this year to fulfill the population control task assigned by the provincial Party committee and the provincial government. [Shandong][13]

[Lt. Governor] Wang Zuwu demanded at the meeting that the Party and government leadership at all levels attach great importance to the matter and strictly control population growth resolutely and relentlessly. [Hebei][14]

Hubei's population must be kept below 26 million by the end of 1990 . . . Strictly ban . . . the birth of a second or [additional] child not included in the plan without any exceptions. This means/that for quite a long time to come, both in the urban and rural areas, a couple can have only one child. [Hubei][15]

[The Shaanxi] provincial authorities have decided that from the middle of [October] to the end of November, the activities of publicizing the documents from the central authorities on firmly grasping birth control and taking remedial measures should be extensively carried out in all urban and rural areas throughout the province All prefectures and cities must really strengthen leadership . . . [16]

From now to the end of this century, Sichuan must control planned parenthood work, not relax it. [17]

The Party committee and government of the Guangxi Region recently issued a joint circular which stressed that "currently the state's family planning policy's principal content is to promote universally one child per couple, late marriage, late birth, and to strictly prohibit unplanned second births, excessive births, and the opening of 'crooked gaps.' "[18]

Assistant Secretary Yue Qifeng of the Hebei Provincial Party Committee said . . . that couples with two or more children should undergo sterilization . . . Those for whom IUDs are suitable should be fitted [with them] and those who are unable to use IUDs must sign a contract to use other forms of contraception and be subjected to periodic inspections . . . Those who have unplanned pregnancies must be resolutely subjected to remedial measures. [19]

If we do not step up family planning work, population will surely get out of control . . . We must mobilize the masses to vigorously . . . implement the measures for birth control and remedial measures. [Yunnan][20]

Meanwhile, the national family planning journal carried articles addressed to the whole country in which the escalation of family planning demands was apparent. In June 1986 a plenary session of the SFPC over which Wang Wei presided was told that because the fulfillment of the Seventh Five-Year Plan targets would be "very difficult," "family planning work must be firmly grasped . . . and not be slackened . . ."[21] In July another article in the same journal asserted that "the population problem is one of the most acute problems in the world" and, taking Anhui as an example, warned:

If the policy were not carried out with effort, the number of births would exceed the projected number. The target of controlling the provincial population at 61 million by the end of this century as decided upon by the State would come to naught. This grim reality shows that family planning is inevitable. It may only be carried out firmly and cannot be slackened. We must resolutely carry out the population policy formulated by the Party Central Committee and the State Council. We must exert our efforts to take charge relentlessly . . . and have steadfast confidence in fulfilling the Seventh Five-Year population plan.[22]

In August, with a forthrightness unusual in domestic communications and even rarer in Chinese statements for foreign consumption, the journal acknowledged:

The population policy created to fulfill this population plan has met with interference from the old view of having children which has had an influence over the masses for thousands of years. Thus, a contradiction has appeared between birth policies and the masses' wishes about having children.[23]

But the article made it clear that the wishes of the masses must not be allowed to deter family planning work, because "our government recognizes from grim reality that birth planning is related to important matters of national wealth and strength, the prosperity of the people, and family happiness." Hence the work must be pushed forward now and in time the masses will come to accept it:

The contradiction between birth policies and the wishes of the masses is not permanent and is not without a solution, because China's population plan and population policy represent the fundamental interests of the people. Following economic and cultural development and the penetration of family planning work, contradictions will gradually be re-solved.[24]

Eliminating Unauthorized Births

In September 1986 an article in the national family planning journal, citing the coming birth peak, the loss of control over population growth in "a few areas," and the concern about exceeding the target population total of 1.2 billion in the year 2000, reiterated the renewed hard line on family planning:

> Fundamentally, from now to the end of this century, family planning work is not to "relax" but to "control." In other words, we must resolutely control the rate of population increase.[25]

In October an article in the *People's Daily* again explained the reasoning behind the new urgency attached to enforcement of family planning requirements:

> At present our family planning work is still facing a stern situation. This is because the coming 10 years and more between now and the end of this century will be a crucial period for our economic development. At the same time it will be a period of another baby boom in our country. Whether we can strictly control population growth will directly determine whether we can smoothly achieve our economic development objectives by the end of this century. In order to ensure the overall interests of our nation, we must continue to do effective work to tighten birth control so as to keep our country's population below 1.2 billion people by the end of this century.[26]

At a national family planning conference on December 2 Wang Wei said that population growth had been accelerating since the beginning of 1986 and that the number of births in 1986 would be a million greater than in 1985.[27] Premier Zhao Ziyang, speaking "in a firm tone," warned family planning officials that they must find a better way to control population growth and said that "the present family planning policy should remain in force for at least the next dozen years."[28] Beginning in January 1987, national and provincial directives insisted that China's family planning policies have not changed and that policies at the local level must be "stabilized."[29] In March an article in a national journal said that

> the fundamental policy of strictly controlling population growth must persist . . . In 1986 some areas slackened the

work of controlling population growth. As a result, the proportion of excessive births is rising . . . According to a sample survey carried out by the State Statistical Bureau, China's birth rate rose from 17.8 per thousand in 1985 to 20.77 per thousand last year and her natural increase rate rose from 11.23 per thousand to 14.08 per thousand. This fact reminds us that family planning work must continue to be grasped tightly.[30]

In April 1987 an article in the *People's Daily* said that the net increase in population in 1986 was 1.86 million more than was authorized in the national population plan and that if this trend continued the excess would be 8 million by the end of the Seventh Five-Year Plan in 1990, which would make it difficult to control the population to 1.2 billion in the year 2000.[31] Although Premier Zhao Ziyang expressed confidence in July that the target of "about 1.2 billion" in the year 2000 could still be attained,[32] others warned that if population growth continued at the 1986 rate, the total could overshoot the target by 84 million.[33]

By the middle of 1987 there was talk of revising the year 2000 target upward to 1.25 billion,[34] but even this figure was in danger of being exceeded.[35] Fears were expressed about China's ability to raise living standards and even to feed its population unless the goal was reached.[36] In December the national family planning journal affirmed that from an ecological standpoint the optimum population for China was between 700 million and one billion, implying a need to maintain below-replacement fertility into the twenty-first century.[37]

The authorities were convinced that China faced "grim realities" in regard to population growth.[38] Talk about a new "birth peak" or "baby boom," an "acute population problem," and a "population explosion" became more frantic than ever.[39] Reports of increasing birth rates came from many provinces. The rise in births was said to be due in part to the growing numbers of young people born between the middle 1960s and early 1970s, who were entering the ages of marriage and childbearing, but it was also attributed to the relaxation of local family planning efforts, which had resulted in earlier marriage and childbearing and increasing numbers of second and higher order births. In many localities population growth was "out of control."[40] The situation was described vividly in an article in the national family planning journal about family planning in Hunan Province, where "the higher-ups yelled vigorously, while the lower levels loosened their hold."[41]

In April 1987 the journal called for "strict control of unplanned births" and demanded that birth quotas be distributed among cou-

65

ples in accordance with "the set population targets."[42] Similar instructions were issued through the *People's Daily* by a spokesman for the State Family Planning Commission in June.[43] In August an editorial in the national family planning journal said that "effective measures" must be adopted to end the "passive state" of family planning work in the "backward areas,"[44] which reportedly constituted more than 30 percent of local areas in China.[45]

Like family planning work, the promotion of late marriage and childbirth had been neglected during the middle 1980s. An official of the SFPC said in June that in the past two years "the proportion of late marriages declined and that of early marriages increased."[46] According to official figures, the percentage of late marriages dropped from 59 in 1984 to 39 in 1986.[47] Late marriage is currently defined as after age twenty-three for women and twenty-five for men, but the authorities have had difficulty in holding young people even to the minimum marriage ages stipulated in the 1981 marriage law—twenty for women and twenty-two for men. In July 1987 another SFPC official said that marriages below the legal age limits accounted for 15 to 20 percent of rural marriages in 1986,[48] and an SFPC document of January 1988 calling for a ban on illegal marriages said that "6.1 million Chinese have married at under the legal age over the past few years." The source added that many rural young people live together after a private ceremony but without marriage registration.[49]

In January 1988 the national family planning journal said that early marriage and cohabitation without marriage had become "a serious social problem."[50] The children of illegal marriages, who were seen by the authorities as "born out of wedlock," were to be treated as "unplanned births" and penalized accordingly.[51] Sichuan Province had issued a "circular" in 1987 which "demanded"

> that all areas truly stop early marriages, early births, and births out of wedlock to control population growth . . . Illegal relationships which should be dissolved must be dissolved . . . Those who are pregnant out of wedlock and have not reached the legal marriage age must undergo remedial operations within the prescribed time.[52]

But the trend toward earlier marriage was not easily halted. A 1988 survey found that the average age at marriage in China had dropped by almost two years for both men and women between 1982 and 1987, resulting in a two-year drop in the age of childbearing.[53] An official of the Chinese Civil Affairs Ministry recently stated that early marriage and childbirth causes about 2.5 million "unplanned" births in China each year.[54]

The Second-Child Loophole

The relaxation of family planning had also resulted in widespread disregard of the narrowly defined categories of couples "with special difficulties" who were to be allowed a second child. More and more couples who could not qualify were declared exempt from the rules and permitted to go ahead. In July 1987 the State Statistical Bureau revealed that the 1984 policy of allowing localities in Liaoning, Shaanxi, and Shandong that had strong family planning organizations to "experiment" with letting rural families with an only daughter have another child had led to an abandonment of restrictions on second births in other areas. By the end of 1986, 70 percent of the villages in Shandong were authorized to approve second births in such cases, but 80 percent of the "unplanned" births in the province in that year occurred in villages that had *not* been so authorized.[55] In Jilin Province the proportion of couples having a second child went from 5 percent in 1984 to 60 percent in 1986.[56] The corresponding national figures were 10 percent and 50 percent.[57]

It was said that because the policies varied from one place to another, "the masses compared the differences and emulated the ones with the largest 'openings.' "[58] Apparently, local cadres in other regions had taken the "experimental" policies as a sign that the central authorities were on the point of abandoning the one-child policy, and this probably contributed to the rumors throughout the country from 1984 onward that everyone was now allowed a second child.

The central authorities demanded that tight control of second births be resumed. A national journal warned in March 1987 that the stipulations for second children had not been changed and must be strictly enforced.[59] The family planning journal said in April that "improving" the policy did not mean expanding the categories of persons allowed a second child and that they must not yield to the masses' desires to have more children.[60] In July local authorities were warned to "adhere strictly to the criteria" for second births,[61] and the same injunction was issued by Acting Premier Li Peng in January 1988.[62]

Accordingly, the provinces spread the word. Hunan complained that many places were allowing everyone to have a second child under the guise of "perfecting the policies" and that controls must now be strengthened.[63] Qinghai warned that some areas allowed too many exemptions from the regulations.[64] Shaanxi ordered that the "indiscriminate granting of exemptions" be stopped.[65] Henan said couples could have a second child "only after going through the correct procedure."[66] Guizhou told its cadres to "refrain from granting exemptions beyond the limits set by the documents."[67] Heilongjiang said second births must be curbed in accordance with the policies.[68]

For all other couples the one-child rule was to be reimposed. The principal means was to insert IUDs in women with one child, sterilize couples with two or more children, and abort all unauthorized pregnancies—the same demands that had led to the massive escalation of coercion in 1983. A Yunnan circular on family planning said, "We must mobilize the masses to vigorously and conscientiously implement the measures for birth control and remedial measures."[69] Hebei Province told its cadres that in 1987 they must

> make efforts to ensure that 90 percent of the women of childbearing age who already have a child use IUDs, 90 percent of the child-bearing women with two children and more receive tubal ligations, remedies [abortions] be given to 90 percent of the unplanned pregnant women, fines be imposed on 90 percent of the women who violate regulations on family planning work, the birth control rate reach 90 percent, and multiple births [births of second and higher parity children] be controlled below 1 percent . . . The Party committees and governments at all levels should conscientiously strengthen leadership over the work. Principal responsible comrades of the Party committees and governments should define management targets for ensuring the fulfillment of the planned population growth targets and the economic construction targets.[70]

Cadres on Hainan Island, Guangdong Province, were told to

> quickly put an end to the passive state in our family planning work . . . We must resolutely promote the work of collecting fees imposed on those who have exceeded the limit set on the number of births for the purpose of promoting the implementation of measures for sterilization . . . Our current emergency task of promoting family planning work must center on energetically stressing remedial measures for unscheduled pregnancies. At the same time, we must pay attention to stressing tubal ligations for those who have already given birth to two children.[71]

> It is necessary to focus on remedial measures regarding pregnancies not covered by the plan and also to do a good job in carrying out ligation surgery after the birth of a second child and inserting intrauterine devices after the birth of a first.[72]

Regional family planning work has been progressing slowly, and the number of completed sterilization operations has been on the low side.[73]

Guizhou told its cadres to take "remedial measures" as the "focal point" of work in 1987 to "ensure the fulfillment of the population plan."[74] Liang Jimin, Director of the General Office of the State Family Planning Commission, said that "abortion remains the chief means of birth control" and that the number of abortions was equal to half the number of births.[75]

Even minorities, who had previously been shown more lenient treatment under the family planning program, were not exempt from these measures. The human rights organization Asia Watch learned from interviews that in Tibet

a pregnant woman, prior to the birth of a [third] child, is given medicine to induce an abortion. Things are done in this way. One doesn't have the freedom to abort or not. If a woman is in a hospital and in the course of an examination [it is seen that she is pregnant], the child is aborted. She is given medicine and an abortion is done without her even being asked.[76]

Tibetans in Qinghai Province complained of forced abortions, large fines for unauthorized third births, and refusal of food ration cards for the children.[77]

In January 1988 the national family planning journal urged that "reliable" birth control measures be carried out and added that

IUDs and ligations still must be taken as the principal means of birth control, especially in rural areas . . . The key is to carry out concrete measures at the basic level. Carrying out reliable birth control measures is an important link in basic level family planning work. In the past we proposed that ligation not be applied indiscriminately. The intention was to stress starting from facts and treating [each case] with discrimination. Now, for the same reasons, we cannot refrain from doing ligations and IUD insertions indiscriminately.[78]

In July 1988 a population journal quoted an undated statement by Deng Xiaoping that

in order to lower the population growth rate, it is all right to use administrative and economic measures. So long as the rate can be lowered, it will be the greatest victory.[79]

Throughout 1988 and into the spring of 1989, provincial directives emphasized tightening controls and strict enforcement of restrictions, quotas, and targets.[80] The return to rigid methods meant the end of the somewhat more "flexible" approach to contraception adopted in 1984, under which some couples were allowed to use contraceptive techniques other than IUDs and sterilization.

New Family Planning Regulations

Another sign of the tightening of control over births was the issuance of more restrictive provincial and local family planning regulations that began in 1986 and continued into 1989. As before, they were instituted at the prompting of the central authorities, modelled on those adopted at higher levels, and required higher level approval before they could be promulgated. The new regulations increased the penalties for violations and were to be vigorously enforced.[81] Sichuan's were formally adopted on July 2, 1987. They called for sterilization of couples with two or more children, "a heavy fine" for having an unauthorized birth, a monthly fine for an unauthorized pregnancy, to be refunded after an abortion was performed, and fines for "illegal" removal of IUDs.[82] The stated aim was to enable local authorities to "rely upon legal procedures to control population growth . . ."[83] Sichuan's cadres were told to "resolutely implement each of the 'Regulations,' strictly block early marriages, early births, births in excess of the planned quota, and other 'large gaps,' and stop all 'crooked gaps' in order to meet the population plan for this year."[84] In September local public security bureaus in Sichuan issued their own circular to emphasize that "where the law applies, it must be adhered to; that the execution of the law must be strict; and that those who violate the law must be prosecuted."[85]

Though the Sichuan family planning regulations punish officials who accept bribes or practice fraud and people who insult, threaten, or beat family planning personnel, they contain no warnings against the use of coercive tactics and no penalties for cadres who resort to coercion. They do provide for appeal to the courts for reconsideration of "erroneous" penalties imposed by the family planning departments, but they give no hint as to possible bases for appeal.[86] Clearly, the regulations do not protect people against such tactics as mass mobilizations, harassments by family planning workers and officials, and group punishments designed to induce other people to ostracize and condemn non-compliant couples, coercive measures which the central authorities have never disapproved.

By September 1989, 17 of the 30 provincial level units in China had adopted new family planning regulations, which were said to be "playing an active role in unifying thoughts, stabilizing birth policies, and tightening family planning work."[87] How severe the terms of subprovincial family planning regulations could be is shown by those adopted by Tianhe District, Dongpu Precinct, Guangzhou Municipality, as of January 1, 1987, as reported in a journal published by Chinese dissidents in the United States. The regulations stipulate that

> any woman who does not have an intrauterine device inserted within four months after giving birth shall be fined 20 *yuan* per month until she accepts the device. If a woman is allowed two children under the law and does not accept an intrauterine device after the birth of the second child, she must be sterilized. Before that measure is taken, she will be fined 50 *yuan* per month . . . If a woman who has one child fails at birth control, the pregnancy must be terminated and the woman sterilized.
>
> If a woman who is eligible to have a second child has that child before she is given permission, or if any woman gives birth to a third child, all members of her family will lose their benefits . . .
>
> A fine will be levied by the government on any woman who has a second or subsequent baby without permission. For the second baby, the fine will be 2,000 *yuan*, for the third baby 3,000 *yuan*, for the fourth baby 4,000 *yuan*, [and] each birth beyond the fourth will be assessed 4,000 *yuan*. If the baby born without government approval is only the second, and the mother voluntarily submits to sterilization, the penalty may be reduced by 80%. If the baby is the third, and the mother submits to sterilization, the penalty may be reduced by 50% . . .
>
> For farm families in violation of the birth control laws, their share of farm profits will be garnished when profits are divided at the end of the year. If the child born illegally is the woman's second, 80% of the income will be impounded. If the child is the woman's third, 100% of the income will be taken. If the child is the second, and the penalty has not been paid but the woman has undergone sterilization, the assessment will be 50%. If the child is the third and these conditions exist, the assessment will be 70%. This assessment will stop when the penalty has been paid up . . .
>
> If an unauthorized baby is the second, third, or subsequent child in a family and sterilization has not been accepted, the family will be denied permission to build a dwelling, their water and electricity will be cut off (or their water and electric rates will be increased five to ten times, depending on the type of residence), grain coupons will not

71

be issued, [and] driver's licenses and private business licenses will be revoked. All these sanctions will end when the sterilization procedure is performed. (The above sanctions apply to all those listed in the family registration book.)

If a cadre or staff member of a collective enterprise or cooperative business unit has an unauthorized second baby, the appropriate punishment will be administered by the employer. Birth control measures must be adopted. Both the man's and the woman's salary will be reduced by 40% and all bonuses will be suspended until the four-year required waiting period is over. If the unauthorized baby is the third or subsequent child, the employment of both parents will be terminated . . .

A woman who illegally removes her intrauterine device, or anyone else who violates birth control regulations or obstructs the work of the committees, should be punished in accordance with the law . . . [88]

The renewed interest in family planning regulations seems to reflect a view expressed early in the 1980s that such laws legitimize the use of compulsory measures. In 1981 a writer in a national newspaper noted that "some people" who opposed the use of coercion in family planning did not approve of the formulation of a national family planning law. The writer argued that enforcement of law is "not the same as coercion."[89] In 1982 and 1983 provincial spokesmen argued that Article 12 of the Constitution making family planning the duty of husbands and wives was "a fundamental law which the people must obey" and a "legal duty that citizens bear to the state."[90] Nevertheless, despite urging from Qian Xinzhong and other Chinese family planning advocates, the national family planning law drafted in 1979 was never adopted.

Since July 1988, another national law has reportedly been under consideration.[91] In February 1989, Peng Peiyun, the new Minister-in-Charge of the SFPC, who had replaced Wang Wei in January,[92] indicated that the SFPC is actively at work on it and that it will go before the State Council "as soon as possible."[93] In March Peng insisted that legislation must be "accelerated" because "without a legal basis, our birth control effort can hardly get anywhere." She added that the legislation was "especially urgent" and that the State Council had decided to draw up "provisional" regulations this year and adopt formal regulations "when the time is right."[94] Peng apparently considered the national law essential in making family planning compulsory, and many other family planning supporters in China took up the demand. But some family planning officials reportedly were "not optimistic about the results of such action." One SFPC official was quoted as saying, "As long as such a great number of people ignore the law, what can the law do to them?"[95]

Controlling the "Floating Population"

The problem of the "floating population," first recognized as a threat to family planning in 1985, became much worse in the next several years. By 1989, it was said that

> almost all of them have at least two children; some even have three or four. They buy grain and coal at negotiated prices, do not have a permanent job, and do not belong to any unit. They work hard to earn as much money as they can, and they can have as many children as they want. They form a social group that is virtually subject to no one's jurisdiction and thereby poses a serious threat to family planning efforts.[96]

Other sources indicated that because the floating population had enough money they did not fear punishment.[97] They constituted what in 1989 was called the "excess-birth guerrilla corps," who left their home communities to live in "excess-birth floating villages" on the fringes of the cities.[98] The floating population often avoided registering their unauthorized children, and by 1988 the number of unregistered children in China was estimated at about one million.[99] They were regarded as a major loophole in the family planning management system and were to be the focus of control efforts from 1988 onward.

The problems were complicated by the rapid rise in their numbers. In 1978 Beijing had only an estimated 300,000, but by 1985 there were 900,000, by 1987 1,150,000,[100], and by 1989 1,310,000.[101] Other major cities also reportedly had large numbers, including 1.1 million in Guangzhou and 1.83 million in Shanghai.[102] A survey of the floating population, estimated at some 50 million nationally,[103] was to be conducted in 1988, after which national birth control regulations designed specifically for them were to be drafted.[104]

Zhejiang Province included a crackdown on the floating population in its new family planning regulations:

> Those [members of the floating population] who violate family planning policies must be treated severely according to regulations. Serious violators are to be punished with cancellation of employment contracts, closing of businesses, or revoking of licenses. Those who conceal their marriage and childbirth status to obtain "family planning certificates"

by deceit and those who intentionally give convenience to and shelter incoming and outgoing violators of family planning policies are to be given either financial or administrative penalties.[105]

Shanghai, Beijing, Tianjin, Fujian, and Qinghai also adopted regulations to control the floating population,[106] as have various provincial level municipalities.

Encouraging Coercion

From 1987 onward there have been increasing indications that the central authorities have decided once again to encourage basic level cadres and officials to use coercive means to attain family planning targets. The inducements include administrative arrangements that require the cadres to fulfill targets at whatever cost, new coercive measures, and abstract exhortations that convey unmistakably the message that any tactics that get results are now permissible.

A number of new tactics have been devised to increase the pressures for plan fulfillment. In September 1987 the national family planning journal described Hunan Province's use of what was called "veto power" to punish townships and districts which failed to do family planning work well. Such units were automatically disqualified from becoming "advanced units" in industrial or agricultural production, and therefore their cadres were ineligible for promotions, bonuses, and other amenities. The journal noted with satisfaction that this method

> greatly heightened the understanding and determination of Party committees at all levels. They could no longer take [family planning work] lightly . . . At present, family planning work throughout the province is progressing smoothly. From January through June of [1987], the number of birth control operations of various types was higher than in the same period of 1986.[107]

Also in September 1987, a Chinese couple receiving advanced training in the United States who were expecting a second child without the permission of their work units in China were ordered to secure an abortion in order to protect the wife's factory from the severe collective punishments it would have to endure if the child were born. The factory's population control office wrote her a letter saying that

> the Walfantia Bearing Factory is now working on a major, government-sponsored expansion. We have successfully

74

passed all the necessary evaluations and reviews. But if our birth control program allows even a single second birth, our factory will not be permitted to advance. All of the strenuous efforts of our 20,000 employees toward this goal will have been in vain. Moreover, our whole factory will be disqualified from any production contests, and the bonuses and benefits of all employees will be negatively affected. From the factory director to the department heads to the cadres in charge of the birth control program, all of us will be punished.

The consequences for you are unthinkable. You would be condemned by all the staff and line employees of the factory. How could you bear the losses you would cause and suffer?

You should seriously reflect on these consequences and come to a speedy decision to fix your problem any way you can. You must not delay! If you have real difficulties, return to China immediately for an abortion . . . [108]

In effect, the Chinese authorities were trying to impose coercive abortion on their nationals within the United States![109] The woman was five months pregnant when this letter was written.

Another new measure tested in Heilongjiang and offered for emulation in April 1988 was designed to restrict the numbers of rural families with only one daughter who could qualify for second births and at the same time enlist their aid in controlling unauthorized births among other families. The policy of allowing second births to only-daughter families, tested in 1984, widely introduced in 1986, and formally adopted early in 1988, was intended to show that family planning policies were "fair and reasonable" and to win support for efforts to control unauthorized second and higher parity births.

As Peng Peiyun explained in February 1989, the policy was meant to strengthen the one-child policy by "lead[ing] the birth behavior of the peasants onto the path allowed by the policy." She added that, since most rural women have two children anyway, if the only-daughter policy could be achieved, "it would be a tightening, not a loosening, of the policy."[110] So far it seems not to have had that effect. However, the authorities have sought ways to narrow the scope of the option as much as possible. The Heilongjiang measure does that somewhat and was said to have been "fully affirmed" by Zhao Ziyang himself.[111] It stipulates that only villages with no unplanned births can permit families with only daughters to have second children and not until their daughters reach six years of age. Reportedly only 37 percent of Heilongjiang's villages have been able to qualify.[112] The rest are not allowed the option.[113]

In September 1988 Liaoning Province described its own policy of designating as "qualified family planning villages" those which met six conditions, including the elimination of "unplanned" births, the adoption of birth control measures by all women of childbearing age, and the establishment of an effective system of population control. Even with these limitations, it was reported that 80 percent of Liaoning's villages were "qualified," but they could immediately lose that status if they had unauthorized pregnancies or births:

> Villages which meet the . . . criteria and conditions are permitted to carry out the policy of giving consideration to families with only one daughter after verification. If there are unplanned pregnancies, quotas for second births will not be issued to the village in question until remedial measures are adopted. If unplanned births are found, quotas for second births will be suspended for one year starting with the month in question. Quotas will be reissued only after effective readjustments.

The heightened group pressures resulting from this policy were alluded to in deliberately vague terms: "By means of this activity, the peasants' view of taking the overall situation in consideration and their group awareness were strengthened."[114]

But if as many as 80 percent of rural villages in a given province can meet the requirements for second births, the numbers of authorized second births would be far greater than the 5 percent allowed under the exceptions recognized before 1984 or the 10 percent (later 20 percent) allowed by the "small gap" announced in Party Document No. 7, since nearly half the one-child families in the qualifying villages would be eligible. Some localities began to look for ways to narrow the opening further.

A district in a Shaanxi county reported in November 1988 that it required only-daughter families to prove that their income was 15 percent above the village average or to undertake certain specified productive activities before they could be given a "quota" for a second child. The local authorities implied that families could easily meet the requirement, ignoring the fact that their efforts would raise the average family income in the village and thus the threshold for qualifying, but it was also disclosed that in the past two years close to half the district's only-daughter families "did not bother to apply" for a quota because they had not met the income "target."[115] A district in a Sichuan county required families seeking a "quota" for their *first* birth to attain a per capita income of 400 *yuan* and per capita food grain of 500 kilograms for a year prior to their application; slightly lower figures were stipulated for families asking for second births. Those who could not qualify had to delay their childbearing for another year.[116] Obviously these policies favor the rich.

At a national family planning conference early in 1989, Premier Li Peng, who supported the Tiananmen student slaughter, demanded that poverty assistance be "combined" with family planning,[117] and in March Peng Peiyun informed a provincial delegation to the National People's Congress that the State Council had decided that this would be done.[118] What they meant was clarified by reports from several provinces whose measures for implementing the new policy were presented for emulation in the national family planning journal. Poverty assistance was to be withheld from poor families that did not practice late marriage and late childbirth and limit themselves to one child.[119] This policy directly penalizes the poor.

Pressures on local officials and cadres were also increased by elaborating the family planning "responsibility system" into a multi-level network of contracts reaching from the top political leadership down to individual couples of childbearing age. Referred to as the "contract and guarantee system" or the "complete family planning management system" or the "double track family planning contract and responsibility system,"[120] the new developments were part of a "reform" in family planning work that was intended to secure total conformity. At a national conference of directors of subnational family planning commissions, the Deputy Director of the SFPC, Chang Chongxuan, said that establishing and improving all types of responsibility systems was "the most important problem that needs to be solved in our work."[121] The contract system was said to "arouse . . . the activism of the basic level [authorities] and of the masses."[122]

> By means of the double track contract and responsibility system, administrative sanctions are combined with the contract and responsibility system. It strengthens the control mechanisms, organizational discipline, policy awareness, the concept of law, information, and per capita value and output. It tightens and implements family planning work.[123]

Under the new management system, contracts were signed between leaders at various levels committing them to fulfill their family planning targets within their terms of office or suffer specified penalties. Regular inspections were to be conducted to make sure the contract terms were met. At the lowest level, individual couples were required to sign contracts with their local authorities guaranteeing the observance of family planning restrictions.

During 1988 and 1989 the new contracts and management systems were installed at provincial and lower levels throughout the country.[124] The purpose of the contracts was to assure that family planning targets were fulfilled at all levels.[125] They stipulated that evaluations of officials and cadres and their remuneration would depend upon whether they met their targets. One province specified that leaders who failed would lose special awards, be criticized in government circulars, and, if the failure persisted, be demoted or "punished in other ways."[126] Another said that heads of city, county, and township governments that did not control population growth could not be considered "competent," regardless of success in other undertakings, and could lose promotions or even be dismissed.[127]

Despite some adjustments, provincial population targets still seem to be based on allocations of the national target of 1.2 billion in the year 2000, even though the central authorities no longer believe that goal attainable.[128] In March 1988, Li Peng reaffirmed the 1.2 billion goal in his report to the First Session of the Seventh National People's Congress.[129] In November Peng Peiyun acknowledged that the 1.2 billion figure had probably been unrealistic when it was first adopted in 1980. She said that a more likely total for the year 2000 was 1.27 billion, but she also confirmed that, at least until the 1990 census was taken, "the . . . 1.2 billion [figure] is still our target."[130] In September 1989, a provincial source indicated that the Party Central Committee and the State Council still "demanded" that this target be met.[131] Retaining the provincial target figures based on the unattainable national target of 1.2 billion meant that provincial and lower level authorities were held accountable for reaching unrealistic goals, even though this has long been a recognized cause of acts of "coercion and commandism" by local cadres.[132]

Some sources claimed that the intensification of the program had already begun to show results. In 1987 the upswing in the national birth rate moderated somewhat and the rise in the natural increase rate in that year was less than in 1986.[133] In 1988 the birth rate began once again to decline, falling to 20.78 per thousand population from 21.04 in 1987.[134] Premier Li Peng claimed that rapid population growth had been brought under control in 1988,[135] and Peng Peiyun reported that there were one million fewer births of third and higher parity and one million fewer unauthorized second births than in 1987.[136]

The reduction was undoubtedly due in part to an increase in the number of birth control surgeries. In the last several years the authorities had expanded the national network of "family planning service stations," which functioned as propaganda distribution points and also as birth control surgery centers. In May 1988, the SFPC announced that sterilizations and IUD insertions together had increased by 40.7 percent in 1987 over the 1986 total.[137] First established in a few areas in 1979, the number of county-level stations had by October 1988 risen to 2,076 with a staff of 22,600. Since their founding, they had reportedly carried out 70 million birth control surgeries,[138] of which the stations in Henan alone accounted for 7,215,000.[139] In December 1988 Shaanxi Province boasted that its 1,000 surgical teams, consisting of 2,000 doctors and nurses working "day and night" in 3,000 surgical centers, had carried out 140,000 in less than two months.[140] In January 1989, Guizhou announced that it planned to do 900,000 such surgeries during the year.[141] A health journal reported that complications and deaths from birth control surgeries were declining and that the total number of persons engaged in "birth control technical services" had risen to over 180,000 full-time and 140,000 "part time workers."[142] At a national family planning conference in October 1988, Peng Peiyun said that the service stations were "an organization and a force we cannot do without" and that the SFPC had decided to appoint a deputy director to take charge of the national service station network. "Currently," she added, "the volume of birth control operations in many rural areas is large."[143] The emphasis on birth control surgeries was reminiscent of the policies of 1983.

The good news about falling birth rates did not, however, give rise to much optimism among the leadership. Peng Peiyun thought that continuing the birth rate decline of the past year or so would be increasingly difficult in the future.[144] She noted that less than one-third of the provincial-level units in the country had reduced their birth rates.[145] An SFPC researcher told a foreign reporter that "In many provinces, the birth control policies are largely ineffective."[146] In March 1989, a Beijing newspaper warned that the numbers of women of childbearing age would increase by about five million each year from 1989 through 1992, hence "we must not lower our guard."[147] In the same month, Li Peng announced that henceforth the State Statistical Bureau would publish the natural increase rates of all provinces each year "in order to strengthen supervision over them,"[148] and in April the national family planning journal presented the newly compiled 1988 provincial figures.[149]

Echoes of 1983

In addition to the new iron-fisted family planning tactics, the mounting insistence that targets be fulfilled, the stiffened penalties for noncompliance, and the crescendo of rhetorical demands that policies be implemented "strictly," "firmly," "resolutely," and "effectively," the central authorities sent out other signals that coercive tactics improvised at the basic level were again acceptable. Though strongly suggestive and obviously open-ended, the demands were couched in abstract terms, presumably so that the central authorities could maintain "plausible deniability" in case they should later wish to disavow the resulting tactics and blame them on the lower levels, as they had often done before.

Local cadres were told to "take action" to achieve quick results in family planning work, as opposed to relying on propaganda and persuasion alone, which was denigrated as "empty talk." Several provincial sources first sounded the "action" theme in the spring of 1987. In March Guangxi told its family planning cadres to "guard against idle talk and do more practical work."[150] In May Hainan Island demanded an immediate "high tide of action to promote family planning work." The instructions made it clear that this involved punishing cadres, Party, and Communist Youth League members who had unauthorized children, imposing financial penalties on other violators, and carrying out sterilization.[151] In June Sichuan issued a call to "take immediate action" to launch a "major propaganda, inspection, and implementation drive throughout the province."[152]

In August and September 1987 the national family planning journal urged family planning cadres to "take action quickly," "resolutely," and "decisively" to change the "passive situation" in areas that were "backward" in family planning work.[153] It warned against leaders who indulge in "more talk than action,"[154] and said that

> action means actively creating public opinion and unifying the thinking of the cadres and the masses. Action itself is the best means of unifying understanding and the best propaganda . . . If action is taken and the work is resolutely carried out to really solve problems, then the news travels quickly and becomes a strong wave which gives a shock to those people who think that it matters little whether you practice family planning or not. The leadership of Dianbai County, Guangdong did just that. Results were quickly achieved. It proved that they had the determination and that they were conscientious and resolute in implementing the guidelines of the Party Central Committee.[155]

"Take real action," said an article in the People's Daily in January 1988, "to solve the problems" of people getting married early, having children early, and having more than one child without permission.[156] Provincial dispatches repeated the call for "action" but did little to clarify the expression except to say that "resolute and effective measures" must be taken and that importance must be attached to obtaining "practical results."[157] In October 1988 the *People's Daily* applauded a Shaanxi urban district that "pushed grassroots family planning work forcefully,"[158] and in November it carried a provincial article warning that unless "forceful measures [were] immediately taken," state birth quotas would be exceeded.[159] The demand for "practical results" was repeated in a national circular on controlling birth rates issued jointly by the State Family Planning Commission and the Party Central Committee Propaganda Department on December 13, 1988,[160] and by Premier Li Peng in his government work report in March 1989.[161] A week later, Peng Peiyun demanded that local leaders take personal charge of family planning work and "try to produce immediate results."[162] In August 1989 Yunnan instructed its cadres to "take every effective measure" to insure fulfillment of targets and plans and Hubei called on its cadres to lower population growth "by all ideological, administrative, legal, economic, and technical means."[163]

More explicit hints were given by SFPC Deputy Director Chang Chongxuan at the January 1988 conference of directors of subnational family planning commissions:

All measures and methods which are favorable to population control . . . and to arousing the activism of the cadres and masses may be tested . . . Methods which are able to arouse everyone's activism, especially the activism of the basic levels and of the masses, must be promoted and be systematized gradually. We must understand clearly that "to arouse activism is the greatest form of democracy . . ."

We must conscientiously solve the problems of excessive births, early marriage, and early childbirth and resolutely correct the loosening [of family planning work] . . . To solve these problems earnestly, we cannot rely on slogans alone. We must have a great deal of determination, a resolute attitude, and solid performance . . .

No matter how the reforms are carried out, make sure that they are favorable to the development of family planning work.[164]

Despite euphemisms, the language in this quotation is relatively undisguised. The meaning of the exhortation to use "all measures and methods which are favorable to population control" would not have been lost on family planning officials who received similar open-ended directives in 1983. In this as in other contexts, forcing cadres and people to comply with unpopular policies through penalties, pressures, and threats is called "arousing their activism." The acquiescence of those coerced by these measures is referred to (rather cynically) as "the greatest form of democracy." Propaganda and persuasion, elsewhere advocated and lauded, are here denigrated as mere "slogans," because the authorities now demand "solid performance."

An even clearer signal was sent in September 1988 by the national family planning journal, which carried an article from Shandong Province defining the meaning of "strict" in family planning directives:

> In our guidance to family planning we persist in giving prominence to the word "strict," strict in controlling the quota, strict in implementing the policies, and strict in carrying out the leadership responsibility system . . . We are determined to use all means to fulfill the population control plan.[165]

Similar rhetorical demands preceded crackdowns on family planning at the beginning of 1979, in the summer of 1981, and in January 1983. Early in 1979, when the one-child limit was made national policy, Deng Xiaoping had demanded that family planning work be "vigorously strengthened."[166] In 1981, Chen Muhua, then head of the family planning office under the State Council, reportedly quoted Deng as saying, "In order to reduce the [rate of] population [growth], use whatever means you must, but do it!" Chen added: "With the support of the Party Central Committee, you should have nothing to fear."[167]

The same message was delivered to family planning cadres in Huiyang Prefecture, Guangdong Province, in 1981 by its acting Party secretary at the start of a coercive abortion drive. He said that "all methods of controlling population were correct" and that it did not matter if some "problems" occurred because the Party would not investigate or hold the cadres responsible.[168] Later Huiyang Prefecture was lauded by the Guangdong provincial authorities for its "great achievements" and the fact that its leaders had "a good grasp" of family planning work and had shown "great determination [and] made a big show of strength."[169] The national authorities praised Huiyang for demonstrating what could be done by "patient and meticulous ideological work."[170]

In the latter half of 1982 the priority in family planning directives shifted from propaganda to practical results, which was interpreted by local cadres as a sign that the central authorities were not greatly concerned about the means by which those results were secured. This interpretation was encouraged by Zhao Ziyang's speech to the

Sixth National Party Congress in June 1983 in which he said that it was necessary to "prevent additional births by all means."[171]

Such thinly disguised invitations to basic level cadres to use coercive means were again being transmitted by the central authorities in 1988 and 1989. In fact, encouragement of coercion went a step further in January 1989 when a Beijing newspaper published an article openly advocating coercion. The author criticized China's family planning officials for "forc[ing] themselves to say" that family planning work should mainly be "carried out by the masses of their own free will" and that "coercion and control should be opposed." This was not practical, he argued, because people were not willing to stop at one child:

> As happy peace must be built on the foundation of powerful military strength, so are the people's voluntary and self-conscious actions to be formed on the basis of the legal and compulsory standard. We should justly and forcefully say that we must punish those who have turned a deaf ear to dissuasion from having additional children . . . and that suitable coercion and control should be implemented in China's family planning . . .
>
> Only if the country adopts effective and compulsory policies and at the same time carries out propaganda and education can the consciousness of society be aroused.[172]

This was the first time that coercive means had been openly endorsed in the Chinese media, but it was not the last. In April the New China News Agency quoted an Agriculture Ministry official who said that the idea of persuading peasants to accept family planning was "an illusion":

> Only coercive measures can be effective in alleviating the problems caused by [the] population explosion . . . From the perspective of future generations . . . temporary coercion is actually a philanthropic and wise policy.[173]

In August 1989 a third article advocating coercion appeared in a Shanghai social science journal. It said that China's one-child policy was faltering and should be replaced by a policy of late childbearing, two births per couple with more than a five-year interval between them, and the elimination of all additional births by means of compulsory abortion. All pregnancies to women aged 24 or under, all second pregnancies occurring less than five years after the first, and all later pregnancies were to be terminated under a new population law "as hard as steel." The author said that a special "population police force" backed by a "population court," both under the supervision of a "population commission," should be established in every county. Local leaders who failed to enforce the abortion rules rigidly were to be "impeached." Those who subverted the law by avoiding abortions, concealing pregnancies, and accepting bribes were to be punished with prison terms or harsher punishments, including death sentences.

The author added that "the coercive measures in the current population policy, such as knocking down houses, felling trees, confiscating . . . cattle, tractors, and other large farm equipment, and refusing . . . registration [of newborns]" were "unscientific" and only served to hinder production and impair the accuracy of birth statistics, whereas compulsory abortion was "entirely in accord with the spirit of the Constitution."[174]

None of these three articles represents official policy, at least not yet. The writers were not recognized official spokesmen and all took the position that they were advocating policies that differed from those currently in force. But the fact that articles advocating coercion appeared openly in China's highly controlled press while no articles opposing coercion were permitted to appear is undoubtedly significant of the official attitude. The coercion articles seem to have been intended to prepare public opinion in China for harsher measures still to come, hence they reflect a further hardening of official attitudes on family planning. This trend has accelerated noticeably since the beginning of 1989 and has continued since the crushing of the Tiananmen uprising in June, as provincial news items in August and September indicate.[175]

Popular Opposition

The Chinese family planning program depends upon coercion because targets cannot be met by relying on education, propaganda, and persuasion alone. Popular opposition to the program remains strong, among local Party and government officials as well as among the people. The extent of the opposition to the one-child policy is, from time to time, frankly acknowledged in the Chinese media. As was noted earlier, opinion surveys in 1985 and 1986 had shown considerable opposition to the one-child limit.[176] In 1988 an SFPC survey found that 72 percent of all couples and 90 percent of rural couples wanted more than one child,[177] and a demographic journal reported other survey results showing that 88 percent of Chinese couples wanted both a boy and a girl.[178] Even in Beijing a survey found that less than 20 percent of a sample of 7,622 married women wanted only one child; 79.7 percent wanted two or more.[179]

In August 1986 the national family planning journal had recognized a "contradiction" between family planning policies and "the wishes of the masses" which had to be resolved in favor of the policies.[180] In July 1987 a Beijing newspaper conceded that "peasants still have a strong desire to give birth early and to have more children."[181] In August 1987 the national family planning journal said that violations of the regulations, if not checked by "firm and effective measures," would become a "wind" that would "become stronger and stronger, resulting in a loss of control over population growth in some areas."[182] An investigation in one Sichuan county found that 70 percent of the women who had had IUDs inserted under the supervision of family planning cadres had later managed to remove them.[183] Bribery and the falsification of records and statistics, offenses involving collusion of the people and the local cadres and officials, were reportedly widespread.[184] Those cadres who enforced the family planning requirements were subject to surreptitious reprisals by the people they offended. An investigation of 381 "vengeful incidents" against cadres in one Jiangsu county found that 32 percent, the largest single category, were related to family planning.[185] This case was not exceptional. In January 1989, an article in the national family planning journal deplored the increasing "contradictions and hostilities between the cadres and the masses":

> When the village cadres tighten family planning control slightly, some of the peasants believe that the cadres are making it hard on them. They find opportunities to take revenge, either deliberately embarrassing the cadres or having members of their family and relatives beat up the cadres. In recent years criminal cases relating to family planning have occurred frequently.[186]

In January 1988 an article in the *People's Daily* said that the reason rural resistance to family planning work was so strong was that peasant families needed manpower for farm work and therefore felt that "they must have baby boys, at least two to three children, the more the better; and the earlier they get married and have children the better." The writer added that

> China's family planning program has been formulated and implemented amidst the contradiction and conflict between these two mentalities . . . But if we give consideration only to the will of individual families in formulating a policy, it will go counter to the long-term overall interests of the state and the nation.[187]

In the same month family planning workers at a conference in Hebei were told that "the people will be motivated and inspired with enthusiasm for doing some work only when great pressure is applied to them."[188] In September 1988 Peng Peiyun acknowledged that "there is still a gap between China's current family planning policy and the wishes of the masses on child-birth."[189]

In view of the continuing popular opposition, the authorities realize their targets cannot be attained by purely voluntary means and are determined to reach them by whatever other means may be required.. They are encouraged in the use of compulsion by the continued support of the program by foreign family planning advocates, who repeat and ostensibly believe the official denials that the program is coercive and insist that the pressures driving the program are becoming more moderate when in fact they are being intensified. In April 1989, as part of a national media blitz marking China's attainment of a population of 1.1 billion, a spokesman on Beijing television said:

> China's family planning program has received the understanding and support of many countries, international organizations, and individuals. We hope to step up cooperation with [them] . . . [190]

A *China Daily* commentator said:

> As [the] population explosion is a problem that has worldwide impact, international support has reached China to back its control endeavors. This support is greatly appreciated, because it reflects sympathy about the pressure on development in China and its cultural dilemma and concern for the future of all mankind.[191]

In October another *China Daily* article, quoting Peng Peiyun, said:

> Although some foreign governments and individuals have held opposing views on China's family planning policy, many other countries and people have shown support for it.
> Starting in 1980 the United Nations Population Fund has donated $10 million a year to China in support of population control, Peng said. During the past few years over 20 foreign delegations, having investigated the country's population control practices, have agreed that the Chinese government has "foresight and sagacity" and that "history will prove [the policy's] validity."[192]

That foreign support would continue was indicated in January 1989 by the UNFPA agreement to fund a third five-year, multimillion-dollar program of assistance to China's population efforts. UNFPA officials disclosed that they and the SFPC had made some changes in the UNFPA's program in China which they hoped would clear the way for a resumption of U.S. government funding. The adjustments required no change in the nature of the Chinese family planning program.[193] The UNFPA would continue to assist the Chinese with contraceptive research and production, which may help to make their coercive measures more effective. In any case, the Chinese authorities can still take foreign assistance and foreign statements praising any aspect of the program as proof that foreigners approve the program as a whole.[194]

UNFPA Executive Director Nafis Sadik reportedly hoped that the changes would enable everyone involved to "save face."[195] However, when the new proposal was laid before the United Nations Population Commission the week after the student massacres in Beijing, the U.S. Agency for International Development announced that it was continuing to withhold funds from the UNFPA because of its involvement in the coercive family planning program in China.[196] After the U.S. Senate adopted a bill to resume U.S. funding of the UNFPA, President George Bush sent a message to House-Senate conferees in October warning that if the fiscal year 1990 foreign operations bill contained that provision when adopted, he would veto it.[197] The president strongly reaffirmed his position at a press conference on November 7, 1989.[198]

Political ferment and disillusionment in China may ultimately undermine the power of the central authorities to sustain coercive measures in family planning, in which case the program will become voluntary by default, but that is apparently not an imminent prospect. Since the Tiananmen slaughter, family planning demands have continued to escalate, and the State Family Planning Commission has announced that further measures will be taken to increase the effectiveness of its work.[199]

5
Conclusions

The Chinese family planning program is being carried out against the popular will by means of a variety of coercive measures. Despite official denials and intermittent efforts to discourage some of the more extreme manifestations, since the early 1970s if not before, coercion has been an integral part of the program.

The central authorities intended only a slight relaxation of family planning policies in 1984. The additional categories of couples allowed a second child as a small gesture toward "reasonableness" affected very few families. The rest were supposed to be held strictly to the one-child limit. Unauthorized second births were not to be allowed and third and higher order births were to be "absolutely prohibited," as in 1983. Although greater flexibility in the choice of contraceptive methods was permitted, the requirements that women with one child have IUDs inserted, that couples with two or more children be sterilized, and that unauthorized pregnancies be aborted were not abandoned. Somewhat greater emphasis was placed on propaganda and persuasion and on tactics that "the masses can accept."

As before, however, the remission was temporary. By summer 1984 the central authorities were already aware that family planning work was faltering, and once again they tried to tighten up. The attempt was rather ineffectual. The incompatibility of exhortations to fulfill stringent targets and at the same time improve relations with the masses by being "fair and reasonable" confused the cadres and implied that the central authorities themselves were ambivalent. Because of the strong popular reaction against the coercive policies of 1983 and the continuing opposition to the one-child policy, the cadres found it easier to ignore unauthorized births than to hold the line against them, and couples of childbearing age rushed to take advantage of their laxity.

For a time the central authorities seemed to be unaware of the extent of the violations. Between December 1984 and March 1985 central policies on family planning softened again, but from April

1985 onward the line steadily hardened. By 1986, with birth rates and population growth rates rising and the target of keeping the population under 1.2 billion in the year 2000 fast becoming unattainable, the central authorities denounced the relaxation and told the local authorities they must regain control of population growth immediately.

During 1987 and 1988 central demands for strict enforcement of family planning requirements increased sharply and the escalation continued in 1989. New measures have been devised to bring pressure on the whole administrative chain of command down to the grassroots level. Severe penalties are prescribed in the newly revised local family planning regulations. Tactics earlier condemned as coercive are once again advocated. Mandatory IUD insertions, sterilizations, and abortions continue. The national family planning journal has issued thinly disguised injunctions to get the job done by whatever means necessary. Admonitions against "coercion and commandism" and injunctions to "improve work style" have virtually disappeared from domestic family planning dispatches. Instead, the emphasis is on "real action," "effective measures," and "practical results." For the first time, articles in the Chinese media are openly advocating coercion in family planning.

Coercion increased under similar circumstances in 1983 and can be expected to increase again. The consequences are by now predictable, and the Chinese leaders must know exactly what they are, having done it all before. Attempts by Chinese officials and by foreign defenders of the Chinese program to represent the changes in China's family planning policies since 1984 as a major and continuing relaxation of program requirements are not in accord with the facts. The Chinese program remains highly coercive, not because of local deviations from central policies but as a direct, inevitable, and intentional consequence of those policies.

Foreign organizations and individuals that indiscriminately laud the Chinese program or provide financial or technical assistance for any aspect of it place themselves in the position of supporting the program as a whole, including its violations of human rights. It is time for a careful review of the issue of human rights in family planning and a reconsideration of the "population crisis" ideology which is undoubtedly part of the explanation for the tolerance that family planning advocates and other humanitarians have shown toward China's use of coercion in family planning.

Appendix A
Family Planning Infanticide

The most coercive measure allegedly used in the Chinese family planning program has never been alluded to in the Chinese media but has been described in several reports by outside sources. This is deliberate infanticide carried out by obstetricians in urban hospitals in China against infants born without official permission. Because these reports have not been confirmed, the extremely repugnant practices they describe have not been cited in the foregoing chapters, but their persistence and their specificity suggest that they may be more than ugly rumors.

The practice was first reported in 1981 by the Guangzhou correspondent of the *Wall Street Journal*, Michael Vink, who wrote that women with unauthorized pregnancies were given injections by hospital doctors that caused them to have stillbirths or to deliver nonviable infants. He also told of cases of doctors killing babies immediately after delivery if they were third children.[1] In 1983 a British medical journalist reported that a hospital in Guangzhou required its doctors to make sure that no infant born without a permission slip from the mother's work unit be allowed to leave the hospital alive. The babies could be destroyed by "any kind of method," including strangulation. Doctors who allowed unauthorized babies to survive could be punished by loss of their jobs.[2] In January 1985, *Washington Post* Beijing correspondent Michael Weisskopf reported an account from Inner Mongolia that since 1981, in accordance with a regulation banning births of second children to Han Chinese, doctors in Hohhot, the regional capital, routinely destroyed unauthorized babies by smashing the skull with forceps as the baby emerged from the womb or by injecting formaldehyde into the fontanel. Doctors who ignored the regulation risked losing their jobs, as in Guangzhou.[3]

In 1987 the New York Chinese dissident journal *China Spring* carried a report by a Chinese doctor studying in Canada that hospital personnel in China destroyed unauthorized infants by injections of

91

alcohol into the fontanel. He also reported that doctors who refused to carry out the procedure could be punished by demotion, salary reduction, or dismissal. He said the practice was followed in Haerbin, Shanghai, and Urumchi, as well as Guangzhou.[4] A similar report was given by a Western physician involved in international human rights activities, who said that when he was in Tibet in 1987 with a medical expedition, he met a woman who said that her baby had been killed by a lethal injection and that she herself had been sterilized against her will in the Lhasa People's Hospital. This was one of several such reports he received.[5]

In January 1989, similar practices were described in an article in a Washington Chinese newspaper by an author identified only as "a mainland scholar." The author reported that newborns were killed by injections of alcohol or ether and by stuffing gauze into their mouths. He asserted that Chinese doctors and nurses were required to carry out such practices against their will. He also alleged that organs from the destroyed infants were used in laboratory research. No specific communities or institutions were mentioned in the article.[6]

Since 1981 *female* infanticide, a spontaneous action by rural Chinese families whose first and only permitted child under the one-child rule proved to be a daughter, has been repeatedly denounced by the Chinese government as barbaric and a violation of the one-child policy.[7] Whether hospital infanticide, which *supports* the one-child policy, is official policy ordered from Beijing through Health Ministry channels, or whether it is a local invention that has been encouraged or at least tolerated by the central authorities, cannot be determined from the evidence available. However, it is significant that the reports come from widely scattered cities in China, that they are quite similar in details, and that the practices they describe have apparently continued over a period of years without official interdiction. It may also be significant that, as two of the above sources imply, these practices began in 1981, the year in which Deng Xiaoping is reported to have told family planning officials to "use whatever means you must, but do it!"[8] If the reports are valid, hospital infanticide is apparently not one of the forms of coercion in the Chinese family planning program that are "stopped as soon as detected" by the authorities.

Appendix B
Policy Trends—Loosening or Tightening?

As this volume was being prepared for publication, the author received copies of two recent articles disputing the conclusion that the Chinese family planning program is currently moving toward greater coerciveness. The first is a Population Council Working Paper by Susan Greenhalgh issued in October 1989 in which she argues that Chinese family planning policies have not gone through cycles of tightening and relaxing but have steadily relaxed.[1] The second is an article by a Chinese demographer at Beijing University in the June 1989 issue of *Population and Development Review* contesting the findings of a 1988 article in the same journal by Karen Hardee-Cleaveland and Judith Banister that since 1986 the policies have again been tightening.[2]

Greenhalgh's "Linear Trend" Thesis

According to Greenhalgh, China's family planning policies since 1983 have followed "a secular trend toward liberalization."[3] She does not deny that the Chinese program is coercive. In fact, she suggests that the one-child policy of 1979 was "probably best pursued through the application of coercive measures."[4] But she insists that the Chinese authorities learned from experience that a strict one-child limit was unattainable and that coercion does not work. Since 1984, she says, policy objectives have changed and family planning requirements have steadily moderated. She does not say coercion is altogether a thing of the past, but her implication is that it need no longer concern us.

Greenhalgh first reached this conclusion in 1986, when she published a short article in the *Wall Street Journal* and a longer article in the journal *Population and Development Review*. In both she asserted that a little noticed but continuous relaxation of program requirements and goals had occurred following the issuance in April 1984 of

93

Party Central Committee Document No. 7.[5] In both articles she also surmised that the relaxation would probably continue to the end of this century.

In 1986 Greenhalgh was the victim of an accident of bad timing. Party Central Committee Document No. 13, issued in May 1986, shortly before Greenhalgh's articles appeared, obviously pointed in the opposite direction, but Greenhalgh was not to be deterred. Her 1989 article maintains her 1986 position in spite of all the evidence to the contrary that has accumulated in the intervening three years.

In opposing the "cyclical" view of changes in China's family planning policies that I have documented in detail,[6] Greenhalgh tries to dismiss the evidence on which it is based and find other evidence that she can construe as supporting her "linear" thesis. She begins by discarding evidence obtained from the Chinese media on grounds that it gives "a biased and partial view of policy formulation and implementation." She particularly deprecates the use of Chinese sources in U.S. government translations because "one has no control over what is translated."[7] Instead, she prefers to rely on what Chinese demographers serving as advisors to the State Family Planning Commission tell foreign visitors about official population policies, which, as reported by Greenhalgh, differs sharply from what the Chinese authorities tell provincial and lower level officials through the public media. Allegedly, the confidential sources indicate moderate expectations and increasingly lenient requirements, even though the demands conveyed in public channels to provincial and lower levels are escalating.

It cannot be denied that information about China's population policies carried in open sources is incomplete. Key policy documents are seldom published in full, and supplementary instructions given at national and provincial meetings and telephone conferences are only summarized, and then often in vague or euphemistic terms that presumably conceal their actual intent from the Chinese people and from foreigners. Greenhalgh says that the Chinese authorities are more likely to conceal moderate than coercive measures, but this is absurd. It is the coercive measures that evoke hostile domestic reactions and foreign criticism and damage the national image.[8]

It is also true that users of translation services have no direct control over what is selected, but no one has yet shown that the selection process involves systematic bias. A much more serious concern is the fact that we have no control over what the *People's Daily* or the New China News Agency or the national family planning journals choose to publish, because they are under control of the Party propaganda machine and bias is their mandate. The same cautions apply still more strongly to the word-of-mouth sources Greenhalgh wants to trust, since Chinese communications directed to foreigners are generally more distorted and manipulative than those aimed at domestic audiences, from whom the authorities have less to hide. Greenhalgh's informants may be fairly candid about some matters, but they surely know what their government *wants* foreigners to be told, and they also know what the risks are in case they reveal something the government does *not* want told to a foreigner who may publish it with attribution. Moreover, published sources can be checked against one another; there is no way of verifying what Greenhalgh or other recipients of confidential leaks claim they were told. In view of Greenhalgh's handling of some of the published evidence, this is cause for concern.

She also tries to dismiss some published policy directives and demands, arguing that the central authorities do not really mean what they say when they call for a one-child limit or the attainment of local targets based on the national target of 1.2 billion in the year 2000. She says her sources assure her that the central authorities really only hope to reach something approaching a two-child limit and a year 2000 figure of around 1.25 billion. It is quite likely that the central authorities, after many disappointments, no longer expect to attain fully their stated objectives, but what then is the true policy? The demands the authorities make on the Chinese people or the results they tell foreigners privately they really expect to get? It is the demands that drive the enforcement system.

Greenhalgh implies that although they manipulate and deceive their own people, the Chinese authorities take sympathetic foreigners wholly into their confidence. The inner truth is reserved for the latter alone. But is this likely? In view of the perennial efforts to mislead world public opinion about coercive family planning measures, one would have to be willfully naive to think so.

At the Population Association meeting in March 1989 at which the original version of Greenhalgh's article was presented, including her argument about biases in the published sources, Judith Banister urged in a comment from the floor that, instead of rejecting these sources, *all* sources should be utilized in order to gain as much information as possible about the policies and the program. Apparently Greenhalgh was not persuaded. The final version of her article still dismisses the published sources. One suspects that her rejection of them is based not so much on their biases as on their content. They do not support her "steady relaxation" thesis.

Her article begins with an essentially irrelevant argument that foreign criticisms of human rights violations in China's family planning program have caused official spokesmen to "speak with two tongues," making it harder to get information from China about family planning. She says that while the *People's Daily* says population policy is being tightened, the English language *China Daily* says it is being relaxed.[9]

Such differences have been commonplace in the Chinese media since 1949, long before the PRC had a family planning program, and they were found in family planning news dispatches before the program came under foreign criticism. Other countries have also been known to resort to official misrepresentations when criticized for human rights violations, but it is unusual for social scientists and humanitarians to place the blame for official secrecy on the critics, which implies that maintaining the flow of information is more important than protesting the violations. In this case, the implication is that a cover-up of human rights violations is preferable to a cover-up of information wanted by demographers, surely a parochial view.

Another tactic Greenhalgh uses to prejudice the case against those with whom she disagrees is to represent their positions in oversimplified form as "models" of policy change and then criticize them for being simplistic. For example, she says they use a "totalitarian model" of Chinese policy making in which "power is highly concentrated in the political center, and the center is capable of both monitoring and controlling events in the provinces."[10] As Greenhalgh undoubtedly knows, the scholars she is attacking cite plenty of evidence that central control in China is not absolute, that widespread popular resistance and cadre noncompliance have greatly hampered the execution of the family planning policies, and that the central authorities have at times been ambivalent and confused. The tactic of demolishing straw men is common in polemic argument, but it is not respectable scholarship and does not enlighten public debate.

There are other examples of false oversimplification in the article, but these are not the main fallacy in Greenhalgh's argument. Its principal deficiency is the erroneous claim that family planning policies in Shaanxi Province, which she takes as a surrogate for national policies, have followed a linear, not a cyclical, pattern of change. The methods she uses cannot sustain the proposition, and she rejects conflicting evidence.

The Shaanxi Regulations

Greenhalgh bases her argument on incomplete documentation from Shaanxi, consisting of family planning regulations for the whole province, for one Shaanxi city, for a township within the city, and for a village, and other information from "local newspapers, journals, and other sources." These materials were obtained during a field research project in the first six months of 1988 undertaken under the joint auspices of the Population Council and Xian's Jiaotong University Population Research Institute, both past recipients of UNFPA grants.[11]

Greenhalgh does not explicitly claim that Shaanxi is typical of China in population matters, though she does note some rough similarities between the province and the country as a whole in birth and fertility rates. Insofar as family planning work is concerned, Shaanxi is definitely not typical. It was among the top third of the provinces in family planning compliance in the late 1970s and early 1980s[12] and is now reportedly among the one-third of China's provinces that are "backward" in family planning work.[13] This seems to suggest that after 1983 family planning efforts in Shaanxi were relaxed more than in other provinces.

Greenhalgh's analysis focuses on national policy "developments" and the Shaanxi provincial and lower level family planning regulations between 1979 and 1986. This limited time frame excludes fluctuations in policy up to 1979 and, of course, the tightening of policies from 1986 onward. Ending the study with 1986 eliminates the evidence of the current escalation that began with Document No. 13. Greenhalgh admits that "field evidence from Shaanxi and articles in the national media indicate a resurgence of campaigns in 1987 and 1988" and that "if these represented but another round in a continuing cycle, we might yet have support for the oscillatory view." But, she adds, these materials are "not analyzed here."[14] One wonders why not, since they bear directly on the question she is supposed to be addressing—the validity of the "oscillatory view"—and may contradict her own "steady relaxation" thesis.

Greenhalgh's analysis also excludes the relaxation in 1980 and the spring of 1981, the tightening of policies in the summer and fall of 1981, the peak of coercion in 1983, and the relaxation in 1984, since these developments were not reflected in the family planning regulations, to which her analysis of policy changes is largely confined. The peak of coercion in 1983 might have received some attention if Greenhalgh had included among her central documents the joint circular of December 6, 1982, which called for the mandatory surgery measures of 1983, but although Greenhalgh is aware of the 1983 policies she does not mention that important policy document or its impact on Shaanxi. This is a critical omission because there are indications that the Shaanxi authorities plunged with exceptional vigor into the 1983 drive.[15]

Since family planning regulations often take some time in the drafting, require higher level approval before promulgation, and are not immediately revised when policies change, they do not accurately indicate either the timing of new policies or the point at which they are superseded by other policies. Many significant policy changes are simply unreflected in the regulations. As one Shaanxi source noted in 1982, "certain stipulations raised by the instructions of the [Party] Central Committee and the State Council are not covered by the provincial regulations."[16] The regulations are therefore inherently unsuitable for tracing changes in family planning policy in Shaanxi.

In the case of the provincial regulations, Greenhalgh has just four sets, the regulations of June 1979, those of May 1981, a supplement of October 1982, and the regulations of July 1986. But she treats the middle two as one set, which means that she has only three time reference points—1979, 1981–82, and 1986. Examining these regulations, she says her evidence does not show a pattern of "tightening-loosening-tightening-loosening, but rather a single oscillation."[17] But of course that was all that her evidence *could* show. With just three time reference points, she has only two time segments, which means she could not possibly trace more than one "oscillation."[18] To discover two she would have needed four time segments—five time reference points. But she avoids the kind of evidence that could have detected so many changes of direction within the period 1979–1986.

In spite of limitations of time frame and content, her provincial evidence indicates a cycle, not a linear trend, but somehow she loses sight of that when she comes to her summing up, where she says that "the overall change was not cyclical, but linear, a finding that challenges the basic tenet of the oscillatory model."[19] She has obviously dismissed the first time segment, 1979 to 1981/82, basing her case on only a single time segment marked by two reference points, 1981–1982 and 1986. Since the shortest distance between two points is still a straight line, the finding of a linear trend was inevitable.[20] However, her claim that she has refuted a proposition her methods could not test is obviously invalid.

If Greenhalgh had really wanted to find out whether there were changes in policy not detectable by her methods, the evidence would surely have been found in the provincial newspapers for the period in question. Greenhalgh claims to have consulted newspapers while in Shaanxi, but she cites only one such source, a *Shaanxi Daily* article of 1984, and that from a U.S. government translation.[21] As a matter of fact, the published sources from Shaanxi *do* show a trend very much like that shown by the national media. It is a pattern of cycles— three of them, in fact—followed by a three-year linear trend of tightening from 1986 through 1989. This evidence, which Greenhalgh ignores, is summarized in the following section.

The Evidence from the Published Shaanxi Sources

Media reports from Shaanxi in the late 1970s show that the province had distinguished itself early in the third campaign as just a little behind the leading provinces in family planning work.[22] How family planning in Shaanxi was affected by the national anti-coercion campaign of 1978 is not indicated in available sources, but because the central circular initiating the campaign had cited Shaanxi's Xunyi County as a national bad example[23] and because leading cadres in another Shaanxi county had already been publicly condemned for similar offenses by the Xian radio station in June 1978,[24] it is likely that coercive family planning measures were in abeyance in Shaanxi during the rest of the year.

When the one-child policy was first announced in January 1979, however, Shaanxi was, as Greenhalgh notes, one of the first provinces to incorporate it into provincial family planning regulations. The Shaanxi regulations, adopted in June, were immediately rendered obsolete when the national policy changed from "one child, two at the most" to "only one child." By September 1979 Shaanxi had also switched to a strict one-child policy,[25] but the new restrictions were not written into the provincial regulations until June 1980 in a set of amendments that Greenhalgh does not mention.[26]

Shaanxi's implementation of the one-child policy must initially have been fairly effective. By 1980 the province's natural increase rate had reportedly fallen to 7.19 per thousand.[27] It was one of twenty provinces that had reached Hua Guofeng's target of under 10 per thousand.[28] Then the reaction against the one-child policy set in, and the central authorities once again denounced "coercion and commandism" in family planning work, identifying it with the political mistake of "leftism," a crime of the "gang of four" that had not been fully eradicated.[29] Shaanxi also participated in the campaign against "leftism," which continued into the spring of 1981.[30] In February 1982, the provincial Party first secretary explained Shaanxi's family planning failures in 1980 and 1981 as due in part to the fact that some people regarded the one-child policy as an example of "leftist ideology" and did not implement it.[31] Evidently Shaanxi had followed the national trend of relaxing family planning demands in 1980 and the beginning of 1981.

By September 1981 the Shaanxi authorities, again following national demands, had become seriously concerned about the relaxation and issued a warning:

Some areas have slackened their leadership over planned parenthood work and the population growth rate naturally has increased by a big margin. We should pay close attention to this situation and must on no account treat it lightly. If we fail to take effective measures to change the situation and let it spread unchecked, we are bound to lose what we achieved during the 1970s . . . We should adopt effective measures to grasp it conscientiously and firmly.[32]

The concern continued at a family planning conference in February 1982, at which an official warned that Shaanxi was facing its "third high tide of births" and that sustaining the decline in natural increase rates was becoming more difficult.[33] The Party first secretary told the conference that despite Shaanxi's "very great success" between 1971 and 1981, the work now lagged far behind the demands of the central authorities:

Although there are objective reasons for this, the main problem [is] one of work. Many places have somewhat relaxed planned parenthood work since the second half of 1980. There has been a rather serious laissez-faire attitude. Population growth in some places results from loss of control. The number of babies born outside the plan in 1981 accounted for 40 percent of the province's births. The momentum of increase in the natural population growth rate after its decline is very strong. The tasks of planned parenthood work are therefore rather arduous.[34]

At the end of October 1982, Shaanxi adopted the already mentioned supplement to its "provisional regulations" of May 1981, which contained new tough language demanding that no third births be allowed regardless of circumstances and that "remedial measures" be used to terminate pregnancies "in excess of the plan." The regulations reflected the harsher tone of central family planning demands during the latter half of 1982.[35]

Before the national circular of December 6, 1982, announcing the "propaganda month" campaign of 1983 had been issued, word of its content must already have reached the provinces. At a November 1982 conference, the provincial Party secretary said that Shaanxi must redouble its efforts during the propaganda month and see that one spouse of every couple with two or more children was sterilized.[36] At the end of December 1982, Shaanxi held a "mobilization meeting" to launch the drive, which was to "create a new situation" in family planning work.[37]

The dispatch did not mention arrangements for rounding up the eligible couples for sterilizations, IUD insertions, and abortions or procedures for organizing the necessary "technical forces," the details of which might have alarmed the rural people prematurely; but by January 15, 1983, a provincial telephone conference was told that in the first two weeks of the new drive 300,000 "propagandists" had gone "deep into the grassroots," and that 12,000 medical personnel in 4,000 operating teams had already performed "over 150,000 contraceptive operations, including 80,000 ligations, without any accidents." "The masses," said the report, disingenuously, "are extremely satisfied."[38] Individual counties reported sterilizing 50 percent of "those who should be sterilized" and completing within a twenty-day period twice as many birth control surgeries as in the whole of 1982.[39]

As 1983 came to a close, Shaanxi again claimed "remarkable achievements in family planning work," and the claim was reflected in the 1983 provincial ligation statistics.[40] The provincial authorities proposed to "mobilize the forces in all quarters" for a second "propaganda month" in January 1984 and held a mobilization rally for the purpose on December 27, 1983.[41] On January 16, 1984, a telephone conference made it clear that once again the stress would be on birth control surgeries.[42]

By April, however, a change of policy was evident. Although the cadres at a provincial planned parenthood conference were told that Shaanxi's natural increase rate must be "kept below 10 per thousand this year," that they must continue to grasp family planning work firmly and register achievements, and that the family planning work force must be strengthened, they were also warned:

> We must lay stress on the policies and must prevent resorting to coercion and commandism and must prevent demanding uniformity in everything. We must publicize the policies on planned parenthood and must do meticulous ideological work so that we can convince people by reasoning.[43]

The two themes of meeting targets and restoring relations with the "masses" were consistent with the ambivalent requirements of Party Document No. 7 issued on April 12. The same two themes were repeated at a provincial family planning conference in October 1984.[44] In March 1985, Shaanxi's newly instituted provincial family planning commission was trying to set up a province-wide family planning information network to improve the monitoring of local activities and discover local innovations that could be adopted elsewhere.[45] In January 1986 Shaanxi was criticized sharply by the central authorities when the results of a State Statistical Bureau survey showed that the province was lagging in family planning work.[46] Shaanxi, like the rest of China, had relaxed too far.

The central criticisms prompted the Shaanxi authorities to promise in May 1986 that they would take ten steps to strengthen family planning work, including convening a new family planning conference, issuing a document strengthening the work, reinforcing family planning organs, and conducting investigations on how to ensure "quality births" as a basis for formulating new regulations.[47] The measures suggest an effort to intensify family planning work in anticipation of the harder line about to be put forward in Party Document No. 13.

New family planning regulations were approved by the provincial people's congress in July 1986 and took effect at once. As described by Xian radio, the new regulations reaffirmed the one-child policy, warned that couples were "strictly forbidden to have a second or more not covered by the plan," and said that "all couples capable of having children must take effective contraceptive measures in accordance with the demands of birth control." The broadcast said:

> The birth control departments at all levels must seriously implement the principles, policies, and rules and regulations on birth control work, and also be responsible for checking on their implementation. They must firm up contraceptive measures and do a good job in providing technical services, drugs, and devices . . .
>
> Regarding pregnancies not covered by the plan, it is necessary to conduct education by persuasion and take remedial measures to terminate the pregnancies. If education by persuasion has no effect, those concerned can be fined and subjected to administrative discipline.[48]

The provincial authorities saw these regulations as a tightening of control over family planning. Greenhalgh, comparing these regulations with those of 1981–1982, misinterprets the 1986 regulations as evidence of a continuous trend toward relaxation; but by limiting her analysis to the regulations, she overlooks the extreme tightening of 1983 and the considerable relaxation of 1984–1985, neither of which was embodied in regulations.

Tightening up continued through the rest of 1986. In August Shaanxi convened a meeting of directors of prefectural and municipal family planning commissions, who decided:

> 1. Leadership at all levels must first study Document No. 13 to unify their understanding of the basic guidelines of strengthening family planning and of controlling population growth strictly.

2. The guidelines of the document must be transmitted quickly to the masses so that the basic guidelines of the document may be known to all families and all people.

3. Areas and units where the work is in a backward state must draw up plans and fix a deadline for changing their backwardness to adopt effective measures to improve their work.

4. Implementation of the guidelines and measures must be achieved level by level. Family planning commissions on all levels must sum up their experiences, find the weak points, and carry out and improve the measures item by item in order that the demands of the document and the various measures may be truly implemented.[49]

In October the provincial authorities announced that they had decided:

From the middle of this month to the end of November, the activities of publicizing the documents of the central authorities on firmly grasping birth control and taking remedial measures should be extensively carried out in all urban and rural areas throughout the province. All prefectures and cities must really strengthen leadership over the organization of these activities as a start in changing the backward outlook of our province's family planning work.[50]

The Shaanxi authorities were not alone in interpreting Document No. 13 as a toughening of family planning requirements. Other provinces and the central authorities concurred.

Shaanxi's new hard line was repeated at a provincial family planning conference in February 1987, which stressed that it was "necessary to continuously and strictly control population growth and to completely fulfill the quota for population control" and added that "the present family planning policies would remain unchanged for at least 15 years."[51] In July 1987 the authorities announced that there were 6,500 fewer births in Shaanxi in the first six months of 1987 than in the same period in 1986, but they warned against "indiscriminate granting of exemptions from the rules" and of a trend toward earlier marriage and childbearing in certain places. They said that Shaanxi's task in controlling population growth was "extremely arduous" and that redoubled efforts would be needed to fulfill the 1987 plan.[52] In September Shaanxi's Lindong County was held up as an example in the national family planning journal because it had taken steps to correct the "loosening" of family planning by "settling accounts" with cadres who had had unauthorized children but had not paid any penalties, including cases that went back to 1984.[53]

In March 1988, Shaanxi convened a meeting of directors of prefectural and municipal family planning commissions to inform them that

> in the next three years it is necessary to adopt comprehensive measures in family planning work, combining administrative measures, propaganda and education, services, and mass support, so as to resolutely level off the peak birth cycle and strive to discard the province's backward label this year and raise the province's family planning work to an upper-middle level in the national table by the year 2000.

They were told to "seriously study and implement" the instructions from the Thirteenth National Party Congress on family planning, to "actively explore reform measures" for controlling population growth, and to "mobilize the enthusiasm of the cadres and the masses."[54]

News items later in 1988 showed that Shaanxi's crackdown efforts were running into problems in some areas. In May a "sweeping operation" was launched against early marriage and cohabitation without marriage,[55] but in September a ten-day inspection tour by members of the provincial people's congress still found evidence in many areas of early marriage and childbirth, "blind births" among the "floating population," failure to mete out rewards and punishments, failure to meet quotas, and falsification of birth statistics.[56] The Shaanxi authorities took steps to intensify their crackdown. They added fulfillment of family planning targets to the contract terms for prefectural and municipal officials,[57] formulated new regulations to control births among the "floating population,"[58] and sent more than 6,000 propaganda teams and 1,000 surgical teams into the countryside to operate "day and night" in 3,000 surgery centers. Between "early October" and November 25, a total of 140,000 sterilizations were carried out.[59]

Despite these efforts the bad news on family planning work continued. In November 1988, the Shaanxi authorities reported a "partial loss of control" over population growth, which they attributed mainly to five causes: (1) the persistence of traditional ideas about births among the people in the mountain areas of the province, (2) the inertia of past patterns of population growth, (3) failure of some localities to implement population policies fully, (4) defective family planning organs, and (5) seriously incorrect statistics which cover up the facts. The authorities warned:

The growth of population is very serious, and many localities throughout the province are basically still in a state of blind population growth. If we continue to fail to grasp this issue now, we will commit historical mistakes . . . If forceful measures are not taken immediately, by the end of this century the numbers of the newborn population will be 2 million more than the quotas planned by the state.[60]

In January 1989 Vice-Governor Sun Daren said that the province had failed to fulfill its population plan for "many years running" and that population growth had "reached the warning line."[61] The 1988 fertility survey reportedly had shown that the population situation in Shaanxi was "grim" and that natural increase in 1987 had reached 20.41 per thousand.[62] In March Shaanxi was said to be one of twelve provinces with an "excessive childbirth rate" of over 20 percent.[63] In August Shaanxi demanded that couples in the "floating population" that had unauthorized children be put out of business and sent back to their villages. If any were found to be pregnant, "remedial measures must be promptly adopted."[64] In the same month, the *Shaanxi Daily* noted that 400,000 babies had been born in the province between January and June 1989, 0.2 percent more than in the same period in 1988. A larger number was expected in the second half of the year, because "we have failed to adopt remedial measures against those pregnant outside the plan." The article suggested that if 20,000 abortions were performed among women with unauthorized pregnancies who were due to deliver before the end of the year, the provincial population plan might yet be fulfilled. The 20,000 abortions would all be of pregnancies in the fourth month or beyond.[65]

This summary of developments in Shaanxi since the 1970s shows that, like the national family planning policies, Shaanxi's have alternately tightened and relaxed over the years and are now tightening once more. When put to the test in Shaanxi with a more adequate body of evidence, Greenhalgh's "steady relaxation" thesis fails.

The Zeng Yi Article

Despite the abundant evidence supporting it, the cyclical view of planning policy is also disputed by Zeng Yi in his article in the June 1989 issue of *Population and Development Review*. The arguments advanced by Zeng are similar to those of Greenhalgh in that they deprecate and dismiss the evidence from the Chinese media and take at face value unpublished statements by "demographers and other scientists" who are said to be in "direct dialogue with the new leadership of the State Family Planning Commission" through recently established advisory committees.[66] As in Greenhalgh's article, these statements resemble the official cover story put forward in Chinese media addressed to foreigners but conflict sharply with what is said in the Chinese media for domestic consumption. Zeng ignores the contradiction and the official pronouncements cited by Hardee-Cleaveland and Banister indicating a tightening of policies.

Zeng's representation of their position is incomplete and amounts to setting up another straw man. He says their case is "largely based on three developments": (1) the replacement of Wang Wei as head of the SFPC by Peng Peiyun; (2) an article in the Beijing newspaper *Bright Daily* criticizing the existing policy-making structure; and (3) "general statements from the leadership and media reports" warning of an impending birth peak and calling on cadres to improve program effectiveness.

This list omits the most important evidence on which Hardee-Cleaveland and Banister base their conclusion: (1) Document No. 13's emphasis on correcting the "loosening" of family planning since 1984 and its stress on "practical results"; (2) official statements in 1987 calling for redoubled efforts, strengthened leadership, and strict control of population; (3) official statements of 1988 reaffirming the 1.2 billion goal, strengthening the family planning cadre forces, and making them responsible for strict implementation; (4) the adoption of a new round of provincial family planning regulations; (5) the resumption of mass mobilization drives for contraceptive surgery; (6) the institution of new mechanisms to offset the loss of grass-roots control in the early 1980s; (7) the institution of new controls on the "floating population"; and (8) the launching of a new campaign to promote late marriage.

The descriptions of official policies attributed by Zeng to Chinese demographers and social scientists contradict what the central authorities say publicly in directives to provincial and lower level family planning leaders and seem on some points to be contrary to fact. Zeng's sources allegedly say that authorizations to have a second child, enlarged since 1984, are being continued, but the national family planning journal has been urging for several years that the rules on second children be followed more strictly so as to reduce second births. The central authorities also commend and publicize local restrictions that render ineligible some couples who would have qualified for a second child under the old rules. In some areas rural only-daughter couples allowed a second child under 1988 policies are now not permitted to proceed until all unauthorized pregnancies in their villages have been terminated or until they attain specified per capita income levels.[67] In Liaoning Province all couples in villages that have a single unauthorized birth lose the second child option for one year.[68] Zeng seems unaware of Peng Peiyun's recent statement that, properly administered, the second child option for only-daughter families would represent a tightening, not a loosening, of family planning policies.[69]

According to Zeng, the central authorities believe that increased birth rates in 1986 and 1987 were not due to policy adjustments but to changes in age structure, declines in age at marriage, and reforms that weakened administrative controls at the grassroots level. All these factors are cited in public statements, but the central authorities also make it clear that they attribute the loss of control primarily to the failure of lower levels to "strengthen leadership" and faithfully execute the policies.[70] Zeng claims that the authorities are still pushing improvement of cadre "work style"; in fact, little is said about "work style" in current national policy statements but several recent provincial sources indicate that the meaning of "bad work style" has been radically altered. As now defined, it no longer denotes abusive treatment of the people but failure to enforce the policies.[71]

Zeng criticizes Hardee-Cleaveland and Banister for citing a signed article in the Beijing newspaper *Bright Daily* as source for their suggestion that the replacement of Wang Wei by Peng Peiyun may have signaled a change in policy from a softer to a harder line. Hardee-Cleaveland and Banister say that *Bright Daily* articles reflect national policy, but Zeng says the article reflects only the opinion of the author. The notion that articles in the controlled Chinese press by individual authors constitute merely expressions of private opinion seems naive. Chinese media people who joined the student protesters in May 1989 declared that they were tired of publishing "lies." Moreover, after the uprising was crushed they were obliged to publish what all the world could recognize as the most blatant lies of all, namely, that nothing happened in Tiananmen Square in June and that only soldiers got hurt. Of course, Zeng's article was probably already in press when these events occurred.

However, Zeng's attempt at the end of his article to imply that *all* of the Chinese sources cited by Hardee-Cleaveland and Banister were "viewpoints of individual authors," even though the majority are statements by national and provincial authorities or articles in the national family planning journals, is simply disingenuous.

Zeng's argument consists of selective references to a few policy changes that, superficially described and in the absence of other information about policy changes, can be used to create the impression that family planning policies are being relaxed. The fact that the considerable accumulation of evidence to the contrary cited by Hardee-Cleaveland and Banister is passed over without comment suggests that the author could not refute that part of their case and therefore chose to ignore it. This too is disingenuous.

Political Influences on Research

The Greenhalgh and Zeng articles illustrate how conflicts of interest among demographers over the Chinese family planning program can compromise the integrity of social science research. In such cases, a political purpose dictates the method and the method guarantees the results. Both Greenhalgh and Zeng prefer to play without a full deck, and since they are dealing the cards, they can slough those that might cost them the game. But to do so is to manipulate the evidence and, incidentally, the audience that trusts what they say about the evidence.

They might have done more careful work if they had expected a more critical and objective response from the professional community they were addressing. But, like everybody else, demographers and family planners seem more disposed to accept than to question arguments, however insubstantial, that support their interests and the causes in which they believe.

Social science research that enters the zone of public controversy is always liable to the distortions of partisanship. The issue of coercion in the Chinese family planning program is not the first case in point nor will it be the last. But this is not an argument for avoiding research on controversial matters that have a bearing on public policy. If social science could not render service to public decision making, it would lose a large part of its raison d'etre. The methods and insights of social science can make a positive contribution to public debate even on controversial issues so long as essential professional standards are observed, including the requirements that an opponent's position be fairly represented and that all relevant evidence and argument be taken into account. However, much of the foreign discussion of the Chinese family planning program, including that among professional social scientists, has not attained the requisite level of completeness and objectivity. This raises again the recurrent question whether social science can really be "scientific" in dealing with issues on which it has its own axe to grind.

Many demographers and virtually all family planners react to the issue of coercion in the Chinese family planning program not as social scientists or humanitarians but as interest groups who think their ox is being gored. Some fall silent when the subject comes up. Some make excuses for the Chinese authorities. Some pretend that the evidence is ambiguous but take care not to examine it closely enough to resolve its ambiguities. Some repeat disingenuous claims and arguments used by the Chinese authorities to deny the compulsory aspects of their family planning program. Some use the format of scholarship and social science to reinforce the deception, compromising the integrity of their discipline and its public credibility. On the whole, the treatment of the coercion issue by family planners and demographers has been neither courageous nor forthright. In the long run this cannot serve anybody's interests well.

Notes

CHAPTER 1: THE COERCION CONTROVERSY

1. The organization was formerly called the "United Nations Fund for Population Activities," and the old abbreviation, UNFPA, is still retained.

2. Marshall Green, "Is China Easing Up on Birth Control?" *The New York Times (NYT)*, April 28, 1986; Susan Greenhalgh, "Chinese Abortions: Point's Been Made So Now Ease Off," *The Wall Street Journal (WSJ)*, July 3, 1986; and Carl E. Taylor, "Family Planning in China," *The Washington Post (WP)*, August 27, 1987, p. A19. The author submitted responses to all three newspapers refuting the misleading allegations in these articles, but the newspapers did not publish the refutations. See also Susan Greenhalgh, "Shifts in China's Population Policy, 1984–86: Views from the Central, Provincial, and Local Levels," *Population and Development Review (PDR)*, New York, Vol. 12, No. 3, September 1986, pp. 491–515; Harish Khanna, "China and Population," *Populi*, New York, Vol. 14, No. 4, 1987, pp. 55–56; an article by Congressman James H. Scheuer of New York entitled "China's Family Planning and the U.S.," *NYT*, January 24, 1987; John Rowley and Jeremy Hammand, "Forty Million Volunteers," *People*, London, Vol. 16, No. 1, 1989, pp. 3–7; H. Yuan Tien, "Second Thoughts on the Second Child: A Talk with Peng Peiyun," *Population Today*, Washington, April 1989, pp. 6–9; and a letter of April 3, 1989, from J. Mayone Stycos, director of the population and development program at Cornell University, published in the "Letters" column, *NYT*, April 20, 1989, p. A26.

3. A recent Hong Kong source cites an estimate of 10 million deaths during the movement against "counter-revolutionaries." It also says that a 1981 issue of the Chinese journal *Jingji guanli (Economic Management)* claimed that 20 million people were executed or died of unnatural causes during what it calls the "anti-rightist" and "people's communication" movements. (Ouyang Minglang, "The Present Situation and Future Prospects of Human Rights in Mainland China," *Cheng ming [Contention]*, Hong Kong, No. 137, March 1, 1989, Joint Publications Research Service [JPRS], No. 89–045, May 15, 1989, p. 31.)

4. The Hong Kong source cited in note 3 doubles these numbers. The U.S. State Department's human rights report for 1987 says that between 7,000 and 14,000 persons were executed in China between 1983 and 1986 as part of a "crime suppression" campaign. U.S. Department of State, *Country Reports*

on Human Rights Practices for 1987 (Washington: U.S. Government Printing Office, February 1988), p. 661.

5. For a report on human rights violations in Tibet up to the beginning of 1988, see The Asia Watch Committee, *Human Rights in Tibet, A Preliminary Report* (Washington: Asia Watch, February 1988).

6. Deng had advocated violent suppression on April 25, 1989, when he reportedly said, "We must not be afraid of people cursing us, of a bad reputation, or of international reaction." (Daniel Southerland, "Troops Roll Through Beijing to Crush Protesters; Scores Reported Killed as Chinese Fight Back," *WP*, June 4, 1989, pp. A1 and A34.) For an assessment of human rights in China as of 1985, see John F. Copper, Franz Michael, and Yuan-li Wu, *Human Rights in Post-Mao China* (Boulder, Colo.: Westview Press, 1985).

7. For a fairly recent reaffirmation of this principle and its application to Chinese dissidents, see Wei Hanjin and Liu Jinting, "It Is Imperative to Discuss the People's Democratic Dictatorship," *Jiefangjun bao* (*Liberation Army Daily*), Beijing, February 3, 1987, Foreign Broadcast Information Service, *Daily Report: China* (FBIS), Washington, No. 29, February 12, 1987, pp. K15–17.

8. The first mention of the principle in connection with family planning policies was in December 1969, but it was frequently used to justify and encourage the use of compulsory measures in in 1975 and 1976. Here are two examples:

> Planned parenthood is a task of prime importance promoted by Chairman Mao for years . . . It is an important field in which . . . the proletariat exercises dictatorship over the bourgeoisie . . . with regard to the question of marriage and birth. (Shijiazhuang radio, Hebei Provincial Service, December 27, 1975, FBIS, No. 3, January 6, 1976, p. K4.)

> A complete dictatorship over the capitalist class must be established where marriage and family planning problems are concerned for the far-reaching development of birth control practice to continue. (Ji Wen, "Late Marriage and Birth Control for the Revolution," *Chunzhong yixue* [*Popular Medicine*], Shanghai, No. 1, January 1976.)

9. The Chinese position, as recently stated in the English language magazine *Beijing Review* (*BR*), is that "China has no objection to the United Nations expressing concern in a proper way over consistent and large-scale human rights violations in a given country, but it opposes interference in other countries' internal affairs under the pretext of defending human rights." ("Government's Stand on Human Rights Explained," *BR*, Vol. 31, No. 48, November 28–December 4, 1988, p. 18.) This statement is clearly designed to narrow the scope, venue, and format of human rights accusations and, in the unlikely event that the United Nations would ever condemn human rights violations in China, to provide for the easy dismissal of the charges on the grounds that they were only a "pretext" for interfering in China's internal affairs.

10. For example, even the U.S. decision in 1987 to continue withholding

funds from the UNFPA on the grounds that the Chinese family planning program was still coercive was labelled a "wanton interference in China's internal affairs." See Qian Wenrong, "Birth Control Allegations Absurd," *BR*, Vol. 30, No. 35, September 7, 1987, p. 12. In 1988, Peng Peiyun, Minister-in-Charge of the State Family Planning Commission, asserted that foreigners who said that China's family planning program violated human rights "either . . . have ulterior motives or they know nothing about China's national conditions." (Yang Chaoling, "Peng Peiyun, Minister of the State Family Planning Commission, on China's Family Planning Situation and Policy," *Liaowang Overseas Edition [LWOE]*, Hong Kong, No. 17, April 25, 1988, FBIS, No. 84, May 2, 1988, p. 34.)

11. Huang Qing, "It Seems to Me," *China Daily (CD)*, Beijing, April 20. 1989, p. 4.

12. Fang Lizhi, "Double Standard in Human Rights," *WP*, February 26, 1989, p. C4; and Daniel Southerland, "Chinese Police Stop Dissident," *WP*, February 27, 1989, p. A11.

13. A statement to this effect was said to have been deleted prior to publication from a book of speeches by Deng issued in March 1987. See Daniel Southerland, "New Book of Deng's Speeches Is Critical of Ex-Party Chief," *WP*, March 24, 1987, p. A24.

14. In 1985 Rafael M. Salas, Executive Secretary of the UNFPA, said that his organization was guided by three principles: respect for national sovereignty, the right of individuals and couples to decide "freely and responsibly" the number and spacing of their children, and that population goals and policies should be integral parts of socioeconomic development. But he explained that sovereignty means that "countries are and must remain free to decide on their own attitudes and responses to questions of population. The United Nations system is not equipped, either by law or by practice, to go behind this principle and judge the moral acceptability of programmes." In regard to the principle of reproductive freedom, Mr. Salas said that "the relationship of individual freedom to the needs of society as a whole is a matter for each country to decide." (Raphael M. Salas, "Population Assistance Is Here to Stay," *Populi*, Vol. 12, No. 4, 1985, p. 6.) These interpretations seem to absolve the UNFPA of any responsibility to make its own determination as to whether or not a national family planning program is coercive, thus permitting it to support coercive programs anywhere so long as the countries in question say they oppose coercion.

In 1986 Mr. Salas said that China's birth control practices were coercive by Western but not by Chinese standards. (Remarks to a public forum in Washington sponsored by the Population Institute, April 8, 1986.) In the same year Nafis Sadik, who succeeded Salas as head of the UNFPA, published an article in which she maintained that "any limitations on the exercise of personal and voluntary choice of methods [in family planning] in itself represents a violation of the right to have access to family planning," but then she added that "judgments about what constitutes free and informed choice must be made within the context of a particular culture and the

113

context of the overall government programme for social and economic development . . ." (Nafis Sadik, "The Importance of Voluntarism," *Populi*, Vol. 13, No. 4, 1986, pp. 17 and 22.) These statements seem to imply that the definition of coercion is up to national governments, which negates the idea of universally applicable human rights in family planning. In effect, the UNFPA opposes coercion in principle but not in practice.

15. "World Population Plan of Action," *PDR*, Vol. 1, No. 1, September 1975, p. 167. But the statement adds that "the responsibility of couples and individuals in the exercise of this right takes into account the needs of their living and future children and their responsibilities toward the community . . ." How this responsibility is to be monitored and by what authority is not indicated, but the statement also assumes that the formulation of "national population goals and policies" is to be "democratic."

16. United Nations Department of Technical Cooperation for Development, *Report of the International Conference on Population, 1984*, Mexico City, August 6–14, 1984 (New York: United Nations, 1984), p. 25.

17. See, for example, Jaime Zipper, "Chinese Expand Medical, Family Planning Services," *Population Chronicle*, New York, No. 8, April 1972, p. 1; Pi-chao Chen, "Population Planning: Policy Evolution and Action Programs," in *Public Health in the People's Republic of China* (New York: The Josiah Macy, Jr., Foundation, 1973), p. 247; Henry S. Bradsher, "China's Sweet Talk Yields to Tough Anti-Baby Policy," *Washington Star-News*, September 12, 1973, p. A26; John S. Aird, "Fertility Decline and Birth Control in the People's Republic of China," *PDR*, Vol. 4, No. 2, June 1978, pp. 243–245; and John S. Aird, "Population Growth in the People's Republic of China," in Joint Economic Committee, Congress of the United States, *Chinese Economy Post-Mao*, Vol. 1: *Policy and Performance* (Washington: U.S. Government Printing Office, November 9, 1978), pp. 442–449.

18. In 1981 Rafael Salas was quoted as saying that "China provides a superb example of integrating population programs with the national goals of development." ("1% Population Growth Goal for Asia," *Popline*, Washington, Vol. 3, No. 11, November 1981, p. 2.) In 1982 Werner Fornos, president of the Washington-based Population Institute, reportedly said that the Chinese program was "one that the world should copy" and in 1984 that "China has shown the world what can be done when people conscientiously tackle the problem." ("*China Daily* Wins Global Media Award," *CD*, March 16, 1982, p. 3; and "Husbands Praised by Population Expert," *CD*, November 24, 1984, p. 1.) At the International Population Conference in Mexico City in August 1984, many delegations reportedly applauded China's family planning program as a model. (Guo Da, "Support for Birth Control," *CD*, November 3, 1984, p. 4.) In April 1984, the Population Institute editorialized that "strict laws and, yes, even coercion to ensure birth control compliance are alternatives to which many nations may have to resort in the near future if they fail to promote voluntary family planning programs now." ("Journal Misses Mark" [editorial], *Popline*, Vol. 6, No. 4, April 1984, p. 2.) In 1985, a World-watch Institute report listed India, Nigeria, Bangladesh, Mexico, Pakistan,

Ethiopia, the Philippines, Syria, South Africa, Peru, Iran, Algeria, Zimbabwe, Zaire, Tanzania, Kenya, Ghana, Bolivia, Uganda, and Senegal as countries that might have to "follow the lead of China" in adopting the one-child policy. ("One-Child Policy Looms as Possible Trend for Future," *Popline*, Vol. 7, No. 2, February 1985, p. 1.)

19. For example, from a UNFPA publication: "In the main, the success of the Chinese family planning programme is due to a clear enunciation of goals and a precise definition of strategies. The entire programme is backed up by strict discipline as well as a national consensus sustained through massive publicity and group dynamics, aided by excellent communications." (Harish Khanna, "China and Population," p. 55.)

20. In its 1981 "status report" on the Chinese program, the Population Crisis Committee said the Chinese program demonstrated "what can be accomplished by an authoritarian government with a rigorous and determined population control policy." The report alluded to the program's "massive education/propaganda program," its incentives and penalties, and its use of "enormous pressure" to terminate unauthorized pregnancies, and warned that the Chinese "model" was probably applicable only to other "highly organized societies." It conceded that "according to some reports" abortion "may be used coercively." ("Status Report on Population Problems and Programs of the People's Republic of China," September 1981.) Subsequent friendly assessments were less candid. On a visit to China in the middle of 1983, the year when coercion in family planning reached its peak, Donald Lubin, then Deputy Secretary-General of the International Planned Parenthood Federation, reportedly said that "the whole of [Chinese] society supported the program," that "the one-child policy has been approved by the people," and that "they saw it as in their interests and they practice it willingly." (XINHUA-English, Beijing, June 12, 1983, JPRS, No. 83–802, June 30, 1983, p. 48.)

21. When the issues are discussed, it is usually in the abstract. An exception is a 1979 monograph by Berelson and Lieberson on the ethical implications of existing governmental policies on fertility, with particular reference to China, Indonesia, and India. At that time, the evidence on coercion in the Chinese program was just beginning to accumulate, and its significance was still underestimated. The authors considered limiting access to methods of fertility control impermissible, incentive systems permissible except under unusual circumstances, and "politically organized peer pressure" permissible only under specified conditions. In general, the ethical status of governmental intervention in human fertility depended on whether the decision to intervene was arrived at with adequate citizen participation and on what sort of considerations entered into it. Some of the tactics used in the Chinese family planning program, details of which later became common knowledge, would not have met the criteria suggested by these authors. See Bernard Berelson and Jonathan Lieberson, "Governmental Intervention on Fertility: What Is Ethical?" Center for Policy Studies, Working Papers, No. 48 (New York: The Population Council, October 1979). In June

1988, at a meeting in Bangkok co-sponsored by UNFPA, the World Health Organization, and several other organizations, such questions as "Where is the boundary between 'incentives' and coercion?" were discussed. The discussants recognized that there are conflicts between "the individual's right of choice and society's goals and responsibilities," but seem to have come to no conclusion as to how these were to be resolved. ("Meeting Focusses on Family Planning Ethics," *Population: UNFPA Newsletter*, Vol. 14, No. 11, November 1988.)

22. In May 1983, when mandatory sterilization for couples with two or more children was the key measure in China's family planning program, a Beijing UNFPA official, questioned by a U.S. correspondent, said, "If there is a very explicit regulation that all couples with a second child must be sterilized, it could cause serious problems for the United Nations." (Michael Weisskopf, "China Orders Sterilization for Parents," *WP*, May 28, 1983, p. A1.) In June 1983 the author sent to Mr. Sjaak Bavelaar, then the UNFPA deputy in Beijing, a translation of an article from a Guangzhou newspaper which quoted Guangdong Vice-Governor Wang Pingshan's statement that sterilization for couples with two children, IUD insertion for women with one child, and abortion for unauthorized pregnancies were mandated by a policy directive of the State Family Planning Commission, adopted with the prior approval of the Party Central Committee and the State Council. The quoted statement would surely have qualified as a "very explicit regulation." There was no reply from Mr. Bavelaar, and, despite whatever "problems" the directive may have caused, UNFPA support for the Chinese program continued.

23. The decision on who was to receive the awards was announced in March 1983. ("Xinzhong, Gandhi Win Population Awards," *Popline*, Vol. 5, No. 3, April 1983, pp. 1 and 4.) When the announcement was made, one of the five members of the UN committee's technical advisory panel, the Nobel laureate economist Prof. Theodore W. Schultz, denounced the choices as a "travesty" and asked that his name be removed from any mention of the awards. (Bernard Nossiter, "Population Prizes from UN Assailed," *NYT*, July 24, 1983, p. 4.) The awards were not actually presented until the end of September 1983. The Chinese authorities not unreasonably interpreted their award as an endorsement of their family planning program. In a 1984 article, the SFPC said: "China's family planning success is recognized and commended by countries around the world. In 1983 our former director of the SFPC, Comrade Qian Xinzhong, won the UN population award. This shows that the UN and the countries of the world approve of the achievements we have made." (State Family Planning Commission, "Zou Zhongguoshi de jihua shengyu gongzuo daolu" ["Take the Chinese Road to Family Planning Work"], *Jiankang bao jihua shengyu ban* [*Health Gazette Family Planning Edition*] [*JKBJHSYB*], Beijing, September 28, 1984, p. 1.)

24. "Perez de Cuellar Issues Warning on Overpopulation," *Popline*, Vol. 5, No. 9, October 1983, p. 4.

25. The group's report affirmed the right of individual couples to make

voluntary informed choices about childbearing, rejected measures that favored one contraceptive method over another, and set limits on the use of incentives and disincentives in government programs. The Assembly was "sharply divided" on whether to publish the report or not and finally agreed to publish it as the working group's report but "not as a reflection of IPPF's present policies and objectives." ("Human Rights Defined," *People*, Vol. 11, No. 1, 1984, p. 36.) The IPPF has consistently regarded the CFPA as a "volunteer" organization, ignoring the evidence that all "mass" organizations in China are instigated and controlled by the Chinese government.

26. Michael Weisskopf, "Shanghai's Curse: Too Many Fight for Too Little," *WP*, January 6, 1985, pp. A1 and A30; Weisskopf, "Abortion Policy Tears at Fabric of China's Society," *WP*, January 7, 1985, pp. A1 and A20; and Weisskopf, "China's Birth Control Policy Drives Some to Kill Baby Girls," *WP*, January 8, 1985, pp. A1 and A10.

27. United Nations Fund for Population Activities, "UNFPA and China: Briefing Note," February 9, 1985, pp. 2–5.

28. XINHUA-English, Beijing, May 6, 1988, FBIS, No. 90, May 9, 1988, p. 33.

29. Ann Scott Tyson, "China, UN Join Forces to Reshape Population Policy," *The Christian Science Monitor* (*CSM*), Boston, January 27, 1989, pp. 1–2. The first two programs each involved expenditures of $50 million; the third is for $57 million, according to XINHUA-English, Beijing, July 2, 1989, FBIS, No. 126, July 3, 1989, p. 2.

30. Liu Wenhui, "Third of the Population Series: China's Family Planning—Successful But Misunderstood," XINHUA-English, April 14, 1989, FBIS, No. 72, April 17, 1989, p. 52.

31. Congress of the United States, *Congressional Record*, Vol. 135, No. 85, June 22, 1989, p. H3059.

32. "China's Views on Major Issues of World Population," *BR*, Vol. 17, No. 35, August 30, 1974, pp. 6–9. China was presumably responsible for the inclusion in the statement of the assertion that "Of all things in the world, people are the most precious," a maxim Mao Zedong used in the 1950s to refute the notion that population growth needed to be controlled. In fact, the Chinese birth control program, already in full swing in 1974, was driven in part by the belief that rapid population growth strained the economic resources of the state. The Chinese position at the Bucharest conference was therefore hypocritical.

33. For a recent articulation, see Xiao Jiabao, "Four Major Crises China Will Face and Countermeasures," *LWOE*, No. 10, March 6, 1989, FBIS, No. 74, April 19, 1989, pp. 28–34. The "population crisis" is the first of the four, followed by a "natural resources crisis," an "environmental crisis," and a "food grain crisis." The current Minister-in-Charge of the State Family Planning Commission, Peng Peiyun, recently said that she did not agree that China faced a "big explosion" or a "big crisis," but she did allow that "we indeed face a grim situation in the population problem . . ." (Ai Xiao, "I Hope That Everyone Will Conscientiously Carry Out Family Planning—An

Interview with Peng Peiyun, Minister of the State Family Planning Commission," *Renmin ribao* [*People's Daily*] [*RMRB*], Beijing, April 14, 1989, FBIS, No. 74, April 19, 1989, p. 35.)

34. Divergent points of view were expressed at a forum sponsored by the American Enterprise Institute in December 1984. See Ben Wattenberg and Karl Zinsmeister, eds., *Are World Population Trends a Problem?* (Washington: American Enterprise Institute for Public Policy Research, 1985).

35. Working Group on Population Growth and Economic Development, *Population Growth and Economic Development: Policy Questions* (Washington: National Academy Press, 1986), pp. 8–9 and 85–93.

36. Among the more considered responses are Paul Demeny, "Population and the Invisible Hand," Center for Policy Studies, Working Papers, No. 123 (New York: The Population Council, May 1986); and Demeny, "Demography and the Limits to Growth," Research Division, Working Papers, No. 2 (New York: The Population Council, 1989).

37. Paper by Samuel H. Preston in Wattenberg and Zinsmeister, *Are World Population Trends a Problem?* p. 10.

38. *P. A. A. Affairs*, Fall 1978, p. 2.

39. One exception is the American demographer, Kingsley Davis, who in 1977 suggested "penalizing overreproductive parents" by "requiring an abortion in the case of an additional pregnancy, by removal of the last child to better circumstances with adoptive parents, [and] by requiring sterilization of one partner . . ." (Kingsley Davis, "World Population Growth and United States Foreign Aid," prepared for hearings before the Appropriations Committee of the U.S. House of Representatives, March 1977.) The Chinese government subsequently adopted two of these measures. In 1982 Davis wrote an article for *People*, the journal of the International Planned Parenthood Federation, deploring popular opposition to government compulsion in family planning, which he likened to legal restrictions on hunting, fishing, speeding, and polluting the atmosphere. He argued that because desired family size in developing countries was generally too high, compulsion was necessary to avoid overpopulation, the dangers of which he took for granted. His article was the first piece by a foreign population specialist to be reprinted in the Chinese press. (Kingsley Davis, "Population Control Not Painless," *CD*, November 13, 1982, p. 4.)

40. In 1987 a UNFPA journal reprinted an article from an Indian newspaper which lauded the Chinese program because its approach was "not sentimental" and because "the lure of the vote does not compel [the] political leadership to keep quiet or to take vague positions." (Harish Khanna, "China and Population," p. 56.) The author's admiration for the decisiveness of totalitarian government and contempt for the popular will are transparent.

41. Statement attributed to Dr. James Grant, Executive Director of UNICEF, in the paper by Samuel H. Preston in Wattenberg and Zinsmeister, *Are World Population Trends a Problem?* p. 13.

42. In affidavits filed in September and October 1985 with the United States District Court for the District of Columbia as justification for bringing

a lawsuit to prevent AID from withholding funds from the U.S. contribution to the UNFPA, Werner Fornos, President of the Population Institute, and George Zeidenstein, President of the Population Council, both affirmed that their organizations had received funds from the UNFPA which were put in jeopardy by the AID action. Fornos said his organization had received $150,000 in fiscal 1985 and was expecting an additional $100,000 if the UNFPA received the remainder of the U.S. contribution. Zeidenstein said the Population Council had received only $700,000 of the $1,243,000 that the UNFPA had committed to it for fiscal 1985 and that another $100,000 was pending. The suit was dismissed by the District Court in October 1985, then appealed to the United States Court of Appeals for the District of Columbia by the Population Institute. The Appeals Court upheld AID's action in August 1986. In effect, however, the UNFPA's grants to domestic U.S. institutions have created what amounts to a paid lobby supported in part by U.S. taxpayers.

43. In 1986, Chen Muhua said that China's 1982 census was "of great significance . . . [in] formulating and implementing its population policy in an even better way." (XINHUA, Beijing, March 6, 1986, FBIS, No. 45, March 7, 1986, p. K19.) Zheng Jiaheng, Deputy Director of the State Statistical Bureau, told a national statistical conference in Beijing in April 1989 that the 1990 census would play a vital role in helping China meet its targets for population control. (Guo Zhongshi, "Preparations Begin for 1990 National Census," CD, April 28, 1989, FBIS, No. 81, April 28, 1989, p. 30.) One purpose of the July 1988 fertility survey was to "provide reliable, comprehensive data for formulating . . . population policy . . ." (SFPC Spokesman, "The Situation of Population Development, Population Policy, and Family Planning Measures of China," China Population Research Leads, Shanghai, No. 3, December 1988, p. 13.) The national survey of population changes during 1988 undertaken in January 1989 was also to be used for "formulating population plans." (Wang Lunwen, "Quanguo 1988–nian renkou biandong qingkuang chouyang diaocha gongzuo huiyi zai Taiyuan zhaokai" ["Work Conference on Nationwide Sample Survey of Population Changes in 1988 Held in Taiyuan"], Shanxi tongji [Shanxi Statistics], Taiyuan, No. 10, October 16, 1988, p. 4.) The same justification is offered for the many other national and provincial population surveys conducted in the past few years. Of course, both censuses and surveys serve many other purposes not related to family planning.

44. At the Third National Population Science Conference in Beijing in February 1981, Chen Muhua, then a vice-premier and head of the SFPC, called upon China's demographers to supply propaganda materials for family planning, to provide "scientific" support for the official population policies, and to support the government's efforts to control population growth. (Chen Muhua, "Fazhan renkou kexue weikongzhi renkou zengzhang mubiao fuwu" ["Develop Population Science to Support Controlling Population Growth"], Renkou yanjiu [Population Research] [RKYJ], Beijing, No. 3, July 1981, pp. 1–7.)

45. For example, senior anthropologist Fei Xiaotong insisted in 1987 that

he had always believed and still believed that population problems were a symptom, not a cause, of China's ills, the solution to which lay in social and economic development rather than in stringent population controls. (Fei Xiaotong, "Zhongguo yao zuohao liangjian renkou dashi" ["China Must Do Two Things Well in Population"], *Zhongguo jihua shengyu bao* [*China Population*] [*ZGJHSYB*], Beijing, October 9, 1987, p. 3.) The demographer Wu Cangping tried repeatedly in the early 1980s to warn the government about the aging of the Chinese population, though he has since been obliged to express support for the current policies. (Wu Cangping, "Some Population Problems That Should Be Deliberated Upon at an Early Date," *Shijie jingji daobao* [*World Economic Report*], Shanghai, No. 165, December 12, 1983, FBIS, No. 8, January 12, 1984, pp. K3–6; and Wu Cangping, "Yingdang zhuyi de liangge renkou wenti" ["Two Problems We Should Pay Attention To"], *Jingji wenzhai* [*Economic Digest*], Beijing, No. 4, 1984, p. 58.)

46. In March 1988, a reporter talked with "some demographers," not otherwise identified, who criticized the government for allowing its one-child policies to be weakened by changes in leadership in the SFPC. They charged that the rise in the birth rates after 1985 was due to policy changes made "regardless of the objections of some demographers." (Liu Jingzhi, "Experts Concerned Are Not Optimistic About China's Population Situation and Think That Interference by Officials Is an Important Reason Why Birth Rate Has Risen Again," *Guangming ribao* [*Bright Daily*] [*GMRB*], Beijing, March 6, 1988, FBIS, No. 53, March 18, 1988, pp. 14–15.) This article apparently offended the SFPC, and the author was obliged to retract the charges six weeks later. (Liu Jingzhi, "Guojia jishengwei zhuangjia zixunzu chengyuan Ma Yingtong shuo woguo kongzhi renkou nengli jin yibu jiaqiang" ["Ma Yingtong, Member of the Consultative Team of the State Family Planning Commission, Says That China's Ability to Control Population Is Further Strengthened"], *GMRB*, April 24, 1988, p. 2.) The press summary of proceedings at a "scholars' forum" on population problems in April 1989 represents all participants as basically supporting the government's position on the seriousness of the population problem in China and the urgency of population control. The summary may, however, be somewhat misleading, or the views expressed at the forum may not have reflected the actual extent of dissent among the participants. (Qu Wei, "China's Population Situation and Measures to Cope with the Problem," *Qunyan* [*Popular Tribune*] [*QY*], Beijing, No. 4, April 7, 1989, JPRS, No. 89–072, July 10, 1989, pp. 32–40.)

47. During 1983, when national policy required all women in China with one child to have IUDs inserted, a new IUD factory was completed with UNFPA support. It was expected to go into full production in 1984. (Executive Director of the United Nations Fund for Population Activities, *1983 Report* [New York: United Nations, 1984], p. 80.) In October 1982 a Chinese demographic journal reported that an investigation in one locality had found a failure rate of over 30 percent for Chinese-made IUDs. (See Yang Jishun and Xu Peng, "The Principal Measure to Implement Birth Control Is the Practice of Contraception," *Renkou yu jingji* [*Population and Economy*] [*RKYJJ*], Beijing,

No. 5, October 25, 1983, JPRS, No. 84,994, December 21, 1983, p. 95.) In 1984 a foreign visitor was told that the failure rate of Chinese IUDs was 20 percent per year. The Chinese IUDs also caused excessive bleeding, pelvic and back pain, and pelvic inflammatory disease. They were inserted without the nylon "tails" used in other countries, undoubtedly (although the source does not say this) because the "tails" would have facilitated unauthorized removals, an implicit admission that the insertions were made without the consent of the recipients. The absence of tails also made it hard for family planning workers to check on whether the IUDs were still in place, so some areas resorted to X-ray or fluoroscope examinations every two to three months, an added risk to the health of the women. (Diana Smith, "Chinese Ring Causes Concern," *People*, Vol. 12, No. 4, 1985, pp. 32–33.)

48. The Chinese authorities have shown considerable interest in new contraceptive technology, including contraceptives that lend themselves to coercive applications. In March 1984 they rewarded the Chinese inventor of an injectable abortifacient that brings on an abortion within five days. ("Yizhong rengong liuchan xin yao Shenyang wenshi" ["A New Artificial Abortion Drug Appears in Shenyang"], *JKBJHSYB*, March 30, 1984, p. 1.) In July 1985 it was announced that the Chinese would shortly begin clinical tests of the abortifacient Ru–486 in collaboration with a French research institution. (AGENCE FRANCE PRESSE, Hong Kong, July 20, 1985, JPRS, No. 85–084, August 20, 1985, pp. 26–27.) A total of five plants for the manufacture of contraceptives were built in China with UNFPA help, including plants in Beijing, Shanghai, and Tianjin. The Beijing plant began production in March 1985. ("Contraceptive Factory Opens," *CD*, March 11, 1985, p. 3.) A "substantial" portion of the UNFPA $50 million allocation to China for 1985–89 reportedly has been used for the production of contraceptives. Some, such as pills and condoms, are not very amenable to compulsory applications, but injectable contraceptives are. Factories established with UNFPA aid are said to be producing enough injectable contraceptives for 2.5 million women each year. (Pramilla Senanayake, "China's Expanding Contraceptive Range," *People*, Vol. 16, No. 1, 1989, p. 36.)

49. The national family planning journal, commenting on the results of the 1988 fertility survey, said that the survey "will play an active role in furthering the analysis of the status of family planning work, in correcting the exaggerations in the reports of family planning statistics, in evaluating current policies, in strengthening scientific management, and in having tight control over family planning work." (Commentator, "Shi shi qiu shi gaohao tongji" ["Seek Truth from Facts and Do Well in Statistics"], *Zhongguo renkou bao [China Population]* [*ZGRKB*], Beijing, November 14, 1988, p. 1.) In 1989, several provinces reported that they had used surveys to check on family planning work. In February Shaanxi concluded from survey results that its situation was "grim" and adopted "countermeasures." (Huang Huiliang, "Renkou xingshi yanjun ren wei yingqi zhongshi" ["The Population Situation Is Grim; Serious Attention Has Not Been Paid"], *ZGRKB*, February 13, 1989, p. 1.) In May a Hubei municipal unit used survey results to "take charge of

key areas and to grasp weak links" and to locate pregnant women so that it could "adopt prompt remedial measures against unplanned pregnancies." (Yang Minghui, "Shishou shi jishengwei sheli dujue duotai shengyu zeren jijin" ["The Shishou Municipal Family Planning Commission Establishes Fund for (Rewarding Those) Responsible for Ending Excessive Births"], *ZGRKB*, May 15, 1989, p. 1.) In August Fujian used a survey to find out which units had failed to implement its new family planning regulations. (Fuzhou radio, Fujian Provincial Service, August 26, 1989, FBIS, No. 168, August 31, 1989, p. 36.)

50. This argument has been advanced by two American demographers who have been fairly open in alluding to the coerciveness of China's program. At a State Department seminar in April 1986, they said: "It seems to us that our best opportunity to influence China's population policy is by helping China to develop not only technical skills but also the understanding of the ethics and practices of the international scholarly community." (Ronald Freedman and William Lavely, "Comments Made at a Seminar at the United States Department of State on Facts and Policy Implications of Local Area Variations in Reproductive Behavior in The People's Republic of China: 1973–76 to 1979–82," April 30, 1986, p. 6.) The same idea was echoed by the American Public Health Association, which reportedly said that failure to restore U.S. funds for the UNFPA would foreclose "any opportunity to work cooperatively with the Chinese to improve the voluntary nature of their programme." ("Health Group Urges US Support for Fund," *Population: UNFPA Newsletter*, Vol. 14, No. 3, March 1988, p. 2.) It could just as plausibly be argued that the PRC leaders are intelligent enough to recognize the international scholarly community's ethical compromise in substituting quiet diplomacy for public condemnation when professional opportunity is at stake, and that they will discount the moral influence of their "foreign friends" accordingly.

51. In 1985, Bongaarts and Greenhalgh proposed that all Chinese families could be allowed to have two children without causing the total population to exceed the year 2000 target of "within 1.2 billion" provided that women were required to delay first births until age 25. The proposal reportedly attracted considerable attention in China but proved impractical because of the difficulty of controlling the timing of births, especially first births, among married couples. Moreover, according to an advisor to the State Council on population matters, Ma Bin, their article contributed to a perception within China that the central authorities were about to abandon the one-child policy, because it stated that the policy was changing although the SFPC was saying that the policy had *not* changed. He credited Greenhalgh and other American demographers with good intentions but warned that "their understanding of the Chinese situation is after all limited." (John Bongaarts and Susan Greenhalgh, "An Alternative to the One-Child Policy in China," *PDR*, Vol. 11, No. 4, December 1985, pp. 491–515; and Ma Bin, "Wei shixian ben shiji zhongguo renkou kongzhi mubiao bixu wending tichang yidui fufu zhi sheng yige haizi de zhengce" ["To Realize China's Population Control Target in This Century,

the Policy of Advocating One Child Per Couple Must Be Stabilized"], *Lun zhongguo renkou wenti—renkou zhanlue renkou guihua renkou zhengce* [*On China's Population Problems—Population Strategy, Population Planning, and Population Policy*] [Beijing: Zhongguo guoji guangbo chubanshe, 1987], pp. 25–34.) In this case, foreign intervention may have contributed to a temporary relapse in policy enforcement that was already under way, but as a result the influence of foreign demographers may have been discredited among family planning hard-liners in China.

52. On the other hand, foreign criticisms of coercion in the Chinese program as a violation of human rights have apparently strengthened the position of those in China who hold similar views. Ma Bin said that it was difficult to prevent third births by abortion "because of the objections to abortion raised by those Chinese and foreigners who believe in reproductive freedom." He told family planning authorities: "Do not waver because of public opinion in foreign countries and do not be disturbed by those who advocate reproductive freedom." (Ma Bin, "To Realize China's Population Control Target . . .") The moderating influence might have been greater but for other foreigners' support for or tacit acceptance of coercion in the Chinese program.

53. Judith Banister, *China's Changing Population* (Stanford, Calif.: Stanford University Press, 1987), pp. 194–195 and 218.

54. This posture is implicitly assumed by those who refer to coercion in the Chinese program as "alleged" or as one interpretation of evidence that can be otherwise interpreted. For the most part, those who adopt this posture have shown little eagerness to come to grips with the actual evidence, something they would probably not have hesitated to do if they thought it could be shown that the allegations were mistaken. An example of this approach is Barbara B. Crane and Jason L. Finkle, "The United States, China, and the United Nations Population Fund: Dynamics of US Policymaking," *PDR*, Vol. 15, No. 1, March 1989, pp. 23–59. This treatise purports to examine the basis of the AID decision to withhold U.S. funds from the UNFPA, but it pointedly avoids dealing with the merits of the stated basis for that decision— namely, that the Chinese program is coercive—preferring instead to deal with the matter exclusively in terms of political decision-making in the United States. In this respect, the authors follow a line advanced in 1986 by Rafael Salas, former executive director of the UNFPA, who denied that the Chinese program was coercive and attributed the withdrawal of U.S. funds to "domestic reasons" in the United States. ("United States Withdraws Support from Fund," *Population: UNFPA Newsletter*, Vol. 12, No. 9, September 1986, p. 1.)

55. "Paying for Abortions," *WSJ*, April 9, 1984, p. 34.

56. In February 1989 Peng Peiyun, the current Minister-in-Charge of the SFPC, cited a "Summary of Minutes" of a meeting of the Standing Committee of the Political Bureau of the Party Central Committee as "an important document guiding our work at present and for a considerable period of time to come." All levels were directed to study it, implement it strictly, and allow

no deviations from it. It has not been published, presumably because it takes a hard line that does not fit with the government's claim to foreigners that the program is voluntary. (Peng Peiyun, "Guanyu 1989-nian de gongzuo" ["On the Work in 1989"], *ZGRKB*, February 24, 1989, p. 1.) At the end of March, a provincial dispatch referred to "important instructions recently issued by the . . . Central Committee and the State Council on tightening birth control and the guidelines laid down by the national conference of directors of family planning [commissions]," but again the document has not been published. (Zhengzhou radio, Henan Provincial Service, March 30, 1989, FBIS, No. 61, March 31, 1989, p. 60.)

57. Here are two examples: "Energetically stress remedial measures for unscheduled pregnancies." (Haikou radio, Hainan Island Service, April 14, 1987, FBIS, No. 77, April 22, 1987, p. P2) "Above plan pregnancies must be discovered and remedied early . . ." (Zhong Kan, "On Sichuan's Current Population Trends," *Sichuan ribao* [*Sichuan Daily*] [*SCRB*], Chengdu, December 22, 1988, JPRS, No. 89–016, February 27, 1989, p. 37.)

58. Chengdu radio, Sichuan Provincial Service, April 13, 1989, FBIS, No. 71, April 14, 1989, p. 47.

59. For example, "Providing good technical services is another important aspect of developing good family planning. [Fewer] birth control measures were used and a lot less birth control operations were performed in 1988 and, if attention is not paid to solving this problem, above-plan pregnancies may increase in 1989 . . . The technical policy of 'IUDs first and tying tubes second' must be carried out well . . . and technical services should be provided before and not after pregnancies occur." (Zhong Kan, "On Sichuan's Current Population Trends.")

60. In July 1981, a reporter from a Hong Kong newspaper went to Huiyang Prefecture, Guangdong Province, to check on reports of a highly coercive campaign waged there in May and June, when 47,000 women with two or more children who were again pregnant were targeted for abortions. He learned that the worst excesses were committed in the prefecture's Dongguan County, where those women who refused or tried to escape were punished by having their water and electricity cut off, their houses sealed, roof tiles lifted off, children chased out of doors, and fines of as much as 840 *yuan* imposed. (Lo Ming, "Xiachua guaishi wuqibuyou" [Laughable and Peculiar Events; Nothing Is Too Strange'], *Zhengming ribao* [*Contention Daily*] [*ZMRB*], Hong Kong, July 28, 1981, p. 1.) In September, a New China News Agency dispatch from Beijing commended Dongguan County because within a month or so it had "persuaded" over 27,000 people to undergo "birth control surgery." (XINHUA, Beijing, September 11, 1981, FBIS, No. 179, September 16, 1981, p. P1.) According to a survey, the average per capita annual income in rural Guangdong in 1987 was 645 *yuan*. (State Statistical Bureau, *China: Statistical Yearbook, 1988* [Hong Kong: International Centre for the Advancement of Science and Technology, Ltd., 1988], p. 137.)

61. Ma Bin, "To Realize China's Population Control Target . . ."

62. That "administrative measures" often stands for coercive tactics is

indicated in an August 1989 source which advocates that the term be limited to measures that have "the support of the people," a phrase that is also subject to ambiguity. (Qie Jianwei, "Fansi: liangnan de kunjing he zhengque de jueze" ["Retrospective View on the Dilemma and on Making Correct Decisions"], *RKYJJ*, No. 4, August 25, 1989, pp. 3–7 and 28.)

63. In 1984 Werner Fornos, whose Population Institute is a recipient of UNFPA funds, went to China at the invitation of the SFPC. He toured four provinces and two municipalities and said that he found relations between family planning workers and parents to be friendly and confident. Fornos, who does not speak Chinese, said he had not detected any coercion in talking with people during his two-week visit. He said that his institute and the China Population Information Center had agreed to publish jointly a magazine for Chinese family planning workers starting early in 1985 and that his institute was considering sending foreign experts to teach at the Nanjing College for Family Planning Administrators. ("Population Specialist Hails PRC Family Planning," XINHUA-English, Beijing, November 23, 1984, JPRS, 84–081, December 28, 1984, pp. 7–8.)

The most recent example is the trip by John Rowley, editor of the IPPF journal *People*, whose report on his October 1988 trip to China was carried in the first 1989 issue of the journal. (John Rowley and Jeremy Hammand, "Forty Million Volunteers".) In it he declares China's program voluntary and insists that it is moderating and is shifting from state management to "volunteer" management—this at a time when the Chinese family planning authorities are trying to establish an all-encompassing system of "top down" management.

64. See Pranay Gupte, *The Crowded Earth* (New York: W. W. Norton and Company, 1984), p. 156.

65. See "Abortion a Woman's Right—Minister," *CD*, July 31, 1984, p. 1; and "Population Policies Explained at Forum," *CD*, August 9, 1984, p. 1.

66. Peng Peiyun, "Why I Am Extending the Two-Child Option," *People*, Vol. 16, No. 1, 1989, p. 12.

67. Peng Peiyun, "On the Work in 1989." The relevant statement reads: "Late marriage and late child bearing, fewer and higher quality births, and one child per couple must be vigorously promoted. In rural areas, simultaneously with promoting one child per couple, the policy of allowing 'households with only daughters' to have a second birth after a spacing of several years must be conscientiously implemented. To conscientiously implement this policy is to lead the birth behavior of the peasant masses onto the path allowed by the policy. Currently, the reality in the rural areas is that the majority of women give birth to two children . . . If the birth of a second child after a spacing of several years by households with only daughters can truly be achieved, it will be a tightening, not a loosening of the policy." In a letter to the Association of Chinese Population Students in America dated June 6, 1988, Peng had written that "we must adhere to the established family planning policies . . . later marriage, later, fewer, and better births, and one child per couple. The only exceptions are a few peasants who . . .

are allowed to have a second birth . . ." ("A Letter from Ms. Peng Peiyun," *ACPSA Newsletter*, No. 4, July 1988, p. 3.)

68. See Daniel Southerland, "1.1 Billion and Counting," *WP*, March 13, 1989, p. A25.

69. Peng Peiyun, "On the Work in 1989."

70. See "Minister Warns of 'Legal Punishment' for Family Planning Offenders," XINHUA-English, Beijing, February 23, 1989, FBIS, No. 20, March 8, 1989, p. 33.

71. Peng Peiyun, "Zuohao jihua shengyu gongzuo tuijin funu jiefang shiye" ("Do Family Planning Work Well to Push Forward the Liberation of Women"), *ZGRKB*, September 12, 1988, p. 1.

72. For example, in November 1985, Wang Wei reaffirmed the "principle" in an address to a national population conference. (Wang Wei, "A Speech at the Fourth National Symposium on Population Science," *Population Research*, Beijing, Vol. 3, No. 3, July 1986, p. 8.) In January 1987, the Chinese representative to 24th Session of the United Nations Population Commission cited the principle as part of a denial that coercive family planning practices in China were caused by the government's policy. ("Statement by Mr. Chang Chongxuan" [mimeo], January 29, 1987, pp. 4–5.)

73. At the present time, about one-third of the local units in the country are said to be "backward" in family planning. Current policy demands that they catch up with the rest. (Yang Chaoling, "Peng Peiyun, Minister of the State Family Planning Commission, on China's Family Planning Situation and Policy," *LWOE*, April 25, 1988, FBIS, No. 84, May 2, 1988, p. 34–35.) The recent policy of allowing some rural families with only daughters to have a second child has not been extended to Sichuan, Jiangsu, and Hebei provinces or the three central municipalities—Beijing, Tianjin, and Shanghai—or is applied there under very tight restrictions. Sources differ on this point. See Pierre-Antoine Donnet, "One-Child Rule Said Relaxed in Rural Areas," AGENCE FRANCE PRESSE, Hong Kong, August 4, 1988, FBIS, No. 150, August 4, 1988, p. 37; and Qu Wei, "China's Population Situation and Measures to Cope with the Problem," *QY*, April 7, 1989, JPRS, No. 89–072, July 10, 1989, p. 35.

74. When the Han population were required to stop at one child, with only exceptional categories allowed to have a second, most minorites were allowed to have two, with exceptional categories permitted to have a third. Similar policies applied to dwellers in remote frontier and mountain regions where life in general was difficult. Now minorities residing in areas in which the majority of the population are Han Chinese must observe the stricter limits required of the Hans.

75. A Sichuan source reveals that the quoted phrases mean somewhat more than they seem to imply. "To unify thinking will mean integrating all ideas with and upholding the [provincial family planning] 'Regulations' wholeheartedly and firmly. To stabilize the policies will mean enforcing the 'Regulations' to the letter and allowing no unauthorized expansion of birth categories or two-birth preferential treatment on any pretext or in any name." (Zhong Kan, "On Sichuan's Current Population Trends.")

76. In spite of the effort to "unify thinking," there is apparently profound disagreement among technical specialists in China at present about how serious China's population problem is and how much coercion should be used. When their views appear in print, however, they all seem to support the official policies. For a recent example, see Qu Wei, "China's Population Situation . . . ," pp. 32–40.

77. Some foreign apologists for the Chinese family planning program use an even narrower definition of "coercion," limiting the term to "outright physical force." See Crane and Finkle, "The United States, China, and the United Nations Population Fund . . . ," p. 24. The purpose, of course, is to exculpate the Chinese authorities from the coercion charge.

78. The claim that cadres who use coercion are quickly punished seems to be reserved for communications directed at foreigners. For one example, see Xin Lin, "A Realistic Population Policy," BR, Vol. 27, No. 30, July 23, 1984, p. 4. Two weeks before this article appeared, a domestic journal for rural cadres recommended a much gentler treatment for the guilty parties: "Those who have used coercion and force must be persuaded to refrain from such practices." (Editorial Department, "Guanyu dangqian jihua shengyu gongzuo de jige wenti" ["Several Questions on Current Family Planning Work"], Nongcun gongzuo tongxun [Rural Work Bulletin] [NCGZTX], Beijing, No. 7, July 5, 1984, p. 21.)

79. "Some Current Problems in Drafting Laws," GMRB, December 22, 1978, FBIS, No. 3, January 4, 1979, p. E7; "Lianxi shiji wenti tantao renkou guilu" ("Relate Real Problems to the Study of Population Laws"), GMRB, November 28, 1978. p. 3; Guangzhou radio, Guangdong Provincial Service, December 21, 1978, JPRS, No. 72,593, January 10, 1979, pp. 80–81; Zhengzhou radio, Henan Provincial Service, May 3, 1979, FBIS, No. 91, May 9, 1979, p. P3; Guangzhou radio, Guangdong Provincial Service, May 9, 1979, p. 68; and Liu Haiquan, "Control Population Growth with the Same Drive Used in Grasping Production and Construction," GMRB, September 13, 1979, JPRS, No. 74,694, December 3, 1979, p. 68.

80. For one example, see the family planning regulations adopted by a district in Guangzhou Municipality cited in chapter 4.

81. For example, provincial and national approval was accorded to Huiyang Prefecture in 1981 for tactics that included a number of physically coercive measures. See John S. Aird, "Coercion in Family Planning: Causes, Methods, and Consequences," in Joint Economic Committee, Congress of the United States, China's Economy Looks Toward the Year 2000, Vol. 1, The Four Modernizations (Washington: U.S. Government Printing Office, 1986), pp. 208–11.

82. In March 1982 a directive from the Party Central Committee and the State Council authorizing "economic restrictions" against people who failed to practice family planning warned that "we should rely primarily on ideological education and encouragement to promote family planning work." ("Central Committee and State Council Urge Better Family Planning," XINHUA, Beijing, March 13, 1982, British Broadcasting Corporation, Summary of World

Broadcasts, London, No. FE/6981/BII, p. 7.) This theme was echoed in other central and provincial instructions through the spring, summer, and fall of 1982, along with warnings to supplement ideological education with "administrative actions," economic penalties, "mobilizations" of women pregnant without permission to undergo "remedial measures" (abortions), and other "resolute and vigorous measures," which, one provincial source revealed, were also in accord with the directives of the central authorities. (Guiyang radio, Guizhou Provincial Service, October 29, 1982, JPRS, No. 82–347, November 30, 1982, p. 85.) In November Bo Yibo, a member of the State Council, in a speech to a national family planning conference, said: "It is wrong to neglect propaganda. However, propaganda alone is not enough. Corresponding measures should be adopted." The "corresponding measures" included IUD insertion, sterilization, and abortion, the three major methods made mandatory in 1983. (Bo Yibo, "Kongzhi renkou yao tong shixian fan liangfan de zhanlue mubiao tong bu jinxing" ["Population Control Must March in Step with the Strategic Target of Quadrupling Output"], *Jiankang bao* [*Health Gazette*] [*JKB*], Beijing, November 28, 1982, pp. 1–2.) And in December, on the eve of the acutely coercive drive of 1983, orders for which had already been issued by the Party Central Committee and the State Council, the Sixth Five-Year Plan, adopted by the Fifth National People's Congress, said that "while we must persist mainly in ideological education, we should at the same time adopt the necessary supplementary economic and organizational measures." ("Sixth 5-Year Plan 'Excerpts' " *RMRB*, December 13, 1982, FBIS, No. 244, December 20, 1982, p. K36.)

83. This practice was disclosed to a Hong Kong reporter during interviews in Huiyang Prefecture, Guangdong Province, during a highly coercive campaign in the summer of 1981. The leader who directed the program told the cadres that the same methods were being used throughout the country. (Lo Ming, " 'Zuo' xing weigai huaiyun youzui" ["The 'Leftist' Nature Has Not Been Changed"], *ZMRB* July 27, 1981, p. 1; and Lo Ming, "Laughable and Peculiar Events . . .")

84. In 1985, commenting on Chinese claims that their program was "voluntary," a *New York Times* correspondent said that "most Western diplomats and experts consider the Chinese statements true only by an Orwellian definition of voluntarism." (John F. Burns, "In China These Days, an Only Child Is the Only Way," *NYT*, May 12, 1985, p. 24E.)

85. "Couples with More Than One Child Seek Shelter Along Borders of Hunan, Hubei, Sichuan, and Guizhou," ZHONGGUO TONGXUN SHE, Hong Kong, January 20, 1989, JPRS, No. 89–014, February 15, 1989, pp. 44–45.

86. See chapter 4.

87. Xie Zhenjiang, "There Is No Route of Retreat," *Jingji ribao* (*Economic Daily*) (*JJRB*), Beijing, January 24, 1989, FBIS, No. 30, February 15, 1989, pp. 36–37.

88. See chapter 2.

89. Permitting exceptions to the one-child limit is said to "create the

impression in people's minds that the central authority makes frequent changes," according to Ma Bin. He adds, "Frequent policy changes cause confusion among the basic level family planning cadres and among the masses. It is extremely damaging to family planning work." (Ma Bin, "To Realize China's Population Control Target . . .")

90. See chapter 4.

91. In 1984, Wang Wei, the Minister-in-Charge of the SFPC, said that up to 1983 women with only one child accounted for only 21 percent of all married women in the reproductive ages, women with two accounted for 24 percent, and those with three or more for 19 percent. He cited these figures as proof that the one-child policy was just a "recommendation." ("Abortion a Woman's Right—Minister," *CD*, July 31, 1984, p. 1.) In November 1988, Peng Peiyun noted in an interview with the English language newspaper *China Daily* that "not all families have only one child each, because more than half of the families have more than one child, and rural couples who have a daughter as a first child are allowed to have a second baby and the ethnic minority people enjoy even more freedom in this respect . . ." (XINHUA-English, Beijing, November 1, 1988, JPRS, No. 88–080, December 19, 1988, p. 49.)

92. For example, in his 1987 *New York Times* article, James H. Scheuer, a member of the U.S. House of Representatives from New York, said that on a trip to China he had found "that the much publicized one child policy was not what it seemed. The national average is actually 2.2 children per family with the strongest adherence to the one child policy occurring in urban areas, where housing is in short supply. The policy is far less rigid in the rural areas . . . Last year nearly 50 percent of the births in China were in families that already had one child." (James H. Scheuer, "China's Family Planning and the U.S.") Some foreign apologists assert that the central authorities are not serious about the one-child limit and use it merely as a propaganda tool to attain a real objective of two children per couple. (See Appendix B.) This would come as news to the grassroots family planning cadres and the couples they supervise.

CHAPTER 2: BIRTH CONTROL IN CHINA, 1949–1983

1. Sun Jingzhi, "Suqing dilixue zhong de chong Mei sixiang" ("Eliminate the Worship-America Ideology in the Field of Geography"), *RMRB*, Beijing, August 2, 1952, April 25, 1952; and E. Stuart Kirby, "China's Population Problem," *Far Eastern Economic Review*, Hong Kong, Vol. 24, No. 17, April 24, 1958, p. 613.

2. "The Bankruptcy of the Idealist Conception of History," September 16, 1949, in *Selected Works of Mao Tse-tung*, Vol. 4 (Beijing: Foreign Languages Press, 1961), pp. 453–454.

3. "Grain Production Increase Is the Primary Task on the Production Front," *RMRB*, April 15, 1953, American Consulate General, Hong Kong, *Survey of China Mainland Press (SCMP)*, No. 551, April 15, 1953, p. 14.

4. Deng Zihui, "Rural Work; Its Basic Mission and Policy," *RMRB*, July 23, 1953, American Consulate General, Hong Kong, *Current Background* (*CB*), No. 255, August 10, 1953, pp. 3 and 13.

5. Bai Jianhua, "600 Million People—A Great Strength for Socialist Construction of China," *RMRB*, November 1, 1954, *SCMP*, No. 926, November 11–12, 1954, pp. 32–34.

6. This fact was not disclosed until several years later. ("Exercise Appropriate Birth Control," *RMRB* [editorial], March 5, 1957, *SCMP*, No. 1487, March 12, 1957, p. 6.)

7. Shao Lizi, "Concerning the Problem of Dissemination of Knowledge about Contraception," *GMRB*, December 19, 1954, *SCMP*, No. 976, January 28, 1955, p. 26.

8. "Deputy Shao Lizi Speaks at National People's Congress," *RMRB*, September 18, 1954, *SCMP*, No. 690, November 2, 1954, pp. 3–5. In an article in another Beijing newspaper in December 1954, Shao said his *People's Daily* article had evoked many critical letters, but the views of his opponents were not published in the Chinese press. (Shao Lizi, "Concerning the Problem of Dissemination of Knowledge about Contraception," *GMRB*, December 19, 1954, *SCMP*, 976, January 28, 1955, p. 26.)

9. Again, the fact that the symposium had taken place was not made public until two years later and the text of Liu's remarks until 29 years later. ("Exercise Appropriate Birth Control"; and Liu Shaoqi, "Tichang jieyu" ["Promote Birth Control"], speech at the symposium of December 27, 1954, *JKB*, November 20, 1983, p. 1.)

10. Mao Zedong, "On the Cooperativization of Agriculture," XINHUA, Beijing, October 16, 1955, *CB*, No. 364, October 19, 1955, p. 8. Mao said that China's frequent natural calamities were "due to the large population."

11. Yu Rongpei, "Mao Zedong shehuixue sixiang yanjiu" ("Research on Mao Zedong's Thoughts on Sociology"), *Shehui kexue zhanxian* (*Social Sciences Front*), Beijing, No. 1, January 25, 1983, p. 240.

12. State Family Planning Commission, "Woguo de jihua shengyu gongzuo" ("China's Family Planning Work"), *Guanghui de chengjiu (xia ce)* (*Glorious Achievements [Volume 2]*) (Beijing: Renmin chubanshe, September 1984), pp. 446–486.

13. Mao's remarks about "extinction" were cited in Kong Xiwu, "Jianyi zhaokai jieyu gongzuo huiyi" ("Birth Control Work Conference Proposed"), *Heilongjiang ribao (Heilongjiang Daily)* (*HLJRB*), Haerbin, June 11, 1957. His comment about "anarchy" in human reproduction was made in a speech at the enlarged plenary session of the Eighth Party Central Committee on October 9, 1957 and published in *Selected Works of Mao Zedong*, Vol. 5, p. 488. His demand that mankind achieve planned increase was reported in State Family Planning Commission, "China's Family Planning Work."

14. "Weishengbu fachu guanyu biyun gongzuo zhishi" ("The Ministry of Public Health Issues a Directive Concerning Contraceptive Work"), *GMRB*, August 13, 1956.

15. "Shao Lizi on Contraception at Hangzhou," *Hangzhou ribao* (*Hangzhou*

Daily), Hangzhou, December 21, 1956, *SCMP*, No. 1458, January 25, 1957, p. 7; "Shandong Provincial People's Council Directive on Scientific Contraception," *Dazhong ribao (Mass Daily) (DZRB)*, Jinan, February 14, 1957, *SCMP*, No. 1487, March 12, 1957, p. 13; "Exercise Appropriate Birth Control" (editorial), *RMRB*, March 5, 1957, *SCMP*, No. 1487, March 12, 1957, p. 6; Yuan Anzhuan and Yang Zhenguo, "Duo fangmian luli dadao jiezhi shengyu de mudi" ("Many-Sided Efforts to Achieve the Objective of Birth Control"), *RMRB*, March 24, 1957; and Wang Zuo and Dai Yuanzhen, "Criticism and Appraisal of the 'New Theory of Population,' " *Jingji yanjiu (Economic Research) (JJYJ)*, Beijing, No. 2, February 17, 1958, American Consulate General, Hong Kong, *Extracts from China Mainland Magazines (ECMM)*, No. 128, May 12, 1958, p. 7.

16. "How to Approach the Problem of Birth Control," *Xin Zhongguo funu (Women of New China)*, Beijing, Nos. 4 and 5, 1955, *ECMM*, No. 2, August 22, 1955, p. 8.

17. Zhou Efen, "How to Treat the Question of Contraception," *Zhongguo qingnian (Youth of China) (ZGQN)*, Beijing, No. 4, February 16, 1955, *SCMP*, No. 1017, March 29, 1955, pp. 29–30.

18. "Shandong Provincial People's Council Directive on Scientific Contraception"; "Shi weishengju zhaokai jieyu zuotanhui jueding jiaqiang biyun de xuanquan he zhidao" ("Municipal Public Health Bureau Holds Birth Control Symposium and Decides to Strengthen Contraceptive Propaganda and Guidance"), *Chichihaer ribao (Chichihaer Daily)*, Chichihaer, March 26, 1957; "Jieyu xuanquan xuyao guangfan jinxing" ("Birth Control Propaganda Needs to Be Carried Out Extensively"), *Xin Hunan bao (New Hunan Daily) (XHNB)*, Changsha, March 17, 1957; "Shenru kaichan biyun xuanquan gongzuo" ("Carry Out Contraceptive Propaganda Work Thoroughly"), *Haerbin ribao (Haerbin Daily)*, Haerbin, March 19, 1957; "Kaizhan woguo renkou wenti de taolun" ("Begin the Discussion of Our Country's Population Problems"), *Wenhui bao (Wenhui Daily) (WHB)*, Shanghai, April 27, 1957; Wang Yizhi, "Women shi zheyang kaizhan biyun xuanquan de" ("How We Carried Out Propaganda on Contraception"), *Xinhua ribao (New China Daily) (XHRB)*, Nanjing, February 15, 1958; and "Further Develop Birth Control in Rural Areas," *GMRB*, May 20, 1958, *SCMP*, No. 1830, August 12, 1958, p. 7.

19. "For Active Dissemination of Contraceptive Knowledge" (editorial), *GMRB*, August 6, 1956, *SCMP*, No. 1352, August 17, 1956, pp. 2–4.

20. "For Active Dissemination of Contraceptive Knowledge"; "Jieyu xuanquan yao zai nongzun guangfan shenrudi kaizhan" ("Birth Control Propaganda Should Be Carried Out Extensively and Deeply in the Rural Areas"), *XHNB*, August 12, 1957; and "Jiji xuanquan yu kaizhan jieyu gongzuo" ("Publicize and Carry Out Birth Control Work Actively"), *HLJRB*, June 6, 1957.

21. "Further Develop Birth Control Work in Rural Areas," *GMRB*, May 20, 1958, *SCMP*, No. 1830, August 12, 1958, p. 7.

22. Sun Jingxia, "Present Problems in the Work of Propaganda on Contraception and Its Technical Guidance," *GMRB*, December 9, 1956, *SCMP*, No.

1452, January 17, 1957, p. 9; Lu Shutian, "Renzhen zuo hao biyun gongzuo" ("Conscientiously Do a Good Job of Contraception"), *HLJRB*, January 7, 1957; "Shandong Provincial People's Council Directive on Contraception"; "Zhonggong Liaoning shengwei Liaoning sheng renmin weiyuanhui guanyu jiji kaizhan jizhi shengyu gongzuo de lianhe tongzhi" ("Joint Notice of the Liaoning Provincial Party Committee and the Liaoning People's Committee Concerning the Active Carrying Out of Birth Control"), *Liaoning ribao* (*Liaoning Daily*) (*LNRB*), Shenyang, June 9, 1958; and "Exercise Appropriate Birth Control."

23. "Contraception and Planned Childbirth Must Be Practiced," *WHB*, January 23, 1958, *SCMP*, No. 1721, February 28, 1958, p. 7.

24. "Dali kaizhan jieyu gongzuo zengqiang minzi jiankang he fanrong" ("Carry Out Birth Control Work with Great Effort to Improve the Health and Prosperity of the Nation"), *LNRB*, June 9, 1958.

25. The official position as stated in 1956 by Health Minister Li Dechuan and Premier Zhou Enlai was that birth control was necessary for the health of women and children, the education of children, and the prosperity of nation, but no mention was made of population problems. (Li Dechuan, "New Tasks for the Protection of Public Health," XINHUA, Beijing, June 18, 1956, *CB*, No. 405, July 26, 1956, p. 15; and Zhou Enlai, "Report on the Second Five-Year Plan," XINHUA, Beijing, September 20, 1956, *CB*, No. 413, October 5, 1956, pp. 285–286.)

26. Zhou Efen, "Jiezha shuluanguan he shujingguan" ("The Ligation of the Fallopian Tubes and the Spermatic Ducts"), *Gongren ribao* (*Daily Worker*) (*GRRB*), Beijing, January 13, 1957.

27. Shao Lizi, "The Problem of Birth Control," XINHUA, Beijing, June 26, 1956, *CB*, No. 405, July 26, 1956, p. 18.

28. Shao Lizi, "Concerning the Problem of Dissemination of Knowledge about Contraception," *GMRB*, December 19, 1954, *SCMP*, No. 976, January 28, 1955, pp. 30–31.

29. One of the most outspoken opponents was the vice-director of the Beijing Public Health Bureau, Li Jiansheng, who led a storm of protest at the Chinese People's Political Consultative Conference meeting in March 1957 when Li Dechuan announced "with the greatest reluctance" the decision of the Ministry of Public Health that abortions would henceforth be granted on request. (Li Jiansheng, "Do Not Perform Artificial Abortion Unless Absolutely Necessary," *RMRB*, March 9, 1957, *CB*, No. 445, April 5, 1957, pp. 6–8; "Health Minister on Birth Control," XINHUA-English, Beijing, March 7, 1957, *SCMP*, No. 1487, March 12, 1957, p. 9; and An Zhonghuang, "Medical Experts Discuss Late Marriage and Contraception in Capital," XINHUA, Beijing, February 25, 1957, *SCMP*, No. 1487, March 12, 1957, p. 12.)

30. Notable among them the President of Beijing University, Ma Yinchu, who in 1960 was dismissed from his post for continuing to advocate the control of population growth and other ideas no longer acceptable to the regime. Ma had argued that destroying a fetus was homicide. ("Rengong liuchan yingxiang funu shenti jiankang" ["Artificial Abortion Affects the

Health of Women"], *Chongqing ribao* [*Chongqing Daily*], Chongqing, September 15, 1957; "Jieyu de bianlun" ["Debate on Birth Control"], Beijing dispatch filed with an unidentified Beijing newspaper, March 10, 1957.) The otherwise indefatigable advocate of birth control of the 1950s, Shao Lizi, initially supported the restrictions on abortion. (Shao Lizi, "Concerning the Problem . . .")

31. "Health Minister on Birth Control," p. 9; "Weishengbu fachu tongjiu jueyu he liuchan zhoushu poushou xianzhi" ("Public Health Ministry Notice on Sterilization and Abortion Without Restriction"), *WHB*, April 12, 1957; and "Public Health Ministry Issues Notification on Abortion and Sterilization," XINHUA, Beijing, May 18, 1957, *SCMP*, No. 1539, May 28, 1957, pp. 2–3.

32. "Chairman Mao's Article for *Red Flag*," XINHUA-English, Beijing, May 31, 1958, *SCMP*, No. 1784, June 4, 1958, p. 9.

33. For a summary of the developments in the so-called "Hebei reform of statistics" in 1958, the falsification of data that resulted from it, and the effort to repair the damage to China's statistical system following the August 1959 Party plenum, which sharply revised downward the statistical claims of 1958, see John S. Aird, *The Size, Composition, and Growth of the Population of Mainland China*, International Population Statistics Reports, Series P–90, No. 15 (Washington: U.S. Government Printing Office, 1961), pp. 55–58.

34. Hu Yaobang, "Man Is the Determining Factor in Our Great Undertakings," XINHUA, Shanghai, April 13, 1958, *SCMP*, No. 1768, May 9, 1958, p. 7.

35. Interview with Judith Banister reported in Stephens Broening, "The Death of 30 Million Chinese," *The Baltimore Sun*, April 26, 1984, p. A19; Ansley J. Coale, *Rapid Population Change in China, 1952–1982*, Committee on Population and Demography, Report No. 27 (Washington: National Academy Press, 1984), pp. 68–70; and Basil Ashton, Kenneth Hill, Alan Piazza, and Robin Zeitz, "Famine in China, 1958–61," *PDR*, Vol. 10, No. 4, December 1984, p. 614.

36. Birth control propaganda was resumed in the spring of 1962. In December 1962 the Party Central Committee and the State Council issued a document entitled "Directive on Conscientiously Promoting Family Planning," but the action was not publicized in the media at the time. (Li Kangmei, "Zhongguo de jihua shengyu" ["Family Planning in China"], *Zhongguo weisheng nianjian [1983]* [*The Public Health Yearbook of China (1983)*] [Beijing: Renmin weisheng chubanshe, February 1984], pp. 160–166.)

37. Bo Ling, "If There Is No Birth Control," *Yangzheng wanbao* (*Evening News*), Guangzhou, August 21, 1963; Zhong Chohuan, "This Is Not an Embarrassing Thing or an Unimportant Matter," *Nanfang ribao* (*Southern Daily*) (*NFRB*), Guangzhou, December 1, 1963, *SCMP*, No. 3128, December 20, 1963, p. 12; and Fu Lianzhang, "The Positive Significance of Planned Family," *Zhongguo funu* (*Women of China*), No. 4, April 1, 1963, *Survey of China Mainland Magazines* (*SCMM*), American Consulate General, Hong Kong, No. 364, May 13, 1963, p. 38.

38. The effects of sex on men before the age of 25 were described as "strong nervous stimulation," "excessive dissipation of bodily fluids," "malfunctioning of the central nervous system," "sexual neurasthenia, low spirits, headaches, . . . discomfort all over the body," emaciation, dizziness, tension, memory loss, premature old age, mental and physical pain, and impotence! ("What's To Be Done If One Has Married Early," Zhongguo qingnian bao [China Youth Gazette] [ZGQNB], Beijing, July 7, 1962, SCMP, No. 2785, July 25, 1962, p. 11; Yang Xiu, "For Late Marriage," ZGQN, No. 11, June 1, 1962, SCMM, No. 322, July 16, 1962, p. 24; Da Yu, "What Are the Disadvantages of Early Marriage?" GRRB, June 28, 1962, SCMP, No. 2777, July 13, 1962, p. 11; "A Problem That Deserves Careful Consideration by Unmarried Young People," ZGQNB, May 10, 1962, SCMP, No. 2745, May 24, 1962, pp. 15–16; and Ye Gongshao, "What Is the Most Suitable Age for Marriage?" ZGQNB, April 12, 1962, SCMP, No. 2745, May 24, 1962, p. 17.)

The admonitions to women warned that pregnancy would deprive them of calcium needed for their own bones, that the growing fetus would "consume" their bodies, that delivery was a "major operation" in which "some blood will be lost," that childbearing was a "torture," that nursing would take "nutriment" from their bodies, and that too early childbearing would "enfeeble" them at an early age. (Ye Gongshao, "What Is . . . Most Suitable?" p. 18; Wang Shuzhen, "Marriageable Age and Childbirth Viewed from the Physiological Angle," Jiefang ribao [Liberation Daily] [JFRB], Shanghai, March 5, 1963; Da Yu, "What Are the Disadvantages?" p. 10; Ye Gongshao, "My Views on the Problem of Young People's Marriage, Love, and Children," ZGQNB, July 21, 1962, SCMP, No. 2795, August 9, 1962, p. 14; Tao Cheng, "A Talk with Young Friends About the Question of Marriage," GRRB, July 28, 1962, SCMP, No. 2800, August 16, 1962, p. 12; "What's To Be Done If One Has Married Early?" "A Problem That Deserves Careful Attention by Unmarried Young People"; and "Early Marriage Is Harmful, Not Beneficial," NFRB, November 15, 1962, SCMP, No. 2871, December 3, 1962, p. 11.)

39. Ye Gongshao, "My Views on Young People's Marriage, Love, and Children," p. 15.

40. Li Kangmei, "Family Planning in China."

41. Analysis on China's One-per-Thousand-Population Fertility Sampling Survey (Beijing: China Population Information Centre, 1984), pp. 159–167.

42. State Family Planning Commission, "China's Family Planning Work."

43. Li Kangmei, "Family Planning in China." The slogan meant late marriage (marriage at age 25 for males and 23 for females), an interval of four years between births, and no more than two children per couple.

44. Yu Rongpei, "An Exploration of Mao Zedong's Thoughts . . ."

45. "Go Quickly into Action to Carry Out the Patriotic Public Health Movement with the Elimination of the Four Pests as Key," WHB, April 21, 1968, SCMP, No. 4179, May 16, 1968, p. 8.

46. "Stem the Evil Wind of Falling in Love and Getting Married Early Among Literary and Art Circles," WHB, July 28, 1968, SCMP, No. 4250,

September 4, 1968, p. 17; "Firmly Destroying Old Habits, Insisting on Late Marriage," *RMRB*, August 31, 1969, *SCMP*, No. 4495, September 15, 1969, p. 5; Jilin Medical College Revolutionary Committee, *Chiyao yisheng peixun jiaocai* (*Teaching Materials for the Fostering and Training of Barefoot Doctors*) (Beijing: Renmin weisheng chubanshe, 1971), pp. 352–355; and "Do a Serious Job in the Work of Family Planning," *NFRB*, December 7, 1973, *SCMP* (Supplement), No. 333, January 21, 1973, pp. 25–26.

47. For example, *NFRB* Commentator, "Seriously Do a Good Job of Family Planning Work," *NFRB*, July 10, 1973, *SCMP* Supplement, No. 325, October 1, 1973, p. 42.

48. For example, ibid., p. 43.

49. The crude birth rate is the total number of births in a given year divided by the average population total for the year. The crude death rate is derived in the same way using the total number of deaths during the year. The natural increase rate is obtained by subtracting the death rate from the birth rate. All three rates are customarily expressed as rates per thousand population rather than as percentages.

50. For example, a provincial conference in Shandong Province in October 1973 was told that "the masses must be fully mobilized" and that "all appropriate measures [for planned parenthood] must be carried out without fail." Backward units were to be quickly transformed into advanced units. (Jinan radio, Shandong Provincial Service, October 7, 1973, FBIS, No. 198, October 12, 1973, p. C7.)

51. A natural increase rate of 26 per thousand represents a population growth rate of 2.6 percent.

52. Hua Guofeng, "Report on the Work of the Government," February 26, 1978, XINHUA-English, Beijing, March 6, 1978.

53. Wang Wei, "Zai jianshe you zhongguo tese de shehuizhuyi zong de jihua shengyu gongzuo" ("Family Planning Work Amidst the Construction of Socialism with Chinese Characteristics"), *JKBJHSYB*, December 18, 1987, p. 2.

54. Couples among the minority nationalities, fishermen and their families, and families living in frontier and mountain areas were allowed two children each.

55. XINHUA, Beijing, January 26, 1979, FBIS, No. 22, January 31, 1979, p. E9.

56. High rates of female infanticide were prevalent before 1949 in many of the poorer rural areas of China, because the birth of a daughter was considered an economic misfortune for the family. The costs of rearing and marrying her off could not be recouped in later years because she became a member of her husband's family and could no longer contribute to the support of her own. Infanticide was a cruel but effective way of addressing these economic anxieties. There is some evidence from the censuses of 1953, 1964, and 1982 that preference for males resulted in somewhat lower survival rates for female children even after 1949, but the extremely high sex ratios among people born prior to 1949 were absent for the next 30 years. The

135

higher sex ratios shown in the 1982 census age data for children born in 1979–82 may be due partly to the undercounting of girls, but the Chinese authorities viewed it as largely the result of infanticide. In 1981–83 the press carried reports of widespread female infanticide, some of which attributed its revival to the one-child policy. For example, see CCP Central Department of Propaganda and State Council Family Planning Leadership Group, "Kong-zhi woguo renkou zengzhang de xuanchuan yaodian" ("An Outline of Propaganda for Controlling Population Growth in China"), *RKYJ*, No. 2, April 1981, p. 2.

57. "Jiujiu nuying" ("Save the Baby Girls"), *ZGQNB*, November 9, 1982, p. 3.

58. "Zong nan qing nu shahai qingsheng nuying qinggong Wan Chuwen panxing shisannian" ("Young Worker Wan Chuwen Sentenced to 13 Years in Prison for Murdering His Own Infant Daughter"), *GMRB*, January 12, 1983, p. 1; Su Zhongheng and Zhang Bowen, "Yanjin nibi nuying" ("Strictly Prohibit the Killing of Girl Babies"), *NFRB*, February 7, 1983, p. 2; "Female Infanticide Evokes Danger of Sexes Imbalance," *CD*, April 9, 1983, p. 3; "Jiangsu Yancheng fasheng duoqi yiqi nuying shijian" ("Cases of Abandoning of Girl Babies Occur Frequently in Yancheng, Jiangsu"), *GMRB*, January 12, 1983, p. 1; Xu Jialiang, "Yumei Zaocheng de beiju" ("A Tragedy Caused by Ignorance"), *ZGQNB*, February 5, 1983, p. 2; and Zhang Wansong et al., "Yinger xingbili shitiao yao qieshi jiuzheng" ("Effective Steps Must Be Taken Against the Disproportion in the Sex Ratio at Birth"), *Shehui* (*Society*), April 20, 1983, p. 29. According to media reports, unwanted female infants were often drowned at birth in buckets of water placed purposefully beside the delivery bed, or they were thrown down wells or into ponds, buried alive, or abandoned under bridges, in fields, by riversides, in railway stations, hospitals, or public toilets. A recent article in a Hong Kong source describing similar practices in Fujian Province suggests that the problem, which has not been given much media attention since 1983, is far from over. The article reports the results of an investigation in Fujian that found many instances of "baby girls being thrown away." They were reportedly discarded "on street corners, in hospitals, at vehicle stations and piers, and elsewhere." Delays in treatment allegedly had caused a "continuous increase in the mortality rate of baby girls in the hospitals." One father was recently executed for beating his three-year-old daughter to death. Fears of an unbalanced sex ratio are again being broached. ("Phenomenon of Discarding Baby Girls Becomes Serious in Fujian," ZHONGGUO TONGXUN SHE, Hong Kong, March 22, 1989, FBIS, No. 56, March 24, 1989, p. 61.)

59. "Investigation Conducted by Anhui Women's Federation Shows the Seriousness of the Situation of Drowning Baby Girls in Rural Areas and the Resulting Disproportion Between Male and Female Babies," *RMRB*, April 7, 1983, FBIS, No. 68, April 7, 1983, pp. K5–6; Jiang Chen and Xiao Du, "Yiqi canhai nuying shi fanzui xingwei" ("The Abandoning and Injuring of Girl Babies Is a Criminal Act"), *RMRB*, January 31, 1983, p. 3; Su and Zhang, "Strictly Prohibit the Killing"; and Pu Yun, "Ling ren buan de shuzi"

("Disturbing Figures"), *Gansu ribao* (*Gansu Daily*), Lanzhou, January 19, 1983, p. 4. The normal sex ratio at birth for European and Asian populations is 105 to 107 male births per 100 female births. Higher ratios suggest that some female births are not being reported. In China some of the unreported female infants are presumably victims of infanticide, while others may still be alive but their births simply not registered. In very small units, there can also be considerable random variation in sex ratio at birth from year to year.

The trend toward high sex ratios for births and for children in the first years of life has apparently continued. A national sample survey of births during 1986 showed 110.94 male births per 100 female for the country as a whole and figures over 115 for Zhejiang, Anhui, Henan, and Jiangsu provinces. (Terence H. Hull, "Recent Trends in Sex Ratios in China," International Population Dynamics Program, Research Note No. 96 [Canberra: The Australian National University, November 17, 1988], pp. 1–18.)

60. XINHUA-English, Beijing, September 23, 1983, FBIS, No. 188, September 27, 1983, p. K9. Qian had succeeded Chen Muhua, the first Minister in Charge of the SFPC, on May 4, 1982.

61. Zhengzhou radio, Henan Provincial Service, May 3, 1979, FBIS, No. 91, May 9, 1979, p. P3; and Guangzhou radio, Guangdong Provincial Service, May 9, 1979, FBIS, No. 92, May 10, 1979, p. P1.

62. Michael Parks, "Sex Is High on List of New Chinese Freedoms," *The Baltimore Sun*, January 25, 1979; and Liu Haiquan, "Control Population Growth with the Same Drive . . ."

63. "Zhonggong Guangdong shengwei fachu jinji tongzhi liji xingdong zhua hao jihua shengyu gongzuo" ("The Chinese Communist Party Guangdong Provincial Committee Issues an Urgent Notice for Immediate Action to Carry Out Family Planning Work Well"), *NFRB*, July 22, 1979, p. 1.

64. "The Future Policies Decided by the Central Work Conference Are Policies on Economic Readjustment and Not Contraction," *Ming Pao*, Hong Kong, June 15, 1979, FBIS, No. 119, June 19, 1979, p. L14; and XINHUA-English, Beijing, September 7, 1980, FBIS, No. 175, September 8, 1980, p. L10.

65. Hua Guofeng, "Report on the Work of the Government," June 18, 1979, XINHUA-English, Beijing, June 25, 1979, FBIS, No. 128 (Supplement), July 2, 1979, p. 19.

66. Beijing radio, Domestic Service, July 5, 1979, FBIS, No. 134, July 11, 1979, p. L25.

67. XINHUA, Beijing, December 22, 1979, FBIS, No. 251, December 28, 1979, p. L7.

68. Chen Muhua, "Shixian sige xiandaihua bixu you jihuade kengzhi renkou zengzhang" ("For the Realization of the Four Modernizations There Must Be Planned Control of Population Growth"), *RMRB*, August 11, 1979, p. 2.

69. Tianjin radio, Tianjin City Service, August 4, 1979, FBIS, No. 153, August 7, 1979, p. R4.

70. Guangzhou radio, Guangdong Provincial Service, August 24, 1979, JPRS, No. 74,196, September 18, 1979, p. 59.

71. For example, Fujian Province boasted that in May and June 1979 the number of abortions in the province was double that for the same period in 1978, and Henan Province claimed that in the first half of 1979 abortions increased by 30.6 percent over the number in the first half of 1978. (Fuzhou radio, Fujian Provincial Service, August 18, 1979, FBIS, No. 163, August 21, 1979, p. O3; and Zhengzhou radio, Henan Provincial Service, August 25, 1979, FBIS, No. 169, August 29, 1979. p. P1.)

72. Details as to what form of expression "alienation" takes are seldom provided, except for occasional references to verbal abuse, physical violence, sabotage of crops, houses, and other property belonging to family planning cadres, and instances of "cold shoulder" treatment. There are undoubtedly many other expressions which the controlled press is not allowed to report. What makes the "alienation" a significant threat to local administration is that it can add greatly to the difficulties of carrying out regular duties and implementing policies and programs that require public cooperation.

73. Xu Dixin, "A Few Problems Concerning Population Science," *JJYJ*, No. 4, April 20, 1981, FBIS, No. 101, May 27, 1981, p. K23.

74. "Xian jihua shengyu gongzuo zhong de liangge wenti" ("Two Problems in the Family Planning Work of Xian"), *RMRB*, February 1, 1980, p. 4; "Shaoguan diqu jihua shengyu gongzuo chengji xianzhu" ("Family Planning Work in Shaoguan Prefecture Has Gained Outstanding Results"), *NFRB*, June 21, 1980, p. 1; "Dui wosheng jihua shengyu gongzuo di jidian xiwang" ("A Few Expectations About Planned Parenthood Work in Guangdong"), *NFRB*, October 6, 1980, p. 1; Hefei radio, Anhui Provincial Service, June 10, 1980, FBIS, No. 114, June 11, 1980, p. O1; XINHUA-English, Beijing, September 29, 1980, p. L23; XINHUA, Beijing, October 14, 1980, FBIS, No. 202, October 16, 1980, p. L4; Commentator, "Take Practical Action to Implement the 'Open Letter,' " *SCRB*, October 17, 1980, FBIS, No. 216, November 5, 1980, p. Q4; "Sustained Efforts Are Needed in Planned Parenthood Work," *RMRB*, January 27, 1981, FBIS, No. 28, February 11, 1981, p. L20; and "Excerpts of Speeches by NPC Deputies at Panel Discussions," *RMRB*, September 12, 1980, FBIS, No. 184, September 18, 1980, p. L13.

75. XINHUA, Beijing, September 25, 1980, FBIS, No. 189, September 26, 1980, pp. L1–4.

76. For example, see Shijiazhuang radio, Hebei Provincial Service, June 30, 1980, FBIS, No. 135, July 11, 1980, p. R2.

77. The new law actually increased the minimum age for marriage by two years, from 20 and 18 for males and females, respectively, to 22 and 20, but it stipulated that young people who had reached the new age limits and wanted to marry must be allowed to do so. In December 1980, the State Council warned that with the adoption of the new law, "all localities must act strictly in accordance with the relevant regulations . . . From the day that the new marriage law comes into force, all regulations that do not conform to the marriage law will become invalid." (XINHUA, Beijing, December 16, 1980, FBIS, No. 244, December 17, 1980, pp. L15–16.) The new law was apparently intended to solve political, administrative, and social problems

caused by the previous regulations, which had resulted in widespread evasion of marriage registration and some cohabitation without marriage, which seems to have troubled the authorities. Besides, some demographers had argued that with fertility so closely regulated, delaying marriage was no longer necessary. See Judith Banister, *China's Changing Population*, pp. 159–161.

78. In the first half of 1981, 6.73 million couples were reportedly married, more than twice the number in the corresponding period of 1980. (Friend of Women, "Woguo renkou de jing, xi, you" ["The Shocking, Heartening, Worrying Aspects of China's Population"], *ZGQN*, No. 6, June 11, 1982, p. 56.)

79. Some areas reported a rise in second births also. According to one report, "the loudspeakers are silent, the [Party] secretaries are mute, and babies are being born." ("Renda daibiao fayan yaoqiu jihua shengyu ying lifa" ["Deputies to the National People's Congress Demand That a Family Planning Law Be Enacted"], *JKB*, December 13, 1981, p. 1.)

80. "Sheng renkou xuehui zhengshi chengli" ("The Fujian Provincial Population Association Is Formally Established"), *Fujian ribao (Fujian Daily)* (*FJRB*), Fuzhou, September 5, 1981, p. 2; Gao Xin, "Jihua shengyu wanwan buke fangsong" ("Absolutely No Relaxation in Family Planning"), *Banyue tan (Semi-Monthly Forum)* (*BYT*), Beijing, No. 17, September 10, 1981, pp. 26–27; "We Must Seriously Study the New Situation in Family Planning"), *RMRB*, August 18, 1981, FBIS, No. 163, August 24, 1981, p. K12; XINHUA, Beijing, December 8, 1981, FBIS, No. 237, December 10, 1981, p. K2; Xining radio, Qinghai Provincial Service, July 1, 1981, FBIS, No. 127, July 2, 1981, p. T1; "Unswervingly Direct Proper and Intensified Efforts Toward Family Planning," *SCRB*, September 25, 1981, FBIS, No. 207, October 27, 1981, p. Q1; and Jinan radio, Shandong Provincial Service, September 24, 1981, FBIS, No. 188, September 29, 1981, p. O4.

81. XINHUA, Beijing, March 13, 1982, FBIS, No. 50, March 15, 1982, p. K5.

82. "Wei shixian wosheng jinnian jihua shengyu renwu zuochu xin gongxian" ("Make New Contributions to the Accomplishment of the Family Planning Tasks of Shandong Province This Year"), *DZRB*, February 15, 1982, pp. 1–4; Guangzhou radio, Guangdong Provincial Service, February 27, 1982, FBIS, No. 43, March 4, 1982, p. P5; Li Hua, "Jihua shengyu zerenzhi de jizhong xingshi" (Several Forms of the Family Planning Responsibility System"), *RKYJ*, No. 2, March 29, 1982, p. 61; Zhao Yugui, "Kongzhi renkou zengzhang cujin 'sihau' jianshe" ("To Control Population Growth and Accelerate the Construction of the 'Four Modernizations' "), *RKYJJ*, No. 2, April 25, 1982, pp. 5–6; "Haixingxian renzhen luoshi jihua shengyu jiang-cheng zhengce" ("Haixing County Earnestly Carries Out the Reward and Punishment Policy for Birth Control"), *Hebei ribao (Hebei Daily)* (*HBRB*), Shijiazhuang, June 14, 1982, p. 3; "Jianding buyi de zhixing dang de renkou zhengce" ("Implement the Party's Population Policy Resolutely Without Wavering"), *XHRB*, July 5, 1982, p. 1; and "What Punishment Should Be Given to Those

Who Violate Planned Parenthood?—Questions and Answers Concerning Planned Parenthood, No. 4," *FJRB*, August 3, 1982, JPRS, No. 82–230, November 15, 1982, p. 39. Among the disciplinary measures were reducing the amount of contract land allotted to noncompliant peasant families, taking away their private plots on which they could raise crops to consume or sell outside the contract, refusing to register unauthorized births, cancelling medical and welfare allowances for urban families, and charging them "social rearing fees" for each unauthorized child.

83. "Unswervingly Carry Out the Party's Population Policy," *XHRB*, July 5, 1982, JPRS, No. 81,928, October 5, 1982, p. 40; "Yongjia Luoqing Cangnan Wencheng Qingtian deng xian renmin daibiao renwei renkou zengzhang shiqi kongzhi zaiyu ganbu zhuade buli jianyi caiqu guodan cuoshi xunsu niuzhuan renkou huisheng" ("The People's Delegates from Yongjia, Luoqing, Cangnan, Wencheng, and Qingtian Counties Express the Opinion That the Loss of Control Over Population Growth Was Due to Failure of the Cadres to Exert Efforts; They Propose That Decisive Measures Be Taken to Reverse Quickly the Rise in Population Growth"), *Zhejiang ribao* (*Zhejiang Daily*) (*ZJRB*), Hangzhou, June 20, 1982, p. 1; XINHUA, Beijing November 21, 1982, FBIS, No. 233, December 3, 1982, p. R3 (reporting a speech at a Beijing municipal family planning conference); and Shijiazhuang radio, Hebei Provincial Service, June 24, 1982, FBIS, No. 152, August 9, 1982, p. R1.

84. Song Youtian, "Guanyu jihua shengyu gongzuo de baogao" ("Report on Family Planning Work"), *Shaanxi ribao* (*Shaanxi Daily*) (*SXRB*, Xian), Xian, March 9, 1982, p. 3; "Zhazha shishi zuo hao jihua shengyu gongzuo" ("Do Well in Family Planning Work in a Down-to-Earth Manner"), *HLJRB*, March 13, 1982, p. 1; Beijing radio, Domestic Service, April 20, 1982, FBIS, No. 77, April 21, 1982, p. K11; "Luoshi shengyu zhengce kongzhi renkou zengzhang" ("Implement Birth Control Policy to Control the Growth of Population"), *FJRB*, May 4, 1982, p. 1; Guangzhou radio, Guangdong Provincial Service, May 2, 1982, FBIS, No. 85, May 3, 1982, p. P3; and "Shengwei shengzhengfu zhaokai dianhua huiyi dongyuan bushu zai quansheng jizhong jinxing yici jihua shengyu xuanchuan huodong" ("The Sichuan Party Committee and the Provincial Government Call a Telephone Conference to Mobilize and Make Arrangements for Carrying Out Concentrated Family Planning Activities Throughout the Province"), *SCRB*, July 11, 1982, p. 1.

85. XINHUA, Beijing, November 1, 1982, FBIS, No. 213, November 2, 1982, p. K20.

86. XINHUA, Beijing, November 6, 1982, FBIS, No. 218, November 10, 1982, p. K21.

87. "Guanyu kaizhan quanguo jihua shengyu xuanchuanyue huodong de tongzhi" ("Circular on Carrying Out the Nationwide Family Planning Propaganda Month Activities"), State Family Planning Commission Document No. 207, December 6, 1982, *Zhonghua renmin gongheguo guowuyuan gongbao* (*People's Republic of China State Council Bulletin*), 1982:21, February 12, 1983, pp. 1063–1070.

88. Qian Xinzhong, "Xie zai jihua shengyu xuanchuanyue qianmian"

("Written Prior to Family Planning Propaganda Month"), *JKB*, December 19, 1982, p. 1.

89. "Essential Points of the PRC 1983 Plan for National Economic and Social Development," *RMRB*, December 20, 1982, FBIS, No. 247, December 23, 1982, p. K18.

90. Commentator, "Family Planning Work Must Be Publicized to Every Household and Individual," *RMRB*, December 23, 1982, JPRS, No. 82,643, January 14, 1983, p. 155.

91. "Zhongyang lingdao tongzhi zhichu shixing jihua shengyu yao san kao zhongzhi dongyuan, falu he jishu cuoshi" ("Central Leadership Comrade Points Out That the Implementation of Family Planning Must Rely on Political Mobilization, Legal and Technical Measures"), *JKB*, January 13, 1983, p. 1.

92. For example: " . . . We should pay attention to practical results . . . It is necessary to combine the work of ideological education with the action of carrying out family planning." ("Carry Out Education on Basic State Policies," *Yunnan ribao* [*Yunnan Daily*], Kunming, January 6, 1983, JPRS, No. 82,880, February 16, 1983, p. 40.) "Family planning cannot in the end produce results if there is only propaganda, mobilization, and ideological education without effective implementation of rules and regulations and of technical measures." (Taiyuan radio, Shanxi Provincial Service, January 14, 1983, JPRS, No. 82,880, February 16, 1983, p. 42.) "Many areas have combined propaganda and education with the implementation of technical measures and achieved marked results in giving sterilization operations in a widespread manner." ("Hebei Holds Telephone Conference on Family Planning Propaganda Month," *HBRB*, January 19, 1983, JPRS, No. 83,105, March 21, 1983, p. 118.)

93. *China Daily* Commentator, "Family Planning," *CD*, December 27, 1982, p. 4.

94. "Zongyang lingdao tongzhi zuijin zhichu jihua shengyu gongzuo bixu jixu zhuahao" ("A Central Leadership Comrade Recently Pointed Out That Family Planning Work Must Continue to Be Done Well"), *JKB*, March 3, 1983, p. 1.

95. Zhao Ziyang, "Report on the Work of the Government," June 6, 1983, XINHUA-English, June 23, 1983, FBIS, No. 122, June 23, 1983, p. K11.

96. Qian Xinzhong, "Bixu jianjue kongzhi renkou zengzhang" ("Population Growth Must Be Controlled Resolutely"), *JKB*, June 30, 1983, p. 1.

97. Early in January 1983 a provincial source reported that Qian had "suggested" that couples with two children should "generally" be mobilized to undergo sterilization because of high failure rates with IUDs and contraceptive pills. (Ju Genhua, "Tichang nongcun yi sheng liangtai de yuling fufu ziyuan zuo jiesha" ["Promote the Voluntary Sterilization of Rural Couples of Childbearing Age Who Already Have Two Children"], *JKB*, January 16, 1983, p. 2.)

98. For example, Guangdong Province reported that it had 7 million couples of childbearing age, of whom 5.2 million had two or more children

and "should be sterilized." But only 2.2 million had undergone the operation by May 1983. The provincial authorities laid out a three-year plan to sterilize another 2.7 million, including 1.7 million more sterilizations in the remainder of 1983. ("Sheng weishengting fachu tongzhi yaoqiu geji weisheng bumen zuohao jihua shengyu jishu gongzuo" ["The Provincial Public Health Department Issues Circular Requesting All Levels to Do Well in Technical Planned Birth Work"], *NFRB*, May 10, 1983, p. 1.)

99. *Zhongguo weisheng nianjian* Compilation Committee, *Zhongguo weisheng nianjian 1985* (*Public Health Yearbook 1985*) (Beijing: Renmin weisheng chubanshe, March 1986), p. 57.

100. "Zhejiang Begins Family Planning Drive," *ZJRB*, November 6, 1983, FBIS, No. 222, November 16, pp. O4–6; Zhengzhou radio, Henan Provincial Service, November 22, 1983, FBIS, No. 229, November 28, 1983, p. P5; Nanjing radio, Jiangsu Provincial Service, December 24, 1983, JPRS, No. 84–018, February 27, 1984, pp. 66–67; and Feng Zongtang and Cheng Jinzhen, "The Provincial Family Planning Work Conference Once Again Points Out That at No Time Should Family Planning Work Be Relaxed," *HBRB*, January 10, 1984, FBIS, No. 14, January 20, 1984, pp. R1–2.

101. "China Set to Invoke New Law on Statistics," *CD*, December 9, 1983, p. 1.

102. "Guojia jihua shengyu weiyuanhui fuzhe tongzhi weiwen jiceng ganbu he dozinuhu" ("Responsible Comrades of the State Family Planning Commission Visit Basic Level Cadres and Households with an Only Child"), *JKB*, January 28, 1984, p. 1.

CHAPTER 3: THE CONFUSING SIGNALS OF PARTY DOCUMENT NO. 7

1. "Quanguo sheng, shi, ziziqu jihua shengyu weiyuanhui zhuren huiyi haozhao jixu dali zhuanhao shengyu gongzuo" ("Conference of Directors of Family Planning Commissions of All Provinces, Municipalities, and Autonomous Regions Calls for Continued Efforts to Carry Out Family Planning Work"), *RMRB*, March 8, 1984, p. 1.

2. Some provinces permitted a second child if the family had had only one son in two or three generations, if only one of several brothers was capable of having children, if the husband settled down in the family of a wife who was an only daughter, if the marriage was between an only son and an only daughter, if the man was a disabled serviceman, if the couple were both returned overseas Chinese, or if the household was considered a hardship household residing in a distant border area or a coastal fishing area. (State Family Planning Commission General Office, "Guanyu jihua shengyu de ruogan zhengce" ["Several Policies Concerning Family Planning"], *NCGZTX*, No. 2, February 5, 1983, p. 47.)

3. Li Honggui, "Wanshan shengyu zhengce shi ge jianbian guocheng" ("It Is a Gradual Course to Perfect the Policy of Family Planning"), *JKBJHSYB*, February 1, 1985, p. 3; and Qu Yibin, "Woguo renkou chushenglu mingxian huisheng de yuanyin ji duice tantao" ("An Enquiry into the Causes of the

Marked Rise in China's Population Birth Rate and Measures to Deal with Them"), *RKYJ*, No. 2, March 29, 1988, pp. 53–56.

4. Long Guangrong, "Renzhen kai hao xiaokou qieshi duzhu dakou" ("Earnestly Do Well in Opening a Small Gap and Effectively Close the Big Gap"), *JKBJHSYB*, October 19, 1984, p. 3. In the early 1950s, third and higher parity births had been estimated at as high as 30 percent of all births. The 1988 fertility survey showed that by 1987, first parity births accounted for 52.72 percent of the total, second parity births for 32.33 percent, and "excessive" (third and higher parity) births for 14.39 percent. (Feng Jenjun, "Qunian renkou zengzhanglu yu qian fen zhi shiliu" ["Last Year's Population Growth Rate Exceeded 16 Per Thousand"], *RMRB*, October 28, 1988, p. 3.) In 1989 the chief of statistics of the State Family Planning Commission estimated that in 1988 "excessive" births amounted to "over 3 million," and "unplanned" (unapproved) second births numbered "several million." In addition, there were more than 2 million "early births," presumably first births that occurred without official permission. Altogether, "unplanned" births were estimated at 8 million. (Yao Minhua, "Renkou xingshi yanjun yao yi fen wei er kan" ["The Grim Population Situation Must Be Viewed by Dividing One into Two"], *ZGRKB*, March 3, 1989, p. 1.) With roughly 23 million births in 1988, this would mean that the "big gap" accounted for more than one-third of all births.

5. Liu Jingzhi, "Guojia jishengwei zhuangjia zixunzu chengyuan Ma Yingtong shuo woguo kongzhi renkou nengli jin yibu jiaqiang" ("Ma Yingtong, Member of the Advisory Team of the State Family Planning Commission, Said That China's Ability to Control Population Is Further Strengthened"), *GMRB*, April 24, 1988, p. 2.

6. Liang Jimin and Peng Zhiliang, "Ying quanmian lijie zhengque guanche jihua shengyu zhengce" ("The Implementation of Family Planning Policies Should Be Understood Correctly and Fully"), *JKBJHSYB*, April 13, 1984, p. 3.

7. Wang Wei, "Ba zhongyang jingshen bian wei ganbu quzhong de zijue xingdong" ("To Turn the Guidelines of the Party Central Committee into Voluntary Action on the Part of the Cadres and the Masses"), *JKBJHSYB*, July 6, 1984, p. 1.

8. Liang and Peng, "The Implementation of Family Planning . . ."

9. "Jihua shengyu gongzuo renwu ren shifen jianqu" ("The Task of Family Planning Is Still Extremely Difficult"), *RMRB*, March 4, 1984, p. 3.

10. "Shi shi qiu shi yin di zhi yi" ("Seek Truth from Facts and Take Appropriate Action to Suit Local Conditions"), *JKBJHSYB*, March 30, 1984, p. 1; Shijiazhuang radio, Hebei Provincial Service, April 8, 1984, JPRS, No. 84–032, May 2, 1984, pp. 74–75; Commentator, "Jihua shengyu gongzuo yao zhuajing zhuahao" ("Family Planning Work Must Be Carried Out Firmly and Well"), *BYT*, April 10, 1984, pp. 7–9; Guangzhou radio, Guangdong Provincial Service, May 8, 1984, FBIS, No. 91, May 9, 1984, p. P1; and Shenyang radio, Liaoning Provincial Service, May 14, 1984, FBIS, No. 95, May 15, 1984, p. S1.

11. An SFPC official told a XINHUA reporter in July 1984 that there had been "no change in the target of controlling the population under 1.2 billion by the end of this century." ("Woguo jinyibu wanshan jihua shengyu de juti zhengce" ["China Takes Further Steps to Refine the Concrete Policies on Family Planning"], *RMRB*, July 4, 1984, p. 3.) Local sources also demanded that targets be met. Guangdong family planning workers were told that "Guangdong's population must be kept below 70 million by the end of the century," the target assigned to Guangdong in the late 1970s in keeping with the national target of 1.2 billion. (Guangzhou radio, Guangdong Provincial Service, April 27, 1984, FBIS, No. 85, May 1, 1984, p. P1.) For other examples, see Kunming radio, Yunnan Provincial Service, April 30, 1984, FBIS, No. 86, May 2, 1984, p. Q3; Changsha radio, Hunan Provincial Service, May 14, 1984, FBIS, No. 96, May 16, 1984, p. P6; Hohhot radio, Nei Monggol Regional Service, June 6, 1984, FBIS, No. 112, June 8, 1984, p. R7; "Zhejiangsheng zhengfu jueding gaige jihua shengyu gongzuo guanli zhidu ba kongzhi renkou guihua baogan luoshi dao ge shi xian" ("The Government of Zhejiang Province Decides to Reform the Management System of Family Planning Work; It Assigns the Targets for Population Control to All Municipalities and Counties"), *JKBJHSYB*, July 27, 1984, p. 1; Nanning radio, Guangxi Regional Service, August 1, 1984, FBIS, No. 151, August 3, 1984, p. P5; Guiyang radio, Guizhou Provincial Service, November 9, 1984, FBIS, No. 220, November 13, 1984, p. Ql; and Taiyuan radio, Shanxi Provincial Service, November 18, 1984, FBIS, No. 226, November 21, 1984, p. R4.

12. Haikou radio, Hainan Island Regional Service, March 20, 1984, FBIS, No. 57, March 22, 1984, p. P2; Urumqi radio, Xinjiang Regional Service, March 24, 1984, FBIS, No. 59, March 26, 1984, p. T3; Kunming radio, Yunnan Provincial Service, March 28, 1984, FBIS, No. 92, April 12, 1984, p. Q2; Shijiazhuang radio, Hebei Provincial Service, April 8, 1984, JPRS, No. 84–032, May 2, 1984, p. 74; Guangzhou radio, Guangdong Provincial Service, April 29, 1984, FBIS, No. 85, May 1, 1984, p. P1; and Guiyang radio, Guizhou Provincial Service, June 14, 1984, FBIS, No. 120, June 20, 1984, p. Q1. Hainan Island boasted in May 1984 that it had overfulfilled the quota of sterilizations assigned by Guangdong Province by 20 percent. (Haikou radio, Hainan Regional Service, May 4, 1984, FBIS, No. May 7, 1984, p. P2.)

13. Xian radio, Shaanxi Provincial Service, April 8, 1984, JPRS, No. 84–035, May 10, 1984, p. 93; Wang Senhao, "Report on Government Work," *Shanxi ribao* (*Shanxi Daily*) (*SXRB*, Taiyuan), Taiyuan, April 30, 1984, JPRS, No. 84–046, June 12, 1984, p. 35; "Zhuzhong gongzuo fangfa guanxin qunzhong jiku" ("Pay Attention to the Work Method and Care for the Sufferings of the Masses"), *JKBJHSYB*, May 18, 1984, p. 3; Peng Zhiliang, "Tan jihua shengyu zhengce yao heqing heli" ("Family Planning Policy Must Be Fair and Reasonable"), *JKBJHSYB*, June 29, 1984, p. 3; Editorial Department, "Guanyu dangqian jihua shengyu gongzuo de jige wenti" ("Several Questions on Current Family Planning Work"), *NCGZTX*, No. 7, July 5, 1984, p. 14; and "Guangxi Zhuangzu ziziqu dangwei diyi shuji Qiao Xiaoguang shuo bixu zuozhong jiejue zhua jihua shengyu pa fan cuowu de sixiang"

("First Secretary Qiao Xiaoguang of the Party Committee of Guangxi Zhuang Nationality Autonomous Region Says That Emphasis Should Be Given to Dispelling the Thought of Being Afraid to Make Mistakes in Carrying Out Family Planning Work"), *JKBJHSYB*, August 17, 1984, p. 1.

14. "Conference of Directors of Family Planning Commissions . . ."

15. XINHUA, Beijing, March 7, 1984, FBIS, No. 49, March 12, 1984, p. K20. While dissociating themselves from the methods used in 1983, the leaders made it clear that they were happy with the results.

16. Changsha radio, Hunan Provincial Service, April 4, 1984, FBIS, No. 67, April 5, 1984, pp. P4–5; Guangzhou radio, Guangdong Provincial Service, April 29, 1984, FBIS, No. 85, May 1, 1984, p. P1; Hohhot radio, Nei Monggol Regional Service, June 6, 1984, FBIS, No. 112, June 8, 1984, pp. R7–8; Lhasa radio, Xizang Regional Service, August 9, 1984, FBIS, No. 156, August 10, 1984, p. Q2; Changsha radio, Hunan Provincial Service, August 10, 1984, FBIS, No. 157, August 13, 1984, p. P3; Li Guangsheng, "Grasp Family Planning Work Firmly and Continuously," *RKYJJ*, No. 4, August 25, 1984, JPRS, No. 84–085, December 11, 1984, p. 67; Lhasa radio, Xizang Regional Service, March 10, 1985, FBIS, No. 47, March 11, 1985, p. Q2; Haikou radio, Hainan Island Regional Service, October 17, 1985, FBIS, No. 204, October 22, 1985, p. P1; Wuhan radio, Hubei Provincial Service, December 30, 1985, FBIS, No. 200, January 2, 1986, p. P3; Changsha radio, Hunan Provincial Service, January 20, 1986, JPRS, No. 86–018, February 13, 1986, p. 81; Huang Jialiang, "Sichuan dusheng zinu lingzhenglu xiajiang youguan bumen dui ci ying yuyi zhongshi" ("Sichuan's One Child Certificate Acceptance Rate Is Declining; Relevant Departments Should Pay Attention to This Situation"), *JKBJHSYB*, June 13, 1986, p. 1; and Kunming radio, Yunnan Provincial Service, September 22, 1986, FBIS, No. 185, September 24, 1986, p. Q2. The last source says, "We must continue to advocate the policy of each couple giving birth to only one child. The idea that the family planning policy will be relaxed and the idea that each couple is allowed to give birth to a second child whether they are cadres, staff, workers, and urban or rural residents is wrong and groundless."

17. "Liaoning sheng lianxi shiji renzhen guance zhongyang qihao wenjian" ("Liaoning Province Conscientiously Implements Party Central Committee Document No. 7 by Relating It to Reality"), *JKBJHSYB*, November 2, 1984, p. 3.

18. Lhasa radio, Xizang Regional Service, March 10, 1985, FBIS, No. 47, March 11, 1985, p. Q2.

19. Guiyang radio, Guizhou Provincial Service, August 9, 1984, FBIS, No. 156, August 10, 1984, p. Q1.

20. Haerbin radio, Heilongjiang Provincial Service, JPRS, No. 84–074, October 30, 1984, p. 62.

21. "First Secretary Qiao Xiaoguang . . ."

22. Haikou radio, Hainan Regional Service, November 1, 1984, FBIS, No. 215, November 5, 1984, p. P2.

23. Hangzhou radio, Zhejiang Provincial Service, November 19, 1984, FBIS, No. 232, November 30, 1984, p. O3.

24. Of course, since by the end of 1983 more than half of the couples of childbearing age with two or more children had already been sterilized, a drop in the number of sterilizations (and abortions) would surely have occurred even without a relaxation in enforcement of the policies.

25. Guiyang radio, Guizhou Provincial Service, August 9, 1984, FBIS, No. 156, August 10, 1984, p. Q1.

26. Haerbin radio, Heilongjiang Provincial Service, August 13, 1984, FBIS, No. 173, September 5, 1984, p. S1.

27. Haikou radio, Hainan Island Regional Service, FBIS, No. 173, September 5, 1984, p. P5. The Hainan authorities complained that their cadres had "done rather poorly this year in fulfilling the planned parenthood ligation surgery task assigned by the provincial authorities. We lag very far behind the average for the whole province. In fact ours is the poorest performance in the whole province." Accordingly they demanded that their cadres "unswervingly implement the planned parenthood policies and strictly ensure that an IUD is inserted after one birth, that ligation is carried out after a second, that prompt measures [meaning abortion] are taken to deal with a pregnancy not covered by the plan, and that a strict ban is enforced on excessive [i.e., third and higher order] births. Both urban and rural areas are to be grasped, with the focus on the rural areas." These comments illustrate the kind of pressure local leaders feel from family planning targets handed down from higher levels. It is this pressure that accounts for much of the coercion in the family planning program, and the responsibility for it rests with the central authorities who set the targets.

28. Nanning radio, Guangxi Regional Service, September 13, 1984, FBIS, No. 180, September 14, 1984, p. P5. The new ruling contained the qualifying phrase "in principle," suggesting that immediate full enforcement was not intended, but clearly the concern was that to allow more leniency in family planning to large minorities would impose on the Han population a greater share of the burden of reaching national population targets.

29. For example, see Nan Gu, "Shaanxi Implements Responsibility System in Population Control," SXRB, Xian, October 22, 1984, JPRS, No. 85–015, February 15, 1985, p. 107; Taiyuan radio, Shanxi Provincial Service, November 18, 1984, FBIS, No. 226, November 21, 1984, p. R4; Nanning radio, Guangxi Regional Service, December 4, 1984, FBIS, No. 236, December 6, 1984, p. P1; Changsha radio, Hunan Provincial Service, December 13, 1984, FBIS, No. 243, December 17, 1984, p. P3; and Zhengzhou radio, Henan Provincial Service, December 14, 1984. FBIS, No. 243, December 17, 1984, p. P2.

30. Wang Wei, "To Turn the Guidelines . . ."

31. Wu Xuping, "Buyi suiyi fangkuan ertai zhibiao" ("It Is Inadvisable to Soften the Terms for a Second Child"), JKBJHSYB, September 21, 1984, p. 3.

32. Long Guangrong, "Earnestly Do Well in Opening . . ."

33. Wang Wei, "Continue to Unify Our Ideology and Take Pains to Implement Document No. 7" (Speech at the National Family Planning Conference on October 10, 1984), RKYJJ, No. 1, February 25, 1985, JPRS, No. 85–068, July 9, 1985, pp. 27–34. The nature of the "mistakes" is not made clear.

In some contexts it refers to acts of coercion, but that meaning seems inappropriate here. The speech contains other ambiguous comments. For example: "Many of our existing regulations are meant to control the public. Let's make them explicit. But our system is designed to enable the masses to give full play to their enthusiasm and creativity, not to restrict them. This is not a conceptual difference but one of guiding ideology." (P. 34.)

34. "Ba zhuajing he zhuahao tongyi qilai" ("Combine Firmly in Charge with Doing a Good Job"), *JKBJHSYB*, October 5, 1984, p. 1.

35. "Zhonggong Guangdong Shengwei shuji Xie Fei shuo jihua shengyu gongzuo yao zhuazhu yaoling zhuazhu guanjian" ("CCP Guangdong Provincial Committee Secretary Xie Fei Says That Family Planning Must Take Charge of the Essential and Crucial Points"), *JKBJHSYB*, October 19, 1984, p. 1. Here the code expression "strengthen leadership" is clearly shown to mean that local leaders must exercise control over the people. "Education" means propaganda, which is always supposed to accompany penalties and coercive measures. The injunction to combine "regular" work with "organizing necessary activities" means that ongoing surveillance and propaganda should be supplemented by periodic "mobilizations" to round up those not in compliance and make them comply. Because resistance is widespread and often includes the cadres themselves, "strengthening leadership" is the essential factor in implementing the program.

36. Wang Ying, "Quanguo jihua shengyu shidian gongzuo qingkuang jiaoliuhui qiangdiao jihua shengyu gongzuo yao shuli" ("National Meeting for the Exchange of Information on Experimental Family Planning Work Stresses the Importance of Establishing the Idea of 'Two Services' "), *JKBJHSYB*, December 14, 1984, p. 1.

37. "Wang Wei tan jihua shengyu gongzuo gaige de liudian shexiang" ("Wang Wei Talks About Six Ideas on Reform of Family Planning"), *JKBJHSYB*, December 21, 1984, p. 1.

38. Dong Taituo and Wang Lingling, "National Propaganda and Education Conference on Birth Control Work Stresses that Propaganda Work Must Adopt Various Forms to Serve the Masses," *JKBJHSYB*, January 4, 1985, JPRS, No. 85–035, April 15, 1985, pp. 60–61.

39. "Jixu duanzheng zhidao sixiang gaohao jihua shengyu gaige" ("To Continue to Straighten Out the Thinking of the Professional Leadership and Carry Out the Reform of Family Planning Well"), *JKBJHSYB*, January 4, 1985, p. 1.

40. "Quanguo jihua shengyu xuanchuan jiaoyu gongzuo huiyi zai Chengdu juxing" ("National Conference on Family Planning Publicity and Education Held in Chengdu"), *RKYJ*, No. 2, March 29, 1985, p. 61.

41. Beijing radio, Domestic Service, January 11, 1985, FBIS, No. 10, January 15, 1985, p. K27.

42. "Jihua shengyu gongzuo yao genshang gaige bufa" ("Family Planning Work Must Catch Up with the Pace of Reform"), *JFRB*, Shanghai, January 24, 1985, p. 2.

43. Lanzhou radio, Gansu Provincial Service, January 25, 1985, FBIS, No. 18, January 28, 1985, p. T1.

44. Nanning radio, Guangxi Regional Service, February 12, 1985, FBIS, No. 31, February 143, 1985, p. P1.

45. Beijing radio, Domestic Service, March 10, 1985, FBIS, No. 63, April 2, 1985, p. Q1. The source adds that during the previous period, when the cadres were more overtly coercive, a saying circulated that "When the farm machinery cadres arrived, they were served eggs; when Party and government cadres arrived, they were served tea and rice; and when family planning cadres arrived, they were hit with shoulder-poles."

46. Beijing radio, Domestic Service, February 17, 1985, JPRS, No. 85–027, March 18, 1985, p. 29; and "Jihua shengyu gongzuo yao guanchuan fuwu quanju de sixiang" ("Family Planning Work Must Be Imbued with the Thought of Serving the Overall Situation"), JKBJHSYB, February 22, 1985, p. 1.

47. "At Present Our Country's Single Child Rate Has Already Reached 35 Million," JKBJHSYB, January 18, 1985, JPRS, No. 85–055, June 6, 1985, p. 33.

48. Guiyang radio, Guizhou Provincial Service, January 6, 1985, FBIS, No. 5, January 8, 1985, p. Q1. The expression "multiple births" is ambiguous. It sometimes seems to include unauthorized second as well as higher parity births; at other times it includes only third and higher parity births.

49. Qin Zixun, "Current Policy on Family Planning," SXRB, Sian, January 11, 1985, JPRS, No. 85–033, April 5, 1985, p. 89.

50. "Tangqi zhen jianli 'wailai' 'waichu' yuling funu guanli zhidu" ("The Town of Tangqi Establishes a Control System Over 'Incoming' and 'Outgoing' Women of Childbearing Age"), JKBJHSYB, February 15, 1985, p. 1. "Mobilization" is a term used to describe various procedures by which people are impelled under direct administrative pressure to do things they would not do on their own initiative. In this case the "mobilizations" were intended to result in abortions.

51. "Shenqiu xian renda yi falu wei baozhang fachu gonggao zhizhi silei pohuai jihua shengyu gongzuo de xingwei" ("The People's Congress of Shenqiu County Takes the Law as Its Authority to Issue a Public Notice on Prohibiting Four Types of Behavior Sabotaging Family Planning Work"), JKBJHSYB, March 1, 1985, p. 1. The "secret" removal of IUDs is seen by the authorities as "sabotage" of family planning because it is carried out by women who want to become pregnant without permission. Obviously they cannot have their IUDs removed on request by the regular medical services, which in many cases had inserted them without their consent. The fourth type of "sabotage" is female infanticide, which, as this notice indicates, was still continuing in spite of official denials.

52. "Jixu shenru quanmian guanche zhongyang qihao wenjian" ("To Continue to Implement Document No. 7 of the Party Central Committee in Depth and Throughout the Country"), JKBJHSYB, April 12, 1985, p. 1.

53. Jiang Zeyu, Director, Sichuan Provincial Family Planning Commission, "Shiqian yinian chu jian chengxiao" ("The Practice of One Year Wins Initial Success"), JKBJHSYB, April 12, 1985, p. 3; Chen Tongxin, "A New

Phase in Shandong Family Planning Work Has Emerged," *JKBJHSYB*, April 12, 1985, JPRS, No. 85–064, June 28, 1985, p. 39; "Jiangsu quansheng jiben peiqi bu tuochan ganbu" ("Jiangsu Basically Completes Staffing Throughout the Province with Cadres Not Detached from Production"), *JKBJHSYB*, May 10, 1985, p. 1; Lu Haimu, "Regularization and Institutionalization of Family Planning Work in Guangdong," *NFRB*, May 11, 1985, JPRS, No. 85–069, July 10, 1985, p. 58; Fuzhou radio, Fujian Provincial Service, May 14, 1985, JPRS, No. 85–059, June 19, 1985, p. 74; "Qiewu 'bao' pianle" ("Be Sure that 'Contracts' Are Properly Done"), *JKBJHSYB*, May 24, 1985, p. 1; Hohhot radio, Nei Monggol Regional Service, July 29, 1985, FBIS, No. 165, August 26, 1985, p. R2; and "Jilinsheng jisheng gongzuo chuxian hao jumian" ("A Good Situation Has Appeared in the Family Planning Work of Jilin Province"), *JKBJHSYB*, August 2, 1985, p. 1.

54. Huang Caigang, "Woguo renkou zheng xiang di chusheng de siwang di ziran zengzhanglu guodu" ("China's Population Transition toward a Low Birth Rate, Death Rate, and Natural Increase Rate"), *JKBJHSYB*, April 26, 1985, p. 1; "Xia juexin gaibian gongzuo houjin zhuangkuang" ("To Have the Determination to Change the Backwardness of the Work"), *JKBJHSYB*, May 3, 1985, p. 1; "Woguo renkou kuai zengzhang jixu dedao kongzhi" ("China's Exceedingly Rapidly Growing Population Is Continuously Being Put Under Control"), *RMRB*, June 8, 1985, p. 1; and XINHUA, Beijing, June 8, 1985, JPRS, No. 85–067, July 3, 1985, p. 51. The statement that the program is becoming increasingly voluntary contains an implicit admission that it has not been and still is not entirely voluntary.

55. Changsha radio, Hunan Provincial Service, April 8, 1985, FBIS, No. 70, April 11, 1985, p. P2.

56. Guiyang radio, Guizhou Provincial Service, April 11, 1985, FBIS, No. 73, April 16, 1985, p. Q1.

57. "Jisheng gongzuo yao shuli he fayang youliang zuofeng" ("Family Planning Work Must Establish and Promote an Excellent Work Style"), *JKBJHSYB*, April 12, 1985, p. 1. In the article the lieutenant governor said the cadres must "take charge" of two things; the first was targets and the second "work style."

58. "Hebei Provincial CCP Committee and Government Hold Forum in Xingtai Calling on Counties Which Lag Behind in Family Planning to Impose a Strict Ban on Conceiving Children Above Quota," *HBRB*, April 27, 1985, JPRS, No. 85–087, September 4, 1985, p. 101.

59. "To Have the Determination . . ."

60. Fuzhou radio, Fujian Provincial Service, May 3, 1985, FBIS, No. 90. May 9, 1985, p. O1; and Fuzhou radio, May 14, 1985, JPRS, No. 85–059, June 19, 1985, p. 74.

61. "Renkou guanli de zhongyang gaige" ("An Important Reform in Population Control"), *JKBJHSYB*, May 10, 1985, p. 1.

62. Xu Junzhou, "Draft Report on Shanxi Province's 1985 National Economic and Social Development Plan Excerpts," *SXRB*, Taiyuan, May 18, 1985, JPRS, No. 85–061, July 11, 1985, p. 74.

149

63. "Excerpts of a Draft Report by Deng Xichen, Director of the Autonomous Regional Planning Committee, on the National Economic and Social Development Plan for 1985, at the Third Plenary Session of the Fifth Autonomous Regional People's Congress on May 2, 1985," *Ningxia ribao* (*Ningxia Daily*) (*NXRB*), Yinchuan, May 24, 1985, JPRS, No. 85–061, July 11, 1985, p. 66. The expression "technical services" is a standard Chinese euphemism for IUD insertion, sterilization, and abortion.

64. At that time no one seemed to know how numerous they were. A few years later they were said to number some 50 million, or five percent of the national population. (XINHUA-English, Beijing, February 26, 1989, JPRS, No. 89–020, March 8, 1989, p. 34.)

65. Qin Si, "The Emergence of Problems in Urban Family Planning and Suggestions to Supplement the Current Regulations," *JKBJHSYB*, February 8, 1985, JPRS, No. 85–037, April 18, 1985, pp. 16–19.

66. Hu Hanjing, Jiayu County, Hebei Province, "Yige buneng yiwang de jiaoluo" ("A Corner Which Ought Not to Be Forgotten"), *JKBJHSYB*, May 17, 1985, p. 3.

67. Zhao Huishan, "Shiying jingji gaige xingshi zhahao liudong renkou guanli" ("Adapt to the Situation of Economic Reform and Take Firm Charge of Controlling the Floating Population"), *JKBJHSYB*, May 17, 1985 p. 3. Other sources report the use of periodic X-ray examinations of women's abdomens to determine whether their IUDs were in place or whether they were pregnant.

68. "Waichu de jihua shengyu wenti zenmeban?" ("What Should Be Done About the Problem of Planned Births for People Who Are Away from Home?"), *JKBJHSYB*, May 24, 1985, p. 1.

69. Xu Yaping, "Plug Up a Loophole in Planned Parenthood Work," *RMRB*, June 4, 1985, FBIS, No. 108, June 5, 1985, p. K3.

70. Jinan radio, Shandong Provincial Service, July 26, 1985, JPRS, No. 85–085, August 22, 1985, p. 11.

71. Yao Li, "Results of Family Planning in Jilin Described," *JKBJHSYB*, August 2, 1985, JPRS, No. 85–104, October 10, 1985, p. 88.

72. "Do Not Neglect Education and Propaganda Work" (commentary), *JKBJHSYB*, September 6, 1985, JPRS, No. 85–108, October 23, 1985, p. 51. This article makes it clear that the central authorities realize that persuasion does not work as well as force when the cadres are dealing with popular resistance to the one-child limit, but, at least in the middle of 1985, when the coercion issue was receiving worldwide attention, the authorities were trying to put distance between themselves and the tactics their targets made necessary at the grass-roots levels.

73. "To Continue to Implement Document No. 7 . . ."

74. Yu Xudong, "Leading Members of the Shandong Provincial Family Planning Commission Visit Grassroots Units for the Purpose of Helping Those Which Lag Behind in Family Planning Carry Out Work," *JKBJHSYB*, April 26, 1985, JPRS, No. 85–087, September 4, 1985, p. 31.

75. "To Have the Determination . . ."

76. "Nei Monggol Praises Family Planning Success," *Nei Menggu ribao* (*Nei Monggol Daily*), Hohhot, July 29, 1985, FBIS, No. 165, August 26, 1985, p. R2; Lanzhou radio, Gansu Provincial Service, October 17, 1985, JPRS, No. 85–116, November 29, 1985, p. 92; and "Zhejiang shengwei shengzhengfu qiangdiao yao zhuanzhi zhidao zhashi zuohao jisheng gongzuo" ("Zhejiang Party Committee and Government Stress the Point of Taking the Opportune Time This Winter and Next Spring to Do Family Planning Work Well"), *JKBJHSYB*, November 1, 1985, p. 1.

77. Liang Jimin, "Zai wanshan shengyu zhengce zhong yao zhengque chuli hao sige guanxi" ("Four Relations Must Be Handled Well When Making Birth Policies More Perfect"), *JKBJHSYB*, December 20, 1985, p. 2.

78. Nanning radio, Guangxi Regional Service, October 17, 1985, JPRS, No. 85–115, November 19, 1985, p. 57.

79. "The Fundamental Family Planning Policy Calling on Each Couple to Bear One Child Remains Unchanged," *Shanxi nongmin* (*Rural Shanxi*), Taiyuan, October 22, 1985, JPRS, No. 86–016, February 1986, pp. 119–120. The article ends with the instruction that "in places where multi-child families predominate, every woman must be asked to wear an IUD following her first birth and following her second birth she or [her husband] must be sterilized . . ."

80. Shijiazhuang radio, Hebei Provincial Service, November 8, 1985, JPRS, No. 85–120, December 17, 1985, p. 107. As is clear from many Chinese sources, "unplanned births" are births that may have been planned and strongly desired by the couples but were not planned or authorized by the authorities.

81. Shenyang radio, Liaoning Provincial Service, October 5, 1985, FBIS, No. 200, October 16, 1985, p. S1.

82. Yao Minhua, "China's Population Control Plan Makes Good Progress During the Sixth Five-Year Plan," *JKBJHSYB*, September 27, 1985, JPRS, No. 86–004, January 15, 1986. p. 25.

83. Su Hang, " 'Liu-wu' renkou fazhan qingkuang yu 'qi-wu' zhanwang" ("Population Growth During the 'Sixth Five-Year Plan' and Prospects in the 'Seventh Five-Year Plan' "), *JKBJHSYB*, October 25, 1985, p. 2.

84. "Seek Truth from Facts . . ."

85. XINHUA-English, Beijing, September 22, 1984, FBIS, No. 187, September 25, 1984, p. K19,

86. Xi Jianwei, "Initial Thoughts on the Formulation of the Population Plan for the Seventh Five-Year Plan," *RKYJ*, No. 4, July 29, 1985, JPRS, No. 85–118, December 11, 1985, p. 10.

87. Rong Shi, "Zhongguo 1982–nian renkou pucha dierchi kexue taolunhui . . ." ("Second Conference on China's 1982 Population Census . . ."), *JKBJHSYB*, January 10, 1986, p. 2. They were right. The total fertility rate, which had fallen from almost 6.5 in the late 1960s to 2.1 in 1983, was reportedly back up to 2.4 by 1988. (Yao Minhua, "China's Population Control Plan . . .")

88. Nanning radio, Guangxi Regional Service, September 27, 1985, JPRS,

No. 85–110, October 25, 1985, p. 103. The item continues that "Party and government leaders at all levels must . . . combine necessary disciplinary measures with economic sanctions, combine family planning work with the implementation of birth control measures . . . [and] . . . make contributions to the cause of family planning by every possible means . . ."

89. Tianjin radio, City Service, October 29, 1985, JPRS, No. 85–117, December 6, 1985, p. 107; Jinan radio, Shandong Provincial Service, December 30, 1985, JPRS, No. 86–016, February 3, 1986, p. 64; Hu Jingui, "Qinghai shengwei shengzhengfu fachu tongzhi 'qi-wu' qijian yao jin yibu zhuajin zhuanhao jihua shengyu gongzuo" ("Qinghai Provincial Party Committee and Qinghai Provincial Government Issue Circular on Taking Charge of and Doing Well Family Planning Work During the Seventh Five-Year Plan Period"), JKBJHSYB, February 21, 1986, p. 1; Zhengzhou radio, Henan Provincial Service, April 11, 1986, FBIS, No. 71, April 14, 1986, p. P1; and XINHUA, Nanjing, March 23, 1986, JPRS, No. 86–041, April 15, 1986, p. 54.

90. "Proposal of the Central Committee of the Communist Party of China for the Seventh Five-Year Plan for National Economic and Social Development" (adopted at the National Conference of the Communist Party of China, September 23, 1985), BR, Vol. 28, No. 40, October 7, 1985, p. xxii.

91. Wang Wei, "Jihua shengyu shi shehui zhuyi jingshen wenming jianshe de zhongyao neirong" ("Family Planning Is an Important Part of the Construction of Socialist Spiritual Civilization"), JKBJHSYB, November 22, 1985, pp. 1 and 3.

92. Liang Jimin, "Four Relations Must Be Handled Well . . ."

93. "Fujian fushengchang Chen Mingyi tichu ding shengchan jihua yao zhongshi renjun chanzhi" ("Fujian Lieutenant Governor Chen Mingyi Proposes That Production Plan Attach Importance to Per Capita Output Value"), JKBJHSYB, November 1, 1985, p. 1; "Shanqu gexiang yao jianjue kongzhi renkou mangmu zhengzhang" ("Counties in Mountainous Regions [in Ningxia] Must Resolutely Control Their Blind Increase in Population"), JKBJHSYB, November 1, 1985, 1; Taiyuan radio, Shanxi Provincial Service, November 11, 1985, JPRS, No. 85–118, December 11, 1985, p. 113; Kunming radio, Yunnan Provincial Service, December 3, 1985, JPRS, No. 86–013, January 24, 1986, p. 141; Shenyang radio, Liaoning Provincial Service, December 11, 1985, JPRS, No. 86–009, January 20, 1986, p. 99; Nanjing radio, Jiangsu Provincial Service, December 13, 1985, JPRS, No. 86–009, January 20, 1986, p. 49; "Heilongjiang sheng jisheng gongzuo huiyi jiejie shiji wenti" ("Heilongjiang Provincial Family Planning Work Conference Resolves Practical Problems"), JKBJHSYB, December 13, 1985, p. 1; "Guojia jishengwei yaoqiu geji lingdao jishi liaojie qingkuang renzhen jiejue wenti" ("The State Family Planning Commission Demands That Leadership at All Levels Solve Problems Earnestly"), JKBJHSYB, December 20, 1985, p. 1; Chengdu radio, Sichuan Provincial Service, December 29, 1985, JPRS, No. 86–013, January 24, 1986, p. 86; Jinan radio, Shandong Provincial Service, December 30, 1985, JPRS, No. 86–016, February 3, 1986, p. 64; and Wuhan radio, Hubei Provincial Service, December 30, 1985, FBIS, No. 200, January 2, 1986, p. P3.

94. Guo Wensheng, "Daoli yu shishi" ("Principles and Facts"), *JKBJHSYB*, January 24, 1986, p. 3.

95. "Shoudu renkou xu jixu jiaqiang kongzhi" ("Beijing's Population Needs Continuing Control"), *JKBJHSYB*, January 24, 1986, p. 3; Zhao Yugui, "Anhui shengwei fushuji Xu Leyi zhichu yao caiqu youxiao cuoshi . . .") "Deputy Secretary Xu Leyi of the Anhui Provincial Party Committee on Adopting Effective Measures . . ."), *JKBJHSYB*, January 24, 1986, p. 1; Li Laiyou, "Jihua shengyu gongzuo yao zhua dao dianzi shang" ("Family Planning Work [in Gansu] Must Be Carried Out Firmly at the Local Level"), *JKBJHSYB*, January 24, 1986, p. 1; "Tianjin Li Ruihuan shizhang qiangdiao jihua shengyu gongzuo buneng fangsong" ("Tianjin Mayor Li Ruihuan Stresses That Family Planning Work Cannot Be Relaxed"), *JKBJHSYB*, January 31, 1986, p. 1; Nanning radio, Guangxi Regional Service, February 21, 1986, JPRS, No. 86–032, March 25, 1986, p. 94; Guiyang radio, Guizhou Provincial Service, February 22, 1986, JPRS, No. 86–032, March 25, 1986, p. 95; "Shanghai shunli wancheng 'liu-wu' renkou guihua" ("Shanghai Successfully Fulfills the Sixth Five-Year Plan for Population"), *JFRB*, February 25, 1986, p. 1; Huang Caikang and Lu Meiqiang, "Guangxi Zhuangzu zizhiqu zhixi Wei Chunshu zhichu Zhuangzu diqu bixu kongzhi renkou zengzhang" ("Chairman of the Guangxi Zhuang Autonomous Region, Wei Chunshu, Points Out That the Zhuang Nationality Region Must Control Population Growth"), *JKBJHSYB*, March 21, 1986, p. 1; Taiyuan Radio, Shanxi Provincial Service, March 22, 1986, JPRS, No. 86–040, April 11, 1986, p. 75; Xining radio, Qinghai Provincial Service, April 13, 1986, FBIS, No. 72, April 15, 1986, p. T2; Huang Jialiang, "Sichuan xianxing zhengce fuhe shiji" ("Current Policy in Sichuan Fits the Realities"), *JKBJHSYB*, April 25, 1986, p. 1; Lanzhou radio, Gansu Provincial Service, May 24, 1986, FBIS, No. 103, May 29, 1986, p. T1; Guangzhou radio, Guangdong Provincial Service, June 1, 1986, FBIS, No. 106, June 3, 1986, p. P3; Nanning radio, Guangxi Provincial Service, June 29, 1986, FBIS, No. 128, July 3, 1986, p. P2; Guiyang radio, Guizhou Provincial Service, July 3, 1986, FBIS, No. 130, July 8, 1986, p. Q1; and Changchun radio, Jilin Provincial Service, July 16, 1986, FBIS, No. 137, July 17, 1986, p. S3–4.

96. Bai Jun, "National Meeting to Commend Advanced Units and Individuals in Family Planning Ends, Calls for Continued Efforts in Family Planning," *RMRB*, March 5, 1986, FBIS, No. 48, March 12, 1986, p. K16.

97. XINHUA-English, Beijing, February 23, 1986, FBIS, No. 40, February 28, 1986, p. K23.

98. Shandong said that its natural increase rate dropped to 9 per thousand, below the target figure of 10.05; Sichuan claimed that its year-end 1985 population total was some 2.75 million less than the planned target; Qinghai, with a much smaller population, was 20,000 below the stipulated figure; Liaoning had 780,000 fewer births than the plan allowed; Shanghai had 157,000 and Zhejiang 360,000 fewer births during the period than "the quota assigned by the state." (Sun Nianjiu, "Shandongsheng zhaokai jihua shengyu gongzuo huiyi" ["Shandong Province Convenes Family Planning Work

Conference"], *JKBJHSYB*, January 31, 1986, p. 1; Wen Xuan, "Sichuan Achieves Marked Success in Controlling Population Growth," *SCRB*, February 21, 1986, FBIS, No. 49, March 13, 1986, p. Q1; Shenyang radio, Liaoning Provincial Service, February 25, 1986, JPRS, No. 86–037, April 8, 1986, p. 108; Xining radio, Qinghai Provincial Service, March 3, 1986, FBIS, No. 43, March 5, 1986, p. T2; " 'Liu-wu' qijian Shanghaishi bi jihua shao sheng shiwu wan duo ren" ["Shanghai Municipality Had More Than 150,000 Fewer Births Than Planned During the Sixth Five-Year Plan"], *JKBJHSYB*, May 2, 1986, p. 1; and " 'Liu-wu' qijian Zhejiang shao sheng san-shi-liu-wan yu ren" ["During the Sixth Five-Year Plan, Zhejiang Had More Than 360,000 Fewer Births"], *JKBJHSYB*, June 6, 1986, p. 3.)

99. XINHUA-English, Beijing, April 3, 1986, FBIS, No. 66, April 7, 1986, p. K15.

100. Changsha radio, Hunan Provincial Service, January 20, 1986, JPRS, No. 86–018, February 13, 1986, p. 81.

101. Guiyang radio, Guizhou Provincial Service, February 22, 1986, JPRS, No. 86–032, March 25, 1986, p. 95.

102. Taiyuan radio, Shanxi Provincial Service, March 22, 1986, JPRS, No. 86–040, April 11, 1986, p. 75.

103. Xining radio, Qinghai Provincial Service, April 13, 1986, FBIS, No. 72, April 15, 1986, p. T2.

104. "Shanghai Municipality Had More Than 150,000 . . ."

105. XINHUA, Chengdu, March 27, 1986, JPRS, No. 86–045, April 21, 1986, p. 35.

106. Zhao Yugui, "Deputy Secretary Xu Leyi . . ."

107. Zhang Zhiqiang, "Guojia tongjiju zai Shaanxi jingxing shengyu qing-kuang diaocha" ("State Statistical Bureau Conducts Fertility Survey in Shaanxi"), *JKBJHSYB*, February 21, 1986, p. 1; and Sun Huilian and Liang Naizhong, "Shaanxi wanshan shengyu zhence zuochu xin guiding" ("Shaanxi Province Formulates New Regulations to Make the Birth Policy More Perfect"), *JKBJHSYB*, April 25, 1986, p. 1.

108. Huang Jialiang, "Current Policy in Sichuan . . . "; and Huang Jialiang, "Sichuan dusheng zinu lingzhenglu xiajiang youguan bumen dui ci ying yuyi zhongshi" ("Sichuan's One-Child Certificate Acceptance Rate Is Declining; Relevant Departments Should Pay Attention to This Situation"), *JKBJHSYB*, June 13, 1986, p. 1. Couples with one child who pledge not to have another are awarded "one-child certificates" which entitle them to various kinds of preferential treatment, including extra plots of land, priority in medical treatment, and priority access to education.

109. Changsha radio, Hunan Provincial Service, May 28, 1986, FBIS, No. 104, May 30, 1986, p. P3.

110. Guangzhou radio, Guangdong Provincial Service, June 1, 1986, FBIS, No. 106, June 3, 1986, p. P3.

111. Guiyang radio, Guizhou Provincial Service, July 3, 1986, FBIS, No. 130, July 8, 1986, p. Q1.

112. Chen Jialin, "Research Survey on the Motives and Needs of Unmar-

ried Youth to Have Children," *RKYJJ*, No. 3, June 25, 1985, JPRS, No. 85–116, November 29, 1985, pp. 47–55.

113. Ling Baicen, "An Investigation on the Childbearing Situation Among One-Child Specialized Households in the Rural Suburbs of Tianjin Municipality," *RKYJ*, No. 4, July 29, 1985, JPRS, No. 85–118, December 11, 1985, pp. 108–109.

114. XINHUA-English, Beijing, April 9, 1986, JPRS, No. 86–051, April 30, 1986, p. 79.

115. See John S. Aird, "Recent Demographic Data from China: Problems and Prospects," in Joint Economic Committee, Congress of the United States, *China Under the Four Modernizations*, Part 1 (Washington: U.S. Government Printing Office, August 13, 1982), p. 203. A general discussion of falsification in Chinese statistics and the underlying causes follows on pp. 204–213.

116. For example, "Banjiang xiang nongxu zuojia manbao chusheng renkou" ("Banjiang Township Resorts to Deception to Conceal the Numbers of Births"), *JKBJHSYB*, August 10, 1984, p. 3; and "Shijiazhuang diqu jishengwei zai zhengdang zhong jiuzheng jihua shengyu tongji bushi wenti" ("Shijiazhuang Prefecture Family Planning Commission Corrects the Problem of Untruthful Family Planning Statistics During Party Rectification"), *JKBJHSYB*, December 12, 1984, p. 1.

117. "Zhuren gai shuzi" ("The Director Changed the Numbers"), *RMRB*, January 29, 1985, p. 1; Chen Yubao, "Zenyang zuohao jihua shengyu tongji gongzuo" ("How to Do Well in Family Planning Statistical Work"), *JKBJHSYB*, February 1, 1985, p. 3; "Zhongxiang xian tongbao piping Duanji xiang yinman duotai" ("Zhongxiang County Issues Circular Criticizing Duanji Township for Concealing Excessive Births"), *JKBJHSYB*, February 8, 1985, p. 1; Xu Daihuang, "Yingdang dui tamen jinxing yange peixun" ("They Should Be Given Strict Training"), *JKBJHSYB*, February 15, 1985, p. 3; and "Yanting xian quanmian jiancha jihua shengyu gongzuo" ("Yanting County Conducts Countywide Inspection of Family Planning Work"), *JKBJHSYB*, December 20, 1985, p. 1.

118. "Guojia jihua shengyu weiyuanhui fachu tongzhi yaoqiu gedi renzhen fuze zuohao jihua shengyu tongji gongzuo" ("State Family Planning Commission Issues Circular to Demand that All Areas Take Responsibility for Conscientiously Doing Family Planning Statistical Work Well"), *JKBJHSYB*, July 26, 1985, p. 1.

119. Xiu Guojin, "One Must Reveal His Own Shortcomings and Speak the Truth; It Is Strictly Forbidden to Falsify and Exaggerate," *LNRB*, August 6, 1985, JPRS, No. 85–116, November 29, 1985, p. 88.

120. He Guangrong, "Zuo shishi jiang shihua bao shishu" ("Do Real Work, Tell the Truth, and Report True Figures"), *JKBJHSYB*, November 11, 1985, p. 3.

121. "Renkou tongji ying qiushi" ("Population Statistics Should Seek Facts"), *JKBJHSYB*, January 24, 1986, p. 3.

122. "Bixu tujie xubao renkou chusheng shuzi de xianxiang" ("Falsification of the Numbers of Births Must Be Eliminated"), *JKBJHSYB*, March 21, 1986, p. 3.

123. "Gedi jihua shengyu tongji xubao chengfeng" ("Falsifying Family Planning Statistics Has Become a Common Practice", *RMRB*, October 24, 1988, p. 3.

124. Qi Bangmi, "The Alarm Bell of Population Tolls Again," *BYT*, December 10, 1988, FBIS, No. 11, January 18, 1989, p. 25. Even assuming the bottom limit of each range and assigning the ranges with the lowest percentages to the largest provinces, the national average undercount could not have been less than 15 percent.

125. "Falsifying Family Planning Statistics . . ." In February 1989, Hubei Province revealed that discrepancies found in its population statistics for 1987 were as high as 40.64 percent, making it the fourth worst province in the country in respect to statistical inaccuracy. (Fan Zhigang, "Guo Deming zhuren he jizhe de sanci duihua" ["Three Conversations Between Director Guo Deming and This Reporter"], *ZGRKB*, February 27, 1989, p. 1.)

126. Tian Xueyuan, Director, Population Research Center, Chinese Academy of Social Sciences, "Renkou zaishengchan leixing de zhuanbian he renkou de shuliang kongzhi" ("Changes in the Pattern of Population Reproduction and Control of the Size of the Population"), *JKBJHSYB*, February 21, 1986, p. 2.

127. Li Yamo, Wang Chengjin, and Sun Shoubao, "Zuohao jihua shengyu gongzuo bimian shengyu gaofeng changfu" ("Do Well in Family Planning Work to Avoid a Repeat of the Birth Peak"), *JKBJHSYB*, April 11, 1986, p. 2.

128. "Jihua shengyu ke shi zhongguo gengkuai fada qilai" (Family Planning Will Enable China to Become Prosperous More Rapidly"), *RMRB*, April 24, 1986, p. 1.

129. Zhang Xinxia, "Xinde shengyu gaofeng de tedian jiqi duice" ("The Characteristics of a New Birth Peak and Countermeasures"), *JKBJHSYB*, May 9, 1986, p. 2.

CHAPTER 4: PARTY DOCUMENT NO. 13 AND THE CRACKDOWN

1. "Guojia jishengwei fachu tongzhi yaoqiu renzhen xuexi guance zhongyang shisanhao wenjian jingshen" ("State Family Planning Commission Issues Circular on Conscientiously Studying and Implementing the Guidelines of Document No. 13 of the Party Central Committee"), *JKBJHSYB*, June 13, 1986, p. 1.

2. Commentator, "Zhengce, guihua yu shengyuguan" ("Policy, Planning, and Views on Having Children"), *JKBJHSYB*, August 22, 1986, p. 1. The phrase "accepted by the masses" has appeared several times in the past few years in contexts where it seems to suggest something less than "supported by the masses." Presumably it means "tolerated" by the masses, in the sense that it can be imposed on them without leading to open rebellion or to an outbreak of acts of reprisal against family planning cadres.

3. Commentator, "Qieshi jiaqiang jihua shengyu ganbu duiwu de jianshe" ("Truly Strengthen the Building of the Ranks of Family Planning Cadres"), *JKBJHSYB*, August 29, 1986, p. 1.

4. Commentator, "Rang quan shehui guanxin yu ge bumen xiezuo" ("Let the Entire Society Be Concerned and Collaborate with Other Departments"), *JKBJHSYB*, September 12, 1986, p. 1.

5. Commentator, "Zhuanbian houjin xu yu 'fu pin' xiang jiehe" ("The Transformation of Backwardness Must Be Linked with 'Helping the Poor' "), *JKBJHSYB*, September 19, 1986, p. 1.

6. Wang Mingyuan, Hebei Provincial Family Planning Commission, "Guance zhongyang 13 hao wenjian zonghe kaolu zhibiao, zhengce he gongzuo wenti" ("To Implement Document No. 13 of the Party Central Committee and to Give Overall Consideration to the Norms, Policies, and Tasks of Family Planning"), *RKYJJ*, No. 6, December 25, 1986, pp. 3–6 and 27.

7. "Anhui sheng jishengwei zuzhi de shi jishengwei zhuren jiehe bendi shiji yanjiu guance yijian" ("Anhui Provincial Family Planning Commission Organizes Prefectural and Municipal Family Planning Commissions to Study Means of Implementation by Linking It with Local Realities"), *JKBJHSYB*, June 27, 1986, p. 1.

8. Nanning radio, Guangxi Regional Service, June 29, 1986, FBIS, No. 128, July 3, 1986, pp. P2–3.

9. "Sichuan shengwei lingdao qiangdian luoshi coushi" ("Sichuan Party Committee Leadership Stresses the Implementation of Measures"), *JKBJHSYB*, July 4, 1986, p. 1; "Tianjin shiwei yaochiu quanshi wushiwan dangyuan shenti lixing daidong qunzhong" ("Tianjin Party Committee Demands That 500,000 Party Members of the Municipality Set Personal Examples to Lead the Masses"), *JKBJHSYB*, August 8, 1986, p. 1; Song Ganheng, "Hunan caiqu cuoshi shazhu renkou huisheng shitou" ("Hunan Adopts Measures to Check the Upswing of Population"), *JKBJHSYB*, August 22, 1986, p. 3; Yin Su, "Hebei shengwei sheng zhengfu yaoqiu geji lingdao zhongshi jisheng gongzuo" ("Hebei Party Committee and Government Demand that Leadership at All Levels Attach Importance to Family Planning Work"), *JKBJHSYB*, August 29, 1986, p. 1; Liang Naizhong, "Shaanxi sheng ba zhongyang jingshen he gexiang cuoshi luodao shichu" ("Shaanxi Province Carries Out the Guidelines of the Party Central Committee and Various Measures in Earnest"), *JKBJHSYB*, August 29, 1986 p. 1; Kang Zizhen, "Haerbin shi jueding jianli jihua shengyu gongzuo lingdao xiaozu" ("Haerbin Municipality Decides to Establish Family Planning Work Leadership Team"), *JKBJHSYB*, October 17, 1986, p. 1; and Lu Qiang, "Guangxi tongzhi gedi renzhen jiancha zhixing zhiding de jihua shengyu guiding" ("Guangxi Notifies All Areas to Check Conscientiously the Family Planning Regulations Formulated Locally"), *JKBJHSYB*, November 7, 1986, p. 1.

10. Guiyang radio, Anhui Provincial Service, July 3, 1986, FBIS, No. 130, July 8, 1986, p. Q1.

11. Changchun radio, Jilin Provincial Service, July 16, 1986, FBIS, No. 137, July 17, 1986, p, S3.

12. Liang Yi, "Hunan sheng shengwei sheng zhengfu yaoqiu tongguo nongcun zhengdang niuzhuan luohou jumian" ("Hunan Provincial Party

Committee and Hunan Provincial Government Demand that the Backward Situation Be Turned Around by Means of Party Rectification in Rural Areas"), *JKBJHSYB*, August 15, 1986, p. 1.

13. Jinan radio, Shandong Provincial Service, August 17, 1986, FBIS, No. 159, August 18, 1986, p. O4.

14. Yin Su, "Hebei Party Committee and Government . . ."

15. Wuhan radio, Hubei Provincial Service, September 26, 1986, FBIS, No. 189, September 30, 1986, p. P4.

16. Xian radio, Shaanxi Provincial Service, October 13, 1986, FBIS, No. 198, October 14, 1986, p. T3. No central document reaffirming the demand for mandatory abortion ("remedial measures") has been made public as of this writing; however, this source reveals that such a document was issued.

17. Chengdu radio, Sichuan Provincial Service, November 1, 1986, FBIS, No. 215, November 6, 1986, p. Q2.

18. Lu Qiang, "Guangxi Notifies All Areas . . ."

19. Yin Su, "Hebei shengwei fu shuji Yue Qifeng shuo zhua jihua shengyu yao jianding buyi jianchi buxie" ("Assistant Secretary Yue Qifeng of the Hebei Provincial Party Committee Says that Family Planning Must Be Carried Out Firmly and Relentlessly"), *JKBJHSYB*, November 21, 1986, p. 1.

20. Kunming radio, Yunnan Provincial Service, January 5, 1987, FBIS, No. 4, January 7, 1987, p. Q2.

21. "Guojia jihua shengyu weiyuanhui weiyuan xuexi qiangdiao renkou zengzhang xu yange kongzhi" ("Members of the State Family Planning Commission Study the Document and Stress the Importance of Strict Control of Population Growth"), *JKBJHSYB*, June 27, 1986, p. 1.

22. Zhao Yugui, "Dai you zhanluexing de da zhengce" ("An Important Policy of a Strategic Nature"), *JKBJHSYB*, July 25, 1986, p. 2. The article also quoted earlier statements by Deng Xiaoping in defense of China's population policy, including one in April at a meeting with Japanese Prime Minister Fukuda in which Deng reaffirmed the goal of keeping the population total under 1.2 billion by the end of the century.

23. Commentator, "Policy, Planning, and Views . . ."

24. Ibid. The article clearly intends that propaganda to change the opinions of the masses is to be combined with efforts to achieve control of population growth, but it also makes clear that the "small contradiction" between the masses and the authorities over family planning cannot be allowed to interfere with the solution of the "large contradiction" between population growth and economic development. In other words, contradictions between the masses and the policy must be resolved in favor of the policy.

25. Zhang Jiaqiang, "Bixu jin yibu kongzhi renkou zengzhang" ("A Further Step Must Be Taken to Control Population Growth"), *JKBJHSYB*, September 12, 1986, p. 2.

26. Commentator, "It Is Still Necessary to Grasp Birth Control Tightly and Well," *RMRB*, October 23, 1986, FBIS, No. 209, October 29, 1986, p. K7.

27. XINHUA, Beijing, December 3, 1986, FBIS, No. 234, December 5, 1987, pp. K11–12.

28. XINHUA-English, Beijing, December 4, 1986, FBIS, No. 234, December 5, 1986, p. K13.

29. Chengdu radio, Sichuan Provincial Service, January 8, 1987, FBIS, No. 6, January 9, 1987, p. Q2; Nanjing radio, Jiangsu Provincial Service, January 17, 1987, FBIS, No. 20, January 30, 1987, p. O1; Changsha radio, Hunan Provincial Service, February 12, 1987, FBIS, No. 31, February 17, 1987, p. P3; Taiyuan radio, Shanxi Provincial Service, February 22, 1987, FBIS, No. 39, February 27, 1987, p. R2; Cao Guiying, "Several Questions Concerning Population and Employment," RMRB, March 16, 1987, FBIS, No. 57, March 25, 1987, p. K24; Xining radio, Qinghai Provincial Service, April 26, 1987, JPRS, No. 87–009, June 18, 1987, p. 94; Xian Radio, Shaanxi Provincial Service, July 10, 1987, FBIS, No. 135, July 15, 1987, pp. T1–2; and Wuhan radio, Hubei Provincial Service, September 5, 1987, FBIS, No. 173, September 8, 1957, p. 29.

30. Gao Ping, "Jihua shengyu zhengce meiyou bian" ("There Is No Change in the Family Planning Policy"), BYT, No. 6, March 25, 1987, pp. 7–9.

31. Lu Mu, "Our Country's Birth Rate Increased Last Year; It Is Imperative To Strictly Control the Birth Rate," RMRB, April 11, 1987, FBIS, No. 73, April 16, 1987, pp. K3–4. In the same month, Zheng Jiaheng of the State Statistical Bureau said that population growth in 1986, the first year of the Seventh Five-Year Plan period, had already far exceeded the planned figure. (Gong Yan, "Director of the State Statistical Bureau Says That China's Population Increased by 3 Million Last Year," Ming Pao, Hong Kong, April 9, 1987, JPRS, No. 87–047, May 26, 1987, p. 77.)

32. XINHUA, Beijing, July 8, 1987, FBIS, No. 131, July 9, 1987, p. K1.

33. XINHUA, Beijing, January 14, 1988, FBIS, No. 10, January 15, 1988, p. 17.

34. Li Yingming, "Qushi, wenti yu duice—woguo renkou wenti zhanwang" ("Trends, Problems, and Solutions—Future Problems of China's Population"), Weilai yu fazhan (Future and Development), Beijing, No. 3, June 15, 1987, pp. 53–55; and Qu Haibo, "Woguo de renkou qushi ji dangqian de zhuyao maodun" ("China's Population Trends and the Principal Contradictions at Present"), ZGJHSYB, July 24, 1987, p. 3. Even as early as October 1986, there were fears that the 1.2 billion target might be exceeded. See Hu Huanyong, "China's Population: Present and Future," QY, No. 2, February 2, 1987, JPRS, No. 87–047, May 26, 1987, p. 72.

35. For example, see Zhang Yan, "A Noteworthy Sign; an Interview with National People's Congress Deputy, Famed Economist Xu Dixin," RMRB, April 4, 1987, JPRS, No. 87–032, August 12, 1987, pp. 75–76; Lu Mu, "Our Country's Birth Rate"; Guo Zhongshi and Wang Dongtai, "Births Increase Threatens Population Targets," CD, July 1, 1987, p. 1; XINHUA-English, Beijing, July 8, 1987, JPRS, No. 87–029, August 5, 1987, p. 88; XINHUA-English, Beijing, January 5, 1988, FBIS, No. 2, January 5, 1988, p. 28; and KYODO, Tokyo, February 15, 1987, FBIS, No. 30, February 16, 1987, p. 20.

36. XINHUA-English, Beijing, June 12, 1987, JPRS, No. 87–018, July 10,

1987, p. 44; XINHUA, Beijing, July 1, 1987, FBIS, No. 128, July 6, 1987, p. K18; Wu Cangping and Zhan Changzhi, "Urgency of Controlling Present Population Growth in Our Country—Beginning with the World '5 Billion Population Day,' " *JJRB*, July 11, 1987, FBIS, No. 147, July 31, 1987, pp. K20–23; and Ai Xiao and Yu Changhong, "Li Peng Addresses Family Planning Meeting," XINHUA, Beijing, January 20, 1988, FBIS, No. 15, January 25, 1988, p. 25.

37. "Woguo lixiang de shengtai renkou shi duo shao?" ("What Is the Optimum Population for China?"), *ZGJHSYB*, December 18, 1987, p. 3.

38. XINHUA, Beijing, August 7, 1987, FBIS, No. 153, August 10, 1987, p. K4; "Jianjue jiuzheng fangsong yu ziliu xianxiang" ("Resolutely Correct the Loosening of Family Planning Work and [Letting It] Run Its Natural Course") (editorial), *ZGJHSYB*, August 7, 1987, p. 1.

39. For example, see Xia Guixiang, "China on the Threshold of Another Baby Boom," *Liaowang (Outlook)* (*LW*), Beijing, No. 7, February 16, 1987, JPRS, No. 87–044, May 20, 1987, p. 102; XINHUA-English, Beijing, February 21, 1987, FBIS, No. 36, February 24, 1987, p. Q2; *HBRB*, Shijiazhuang, March 17, 1987, FBIS, No. 66, April 7, 1987, pp. R1–2; Gao Ping, "There Is No Change"; XINHUA-English, July 8, 1987, JPRS, No. 87–029, August 5, 1987, p. 87; XINHUA-English, January 5, 1988, FBIS, No. 2, January 5, 1988, p. 28; and KYODO, Tokyo, February 15, 1988, FBIS, No. 30, February 16, 1988, p. 20.

40. For example, see Taiyuan radio, Shanxi Provincial Service, February 22, 1987, FBIS, No. 39, February 27, 1987, p. R2; and Lanzhou radio, Gansu Provincial Service, May 5, 1987, JPRS, No. 87–009, June 18, 1987, p. 92; "Weishenme jiuzheng youxie difang de fangsong yu ziliu xianxiang yao jianjue" ("Why Must [We] Be Firm in Correcting the Loosening of Family Planning Work and the Situation of [Letting It] Run Its Natural Course?"), (editorial), *ZGJHSYB*, August 28, 1987, p. 1; *South China Morning Post* (*SoCMP*), Hong Kong, July 26, 1987, JPRS, No. 87–041, September 1, 1987, p. 50; and Ai Xiao, "Worries about Population," *RMRB*, January 14, 1988, FBIS, No. 12, January 20, 1988.

41. Liang Yi, "Hunan xia daliqi jiuzheng fangsong he ziliu xianxiang" ("Hunan Puts Great Efforts into Correcting the Loosening of Family Planning Work and the Situation of Letting It Take Its Natural Course"), *ZGJHSYB*, September 4, 1987, p. 1.

42. "Wending zhengce wanshan zhengce" ("Stabilize the Policy and Improve the Policy"), *ZGJHSYB*, April 3, 1987, p. 1.

43. "State Family Planning Commission Answers Reporter's Questions on Population Growth Control," *RMRB*, June 14, 1987, FBIS, No. 120, June 23, 1987, pp. K10–12.

44. XINHUA, Beijing, August 7, 1987, FBIS, No. 153, August 10, 1987, p. K4.

45. Lu Mu, "Our Country's Birth Rate . . ."

46. "State Family Planning Commission Answers . . . ," p. K11; and XINHUA-English, Beijing, July 8, 1987, JPRS, No. 87–029, August 5, 1987, p. 87.

47. Colina MacDougall, "Growth Rate Exceeds Target," *Financial Times,* London, December 18, 1987, p. 16.

48. Wen Jia, "Law to Cut Births, End Early Weddings," *CD,* July 30, 1987, p. 3.

49. "State Takes Aim at Illegal Marriages," *CD,* January 9, 1988, p. 1.

50. Liu Fengqin, "Renzhen guanche 'hunyin fa' yanjing weifa hunyin" ("Earnestly Implement the 'Marriage Law' and Strictly Prohibit Marriages in Violation of the Law"), *ZGJHSYB,* January 8, 1988, p. 1.

51. "Zhizhi zaohun zaoyu" ("Prohibit Early Marriage and Early Childbirth"), *ZGJHSYB,* January 8, 1988, p. 1; and Zhao Yugui, "Woyang xian caiqu jianjue cuoshi zhizhi zaohun zaoyu weihun shengyu jian chengxiao" ("Woyang County Adopts Resolute Measures to Stop Early Marriages, Early Childbirths, and Childbirths Out of Wedlock"), *ZGJHSYB,* February 19, 1988, p. 1.

52. Li Huachang, "Sichuan sheng zhengfu yaoqiu gedi caiqu deli cuoshi zhizhi zaohun zaoyu he faihun shengyu" ("The Sichuan Provincial Government Demands That All Areas Adopt Effective Measures to Stop Early Marriages, Early Births, and Births Out of Wedlock"), *ZGJHSYB,* September 13, 1987, p. 1.

53. XINHUA-English, Beijing August 5, 1988, FBIS, No. 52, September 2, 1988, pp. 56–57.

54. Wang Deyi, "Jinhuo hunyin guanli jiang zhuzhong fagui jianshe" ("In Future Marriage Control Will Pay Attention to Establishing Laws and Regulations"), *ZGRKB,* March 10, 1989, p. 1.

55. "Increase in Births Threatens China's Population Target," *CD,* July 1, 1987, p. 1.

56. Qu Yibin, "Woguo renkou chushenglu mingxian huisheng de yuanyin ji duice tantao" ("An Enquiry into the Causes of the Marked Rise in China's Population Birth Rate and a Measure to Deal with Them"), *RKYJ,* No. 2, March 29, 1988, pp. 53–56.

57. Hu Angang, "Why Has China Lost Control of Its Population Growth in Recent Years?" *LW,* No. 10, March 6, 1989, JPRS, No. 89–066, June 27, 1989, p. 51.

58. Ibid.

59. Gao Ping, "There Is No Change . . ."

60. "Stabilize the Policy . . ."

61. Qu Haibo, "China's Population Trends . . ."

62. Ai Xiao and Yu Changhong, "Li Peng Addresses Family Planning Meeting."

63. Changsha radio, Hunan Provincial Service, April 22, 1987, FBIS, No. 78, April 23, 1987, p. 26.

64. Xining radio, Qinghai Provincial Service, April 26, 1987, JPRS, No. 87–009, June 18, 1987, p. 93.

65. Xian radio, Shaanxi Provincial Service, July 10, 1987, FBIS, No. 135, July 15, 1987, p. T2.

66. Zhengzhou radio, Henan Provincial Service, July 10, 1987, FBIS, No. 133, July 13, 1987, p. P4.

67. Guiyang radio, Guizhou Provincial Service, August 7, 1987, JPRS, No. 87–050, October 7, 1987, p. 45.

68. "Heilongjiang's Sun Weiben on Family Planning," *HLJRB*, September 25, 1987, FBIS, No. 200, October 16, 1987, p. 34.

69. Kunming radio, Yunnan Provincial Service, January 5, 1987, FBIS No. 4, January 7, 1987, p. Q2.

70. "Hebei's Xing Chongzhi Speaks on Family Planning," *HBRB*, March 17, 1987, FBIS, No. 66, April 7, 1987, p. R2.

71. Haikou radio, Hainan Island Service, April 14, 1987, FBIS, No. 77, April 22, 1987, pp. P1–2.

72. Haikou radio, Hainan Island Service, May 1, 1987, FBIS, No. 85, May 4, 1987. p. P1.

73. Haikou radio, Hainan Island Service, May 18, 1987, FBIS, No. 97, May 20, 1987, p. P2.

74. Guiyang radio, Guizhou Provincial Service, August 7, 1987, JPRS, No. 87–050, October 7, 1987, p. 45.

75. Colina MacDougall, "Growth Rate Exceeds Target." According to official figures, in 1986, the year in which this was true, there were 21.85 million births and 11.58 million abortions, up from 8.89 million abortions in 1984, and the third highest annual total after the 14.37 million in 1983 and 12.42 million in 1982. See table in chapter 3.

76. The Asia Watch Committee, *Human Rights in Tibet*, p. 55.

77. Daniel Southerland, "Anti-Chinese Unrest Spreads to Province North of Tibet," *WP*, March 11, 1988, p. A21.

78. Ji Xinfang, "Nongcun yao yi gong nei jieyuqi he jieza cuoshi wei zhu" ("Rural Areas Must Take IUDs and Ligations as the Principal Means") (commentary), *ZGJHSYB*, January 29, 1988, p. 2.

79. Tian Wenguang, "Dali tuixing nongcun jihua shengyu yanglao baoxian" ("Vigorously Promote Rural Family Planning and Old Age Insurance"), *RKYJ*, July 29, 1988, p. 57.

80. XINHUA-English, Beijing, March 17, 1988, FBIS, No. 53, March 18, 1988, p. 33; "Beijing's Li Commends Birth Control Model Units," *Beijing ribao* (*Beijing Daily*), Beijing, March 24, 1988, FBIS, No. 63, April 1, 1988, p. 58; XINHUA-English, Beijing, March 26, 1988, FBIS, No. 60, March 29, 1988, p. 38; Guangzhou radio, Guangdong Provincial Service, April 16, 1988, FBIS, No. 74, April 18, 1988, p. 56; Chengdu radio, Sichuan Provincial Service, July 31, 1988, FBIS, No. 57, August 3, 1988, p. 58; Xining radio, Qinghai Provincial Service, September 27, 1988, FBIS, No. 190, September 30, 1988, p. 52; Hou Jie, "Xiang zhua jingji gongzuo nayang zhua jihua shengyu gongzuo" ("Take Charge of Family Planning Work in the Same Way as with Economic Work"), *ZGRKB*, September 23, 1988, p. 1; Han Chuanjiang, "Yao jianding buyi gaohao jihua shengyu gongzuo" ("Family Planning Work Must Be Done Well [and] Resolutely"), *ZGRKB*, October 3, 1988, p. 1; Yue Zhifang, "Gaige jiceng guanli jizhi yange kongzhi renkou zengzhang" ("Reform the Mechanisms of Basic Level Control and Strictly Control Population Growth"), *ZGRKB*, October 7, 1988, p. 1; and Li Laiyou, "Congyan congjin gongzuo yanjin jihuawai

shengyu" ("Carry Out the Work Strictly and Stringently to Restrict Unplanned Births"), *ZGRKB*, October 7, 1988, p. 1.

81. For example, see Xian radio, Shaanxi Provincial Service, July 10, 1987, FBIS, No. 135, July 15, 1987, p. T2.

82. "Sichuan Provincial Family Planning Regulations, Adopted by the 26th Meeting of the 6th Provincial People's Congress Standing Committee on July 2", *SCRB*, July 4, 1987, JPRS, No. 87–044, September 8, 1987, pp. 77–83.

83. Wang Yi, "Sichuan sheng banbu 'jihua shengyu tiaoli' " ("Sichuan Province Promulgates 'Regulations on Family Planning' "), *RMRB*, July 12, 1987, p. 3.

84. Huang Jialiang, "Sichuan renkou huisheng shitou kaishi dedao kongzhi" ("Sichuan Population Upswing Is Being Put Under Control"), *ZGJHSYB*, September 4, 1987, p. 1. The expression "crooked gaps" refers to allowing couples to have a second child even though they do not meet the very strict requirements.

85. Hou Wenfang, "Sichuan sheng zai zhua jing zhua hao jihua shengyu gongzuo zhong chongfen fahui ge bumen he shehui zuzhi zuoyong" ("In Family Planning Work, Sichuan Province Develops Fully the Role Played by All Departments and All Social Organizations"), *ZGJHSYB*, September 4, 1987, p. 2.

86. "Sichuan Provincial Family Planning Regulations," pp. 82–83.

87. Commentator, "Zouxiang fazhi de lianghao kai duan" ("Heading Toward a Good Beginning for a Legal System"), *ZGRKB*, September 4, 1989, p. 1.

88. "Birth Control Regulations of Canton Municipality's Tianhe District, Dongpu Precinct," *China Spring Digest* (*CSD*), New York, Vol. I, No. 5, September–October 1987, pp. 60–62. According to survey data, the average monthly wage in Guangzhou in 1987 was 118 *yuan*, with a range of 65 to 200 *yuan*, or from 780 to 2400 *yuan* for the year. Fines of 20 and 50 *yuan* a month (which add to 240 to 600 *yuan* in a year) would impose some hardship on one-wage-earner families whose income was at the lower end of that range but not those in the middle to upper end. However, fines of 2000 to 4000 *yuan* and fines of 80 or 100 percent of income would be severe for all families, putting some into debt for years to come.

89. Xu Xuehan, "Tiaozheng woguo renkou zaishengchan de guanjianxing juece" ("The Key Policy Decision in the Readjustment of China's Population Reproduction"), *GMRB*, August 29, 1981, p. 3.

90. Fuzhou radio, Fujian Provincial Service, December 18, 1982, FBIS, No. 249, December 28, 1982, p. O2; "Quanguo jihua shengyu xuanchuanyue chengji da xiaoguo hao" ("The Nationwide Family Planning Propaganda Month Obtained Great Success and Good Results"), *JKB*, February 27, 1983, p. 1; Liu Jinglong, "Guanyu zai Huizi shixing jihua shengyu de qianjian" ("My Views on Implementing Family Planning Among the Hui People"), *NXRB*, March 21, 1983, p. 2; Liu Haiquan, "Formulation of Regulations for Planned Parenthood Is Effective in Controlling Population Growth in Sichuan," *SCRB*, May 12, 1983, JPRS, No. 84,176, August 23, 1983, p. 31; and

Guangzhou radio, Guangdong Provincial Service, August 8, 1983, FBIS, No. 155, August 10, 1983, p. P1.

91. Cheng Gang, "China Faces Another Baby Boom," *BR*, Vol. 31, No. 27, July 4–10, 1988, p. 26.

92. Wang was identified with the slight moderation in family planning requirements in 1984 and had reportedly underestimated the numbers of additional births that would be authorized by his policy of permitting a "small gap" to be opened for second births. ("Peasants' Revolt," *The Economist*, London, January 30–February 5, 1988, p. 27.) His replacement, Peng Peiyun, was a former Party secretary from Anhui Province and more recently Vice-Minister of Education, who had had no previous special connection with family planning. (*China News Analysis*, No. 1372, November 15, 1988, p. 5; and XINHUA, Beijing, January 21, 1988, FBIS, No. 13, January 21, 1988, p. 6.)

93. Beijing radio, Domestic Service, February 21, 1989, FBIS, No. 36, February 24, 1989, p. 30; and XINHUA-English, Beijing, February 23, 1989, JPRS, No. 89–020, March 8, 1989, p. 33.

94. Xu Jiangshan and Zheng Zhanguo, "Local Broadcast News Service," XINHUA, Beijing, March 28, 1989, FBIS, No. 65, April 6, 1989, p. 35. Vice-Minister of Public Health Cao Zeyi told a meeting of National People's Congress deputies from Zhejiang that legislative work on family planning was of "great importance" because "rural family planning cannot be put in practice if there [are] no restrictive measure[s]." ("Zhejiang Deputies on Family Planning," *ZJRB*, March 24, 1989, FBIS, No. 65, April 6, 1989, p. 41.) Peng Peiyun told a Chinese reporter in April that work on the family planning law had been "speeded up" and that the law was expected to be available before the end 1989. (Ai Xiao, "I Hope That Everyone Will Consciously Carry Out Family Planning—An Interview with Peng Peiyun, Minister of the State Family Planning Commission," *RMRB*, April, 14, 1989, FBIS, No. 74, April 19, 1989, p. 36.)

95. XINHUA-English, Beijing, April 13, 1989, FBIS, No. 71, April 14, 1989, pp. 17–18. Curiously, in an interview with a foreign demographer, Peng herself expressed skepticism about the effectiveness of such a law and doubted whether the time was ripe for it, but this may be simply another case of Peng's sending different signals to foreign than to domestic audiences. (H. Yuan Tien, "Second Thoughts on the Second China: A Talk with Peng Peiyun.")

96. XINHUA, Beijing, March 3, 1989, FBIS, No. 50, March 16, 1989, pp. 42–43.

97. For example, Yao Minhua, "Jiangsu shifenzhiyi renkou liudong gei jihua shengyu dailai xin mafan" ("One-tenth of Jiangsu's Population Is on the Move; They Cause New Problems for Family Planning Work"), *ZGRKB*, February 27, 1989, p. 1.

98. Guo Xiao, "The 'Population Explosion' Is Drawing Near," *JJRB*, January 10, 1989, FBIS, No. 22, February 3, 1989, p. 51; and "Curb the Excessively Fast Population Growth," *RMRB*, April 14, 1989, FBIS, No. 72, April 17, 1989, p. 51.

99. Zhang Xinyang, "Woguo yue baiwan haizi wu hukou" ("About One Million Children in China Are Without Household Registration"), *RMRB*, June 30, 1988, p. 3. Though they accounted for only five percent of the population, they were said to contribute ten percent of the country's births, all of them "unplanned." ("Yanhai kaifang qu jingji huodong renkou biandong yu guanli zhaokai yantaohui zongshu" ["A Summary of the Conference on Changes in and Control of the Economically Active Population in the Open Coastal Areas"], *ZGRKB*, May 12, 1989, p. 3.)

100. Chang Ke, "Da chengshi liudong renkou wenti yu duice" ("Problems of and Measures in Dealing With the Floating Population in Large Cities"), *Chengxiang jianshe (Urban and Rural Construction)*, Beijing, No. 5, 1988, p. 18.

101. "Population in Beijing Municipality Exceeds 10 Million," *RMRB*, January 11, 1989, FBIS, No. 14, January 24, 1989, p. 70.

102. XINHUA-English, Beijing, February 26, 1989, JPRS, No. 89–020, March 8, 1989, p. 34.

103. A recent source puts the figure at 70 million. (Zhou Dengke, "The Disaster of the Great Movement of Rural Manpower," *Jingjixue zhoubao* [*Economics Weekly*], Beijing, May 28, 1989, JPRS, No. 89–074, July 19, 1989, p. 28.)

104. XINHUA-English, Beijing, January 17, 1988, FBIS, No. 12, January 20, 1988, p. 48.

105. Zheng Defang, "Zhejiang sheng renmin zhengfu banfa xin guiding liudong renkou shengbao gong shang dengji xu chi jihua shengyu zheren shu" ("Zhejiang Province Promulgates New Regulations; Floating Population Must Have Family Planning Certificates When Applying for Industrial and Trade Licenses"), *ZGJHSYB*, July 24, 1987, p. 1.

106. Qingdao Municipality requires that women registered in the city who are among the "floating population" residing in other localities report every three months to a local hospital for a gynecological examination. If they are not pregnant, the hospital will issue them certificates to be turned in to their residence unit in Qingdao. If they fail to do so either their grain rations will be stopped or they must proceed at once to transfer their registration to the locality in which they actually reside, which would bring them under its surveillance for family planning purposes. Women moving into Qingdao as "floating population" must adopt "appropriate birth control measures" before they can receive a settlement permit. They will be penalized by the Qingdao authorities if they have "unplanned" pregnancies. (Shi Hailong, "Zhongshi dui liudong renkou jihua shengyu de guanli—Qingdao shi de shilian" ["Attach Importance to Control over Family Planning among the Floating Population—the Practice of Qingdao Municipality"], *ZGJHSYB*, December 18, 1987, p. 3.)

107. Liang Yi, "Hunan Provincial Party Committee . . ."

108. Quoted in Steven W. Mosher, "The Long Arm of 'One-Child' China," *WP*, April 10, 1988, p. B4. The collective penalties mentioned here are in addition to penalties meted out to the offending couple. The letter also points out that a couple in another work unit who had an unauthorized child were

fired from their jobs and put on probation for one year, during which they received only 5 *yuan* a month for living expenses.

109. In July 1989 a Beijing family planning meeting said that it was "basic policy" that Chinese students studying abroad should not be allowed to "enjoy special treatment" because family planning is an obligation for all Chinese citizens. ("Beijing Mayor Speaks on Family Planning Policy," *Beijing ribao* [*Beijing Daily*], Beijing, July 23, 1989, FBIS, No. 162, August 23, 1989, p. 79.)

110. Peng Peiyun, "Guanyu 1989–nian de gongzuo" ("On the Work in 1989"), *ZGRKB*, February 24, 1989, p. 1.

111. Haerbin radio, Heilongjiang Provincial Service, April 20, 1988, FBIS, No. 82, April 28, 1988, p. 59.

112. Meng Fangang and Chen Fenglan, "Heilongjiang sheng kaizhan cang wu jihua wai shengyu cun huodong qude chengxiao" ("Heilongjiang Province Carries Out Activities to Create Villages with No Unplanned Births and Obtains Results"), *ZGRKB*, October 7, 1988, p. 2.

113. It was recently reported that Henan Province once had a similar policy, under which families qualifying for a second child would lose the privilege if an unauthorized family had a second child, but "irritated farmers just ignored the policy," says the source, "and the local government had to withdraw it." ("Fourth and Last of Population Series: Family Planning Debate," XINHUA-English, Beijing, April 16, 1989, FBIS, No. 72, April 17, 1989, p. 53.)

114. Yin Su and Li Zheng, "Liaoning kaizhan cangjian 'jihua shengyu hege cun' quanmian guanche jihua shengyu xianxing zhengce" ("Liaoning Carries Out Activities for Establishing 'Qualified Family Planning Villages' and Implements the Current Family Planning Policy Fully"), *ZGRKB*, September 30, 1988, p. 1. The phrase "overall situation" refers to the the alleged urgency of reducing population growth for the sake of economic development. The phrase "group awareness" refers to the pressures among the people generated by collective punishments.

115. Fan Zhigang, "Yu shenqing ertai shengyu zhibiao xian dadao guiding jingji zhibiao" ("To Apply for a Quota for a Second Birth, One Must First Meet the Stipulated Economic Target"), *ZGRKB*, November 14, 1988, p. 1. The journal applauded the policy as one which would help to create favorable economic conditions for the second child and commended it for emulation elsewhere. (Commentator, "Zhege 'tiaojian' ti de hao" ["This 'Prerequisite' Is a Good One"], *ZGRKB*, November 14, 1988, p. 1.)

116. Xiang Kening and Dong Hanshu, "Tansuo gaige renkou yu jingji xietiao fazhan xin lu" ("Explore New Ways of Reforming the Coordinated Development of Population and the Economy"), *ZGRKB*, September 2, 1988, p. 3. Other counties in Sichuan have linked poverty assistance with attainment of food grain and family planning targets. (Lu Xiaobin, "Sichuan sheng ba tuo pin zhi fu yu jihuan shengyu youji jiehe" ["Sichuan Province Unites Getting Rid of Poverty and Becoming Rich with Family Planning"], *ZGRKB*, February 27, 1989, p. 1.)

117. "Fupin yu jihua shengyu jiehe wanquan yinggai" ("It Is Absolutely a Must to Combine Assisting the Poor with Family Planning"), *ZGRKB*, May 15, 1989, p. 1.

118. "Peng Peiyun Stresses Need to Enact Law on Family Planning."

119. Investigation Team, Department of Policy, Law, and Regulations, State Family Planning Commission, "Guoyi 'you jin you yin buru you ren' xianzai 'you jin you yin caineng sheng ren' " ("In the Past, 'Having Gold and Silver Is Not as Good as Having Children'; Now [It Is] 'First Have Gold and Silver Then Have Children' "), *ZGRKB*, May 12, 1989, p. 1; and SFPC, "Shandong sheng wei sheng zhengfu gaodu zhongshi jiji xingdong zhiding fupin he jihua shengyu xiang jiehe de juti cuoshi" ("Shandong Provincial Party Committee and Government Pay Serious Attention to Vigorous Action and Formulate Concrete Measures to Combine Poverty Assistance with Family Planning"), *ZGRKB*, May 15, 1989, p. 1. The policy was based on the argument that the poor tended to have too many children, dissipating the effects of poverty relief, hence the linking of relief with family planning was logical. Poverty assistance is administered on the basis of per capita income and per capita food grain.

120. Daye Steel Factory Family Planning Commission, "Women shi zenyang loushi mubiao guanli de" ("How Did We Achieve the Goal by Management?"), *ZGJHSYB*, February 22, 1988, p. 2.

121. "Yi gaige tong lan quanju jianjue wancheng jinnian gongzuo renwu" ("Have Overall Control over the Situation by [Carrying Out] Reform and Resolutely Accomplish the Tasks for This Year"), *ZGJHSYB*, January 29, 1988, pp. 1–2. The reform in family planning work in 1985 made it a little more lenient. (See "Third Interpretation" in chapter 3.) The reform of 1988 is in the opposite direction. Both reforms were part of national reform programs which included features that could make family planning work more difficult. Several Chinese sources warned against a possible weakening of family planning work as a result of other aspects of the current reform, which apparently included an effort to separate Party and government institutions. Zhao Youchun, "Nanjing shi shizhang he xianshang qianshu renqi mubiao zerenshu" ["The Mayor of Nanjing Municipality Signs Goal Responsibility Contracts with County Heads"], *ZGJHSYB*, December 25, 1987, p. 1; and Fuzhou radio, Fujian Provincial Service, February 27, 1988, FBIS, No. 45, March 8, 1988, p. 43.)

122. "Have Overall Control . . ."

123. Xu Cunde, "Lue lun jihua shengyu shuang gui hetong zeren zhi" ("A Brief Discussion of the Double Track Family Planning Contract and Responsibility System"), *ZGRKB*, March 27, 1989, p. 3.

124. Fuzhou radio, Fujian Provincial Service, February 27, 1988, FBIS, No. 45, March 8, 1988, p. 44; Shenyang radio, Liaoning Provincial Service, February 28, 1988, FBIS, No. 42, March 3, 1988, p. 38; Lanzhou radio, Gansu Provincial Service, March 4, 1988, FBIS, No. 43, March 4, 1988, p. 47; Jinan radio, Shandong Provincial Service, March 14, 1988, FBIS, No. 51, March 16, 1988, p. 37; Zhengzhou radio, Henan Provincial Service, March 16, 1988,

FBIS, No. 52, March 17, 1988, p. 46; Guangzhou radio, Guangdong Provincial Service, April 16, 1988, FBIS, No. 74, April 18, 1988, p. 56; Haerbin radio, Heilongjiang Provincial Service, April 20, 1988, FBIS, No. 82, April 28, 1988, p. 59; Nanning radio, Guangxi Regional Service, May 27, 1988, FBIS, No. 104, May 31, 1988, p. 44; Hohhot radio, Inner Mongolia Regional Service, September 23, 1988, FBIS, No. 188, September 24, 1988, p. 75; Xining radio, Qinghai Provincial Service, September 27, 1988, FBIS, No., 190, September 30, 1988, p. 52; Huang Huiliang and Wang Guojun, "Shaanxi sheng zhengfu yu ge de shi qianding zerenshu" ("Shaanxi Provincial Government Signs Responsibility Pacts with Prefectures and Municipalities"), ZGRKB, October 7, 1988, p. 1; "Sichuan di shi lingdao qianding jihua shengyu zerenshu" ("Prefectural and Municipal Leaders in Sichuan Sign Family Planning Responsibility Contracts"), RMRB, November 26, 1988, p. 3; and Shijiazhuang radio, Hebei Provincial Service, November 14, 1988, FBIS, No. 229, November 29, 1988, p. 57.

125. "Innovation in the Course of Exploration in Family Planning Work," GMRB, February 21, 1988, FBIS, No. 51, March 16, 1988, p. 25; and Daye Steel Factory Family Planning Commission, "How Did We Achieve . . ."

126. Huang Huiliang and Wang Guojun, "Shaanxi Provincial Government Signs . . ."

127. Shijiazhuang radio, Hebei Provincial Service, September 16, 1988, FBIS, No. 197, October 12, 1988, p. 64.

128. For some provinces, such as Hunan, Shaanxi, Guangxi, and Heilongjiang, the recent year 2000 target population totals are somewhat higher than those announced in the early 1980s. For Guangdong, the target of 70 million announced in 1980 and 1984 was reduced to 65 in 1989, probably because Hainan Island has now become a separate province. Sichuan's target of 120 million has remained unchanged from 1981 to 1989. It is not possible to determine from sources now available whether the increases in some provincial targets are wholly offset by reductions in others so that the sum equals the national target of 1.2 billion.

129. XINHUA-English, Beijing, March 25, 1988, FBIS, No. 58, March 25, 1988, p. 18.

130. XINHUA-English, Beijing, November 1, 1988, JPRS, No. 88–080, December 19, 1988, p. 48. In March 1989 a Chinese journal said the 1.2 billion mark would be surpassed by 1994 and by 2000 the population would probably exceed 1.3 billion. (Xiao Jiabao, "Woguo jiang yudao de si da weiji jiqi duice" ["Four Great Crises China Will Meet and Measures to Deal with Them"], LW, No. 10, March 6, 1989, p. 24.)

131. Changsha radio, Hunan Provincial Service, September 7, 1989, FBIS, No. 173, September 8, 1989, p. 46.

132. In September 1988 an article in a national population journal warned that setting population targets too low causes "rash actions on the part of the cadres," concealment of childbirths by some couples, and falsification of statistical reports. (Xu Gailing, "Zai tan woguo renkou yuce de wenti" ["An Enquiry into the Problems of China's Population Projections"], RKYJ, No. 5, September 29, 1988, pp. 34–36.)

133. In February 1989, Peng Peiyun noted that recent figures showed that "since 1986 the upswing in the birth rate has moderated." (Lu Xiaobin, "Peng Peiyun zhuren fenxi muqian woguo renkou xingshi . . ." ["Peng Peiyun Analyzes Current Population Situation in China . . ."], ZGRKB, February 24, 1989, p. 1.) In May 1988, the SFPC announced that "the general situation regarding China's population growth [in 1987] was better than expected." ("China Publishes Population Statistics for 1987," RMRB, May 14, 1988, FBIS, No. 96, May 18, 1988, p. 39.)

134. "Population Growth Slows Slightly," CD, March 9, 1989, JPRS, No. 89–030, April 6, 1989, p. 21.

135. "Li Peng zhichu . . . renzhen zhixing jihua shengyu zhengce kongzhi renkou zengzhang nenggou zuodao" ("Li Peng Points Out That . . . It Is Possible to Control Population Growth by Implementing Family Planning Policy Conscientiously"), ZGRKB, March 3, 1989, p. 1.

136. Fan Zhigang, "Quanguo jihua shengyu gongzuo qude xin jinzhan" ("Family Planning Work in China Made New Progress), ZGRKB, February 24, 1989, p. 1. The SFPC statistical chief reported that "In 1988 the work was tightened with good results. More than two million fewer births occurred in 1988 than in 1987." (Yao Minhua, "Renkou xingshi yanjun yao yi fen wei er kan" ["The Grim Situation in Population Must Be Viewed by Dividing One into Two"], ZGRKB, March 3, 1989, p. 1.)

137. "China Publishes Population Statistics for 1987," p. 40.

138. XINHUA, Beijing, October 21, 1988, JPRS, No. 88–080, December 19, 1988, p. 49. The figure for technical service stations apparently does not include those below the county level. In Sichuan Province alone, these numbered 2,640 and had a staff of 6,500. (Hou Wengfang, "Shinian gaige zhoing de Sichuan renkou yu jihua shengyu gongzuo" ["Population and Family Planning Work in Sichuan During the Ten Years of Reform"], ZGRKB, January 30, 1989, p. 1.)

139. Lu Xiaobin, "Woguo yi jian liangqianyuge xianji jihua shengyu fu-wuzhan" ("China Has Established More Than 2,000 County-Level Family Planning Service Stations"), ZGRKB, October 21, 1988, p. 1.

140. Xian radio, Shaanxi Provincial Service, December 8, 1988, FBIS, No. 237, December 9, 1988, p. 54.

141. Wan Qinghua, "Jieyu shoushu fei jizeng jisheng bumen bukan zhongfu" ("Charges for Birth Control Operations Increase Sharply"), ZGRKB, January 20, 1989, p. 1.

142. Hao Xinping, "Woguo weisheng keji renyuan wei zongzhi renkou zuo gongxian" (China's Health Scientists and Technicians Make Contributions to Population Control"), JKB, January 10, 1989, p. 1.

143. Peng Peiyun, "Qieshi jiaqiang jiceng jianshe ba jihua shengyu fuwu-zhan banhao" ("Earnestly Strengthen Construction at the Grassroots Level; Administer Well the Family Planning Service Stations"), ZGRKB, October 28, 1988, p. 1. Peng seemed to concede that they were not a uniformly popular institution. Some had been organized in 1979 and more in 1982 and 1983, when they were used in compulsory abortion, sterilization, and IUD inser-

tion drives. Alluding to the negative public reaction to the "service stations," Peng said obliquely that they "went through a tortuous process" and that there were inevitably "some different views on the service stations in the past."

144. Lu Xiaobin, "Peng Peiyun Analyzes Current . . ."

145. Guo Lingchun, "Woguo mianlin qian suo wei you yanjun renkou xingshi" ("China Faces an Unprecedentedly Grim Situation in Her Population"), *RMRB*, December 12, 1988, p. 3.

146. Marlowe Hood, "Birth Control Program 'Ineffective' in Provinces," *SoCMP*, November 2, 1988, FBIS, No. 212, November 2, 1988, p. 40. But claims about the ineffectiveness of family planning made to foreigners sometimes seem to be intended to soften the ruthless image of the Chinese family planning program.

147. XINHUA-English, Beijing, March 12, 1989, JPRS, No. 89–030, April 6, 1989, p. 22.

148. "Li Peng Points Out That . . ."

149. "1988–nian gediqu zong renkou, zizenglu, duohailu" ("Total Population, Natural Increase Rates, Planned Birth Rates, and Excessive Child Rates for All Areas"), *ZGRKB*, April 14, 1989, p. 1.

150. Nanning radio, Guangxi Regional Service, March 10, 1987, FBIS, No. 47, March 11, 1987, p. P1.

151. Haikou radio, Hainan Island Service, May 18, 1987, FBIS, No. 97, May 20, 1987, p. 2–3.

152. Chengdu radio, Sichuan Provincial Service, June 12, 1987, FBIS, No. 113, June 12, 1987, P. Q1.

153. "Resolutely Correct the Loosening . . ."

154. "Why Must [We] Be Firm . . ."

155. "Jianjue jiuzheng youxie difang de fangsong yu ziliu xianxiang yao jian zhu yu xingdong" ("The Key to Resolutely Correcting the Loosening of Family Planning Work and the Situation of Letting It Take Its Natural Course Must Be Seen in Action") (editorial), *ZGJHSYB*, September 4, 1987, p. 1.

156. Ai Xiao, "Worries About Population."

157. Guangzhou radio, Guangdong Provincial Service, August 26, 1987, FBIS, No. 169, September 1, 1987, p. 33; "Xue Ju on 'Grim Reality' of Family Planning," *ZJRB*, September 27, 1987, FBIS, No. 197, October 13, 1987, p. 32; Nanning radio, Guangxi Regional Service, October 6, 1987, FBIS, No. 196, October 9, 1987, p. 23; Hohhot radio, Nei Monggol Regional Service, October 28, 1987, FBIS, No. 209, October 29, 1987, p. 46; Zhengzhou radio, Henan Provincial Service, December 1, 1987, FBIS, No. 235, December 8, 1987, p. 33; Shijiazhuang radio, Hebei Provincial Service, January 15, 1988, FBIS, No. 22, February 3, 1988, p. 23; Haikou radio, Hainan Island Service, February 17, 1988, FBIS, No. 32, February 18, 1988, p. 21; Guiyang radio, Guizhou Provincial Service, September 24, 1988, FBIS, No. 188, September 28, 1988, p. 71; Zhengzhou radio, Henan Provincial Service, January 21, 1989, FBIS, No. 15, January 25, 1989, p. 53; and Lanzhou radio, Gansu Provincial Service, May 9, 1989, FBIS, No. 90, May 11, 1989, p. 53.

158. Jing Xianfeng, "Yangling qu zhuangshe cunji jihua shengyu fu zhuren" ("Yangling District Puts a Deputy Director in Charge of Family Planning Work at the Village Level"), *RMRB*, October 20, 1988, p. 3.

159. Jing Xianfeng, "Shaanxi Provincial Government Issues Warning to Leaders at All Levels on the Partial Loss of Population Control," *RMRB*, November 20, 1988, FBIS, No. 229, November 29, 1988, p. 64.

160. "Circular on Further Effort to Control Birth Rate," *RMRB*, December 13, 1988, FBIS, No. 249, December 28, 1988, p. 44.

161. Li Peng, "Report on the Work of the Government," Beijing radio, March 20, 1989, FBIS, No. 53, March 21, 1989, p. 26.

162. Xu Jiangshan and Zheng Zhangguo, "Local Broadcast News Service."

163. Kunming radio, Yunnan Provincial Service, August 24, 1989, FBIS, No. 164, August 25, 1989, p. 44; and Wuhan radio, Hubei Provincial Service, August 26, 1989, FBIS, No. 166, August 29, 1989, p. 53.

164. "Have Overall Control . . ."

165. Jiang Chunyun, Assistant Secretary, Shandong Provincial Committee of the CCP, "Zai jingji fazhan zhanlue zhong bixu jianchi 'renjun' yishi" ("In Carrying Out the Strategy for Economic Development, We Must Persist in Having 'Per Capita' Awareness"), *ZGRKB*, September 9, 1988, p. 1.

166. Wang Wei, "Zai jianshe you zhongguo tese de shehuizhuyi zhong de jihua shengyu gongzuo" ("Family Planning Work with Chinese Characteristics While Building Socialism"), *ZGJHSYB*, December 12, 1987, p. 2.

167. Bao Fu, "Massacre of the Innocents in China," *CSD*, Vol. 1, No. 1, January-February, 1987, p. 45.

168. Lo Ming, "The 'Leftist' Nature Has Not Been Changed."

169. Guangzhou radio, Guangdong Provincial Service, August 20, 1981, FBIS, No. 162, August 21, 1981, p. P1; Guangzhou radio, August 28, 1981, FBIS, No. 169, September 1, 1981, p. P5; Guangzhou radio, August 29, 1981, FBIS, No. 169, September 1, 1981, p. P6; and "Jianchi ba jihua shengyu he gongnongye shengchan zhe liangjian dashi yiqi zhuahao" ("Persist in Grasping Family Planning Work and Agricultural and Industrial Production Simultaneously and Well"), *NFRB*, August 29, 1981, p. 1.

170. XINHUA, Beijing, September 11, 1981, FBIS, No. 179, September 16, 1981, pp. P1–2.

171. Zhao Ziyang, "Report on the Work of the Government" (delivered on June 6, 1983), XINHUA-English, Beijing, June 23, 1983, FBIS, No. 122, June 23, 1983, p. K11.

172. Xie Zhenjiang, "There Is No Route of Retreat," *JJRB*, January 24, 1989, FBIS, No. 30, February 15, 1989, p. 37.

173. "Fourth and Last of Population Series," pp. 52–53. The dispatch argued that while coercion would "intensify the conflict between the farmers and the grassroots family planning workers," to ease family planning efforts would undo the work of the past 16 years. The main point of this article was that there was a major debate now going on about the future course of family planning. Some participants demanded a speed-up in family planning, the retraction of the option for rural only-daughter families of having a second

child, and the use of coercion to enforce the one-child limit. Others argued that the second-child option should be extended to all rural families, not just those with one daughter. The SFPC was said to occupy a middle position between these two views.

174. Kuang Ke, "Renkou chusheng lifa chuyi" ("Some Suggestions on Legislating Childbirths"), *Shehui Kexue* (*Social Sciences*), Shanghai, No. 8, August 15, 1989, pp. 35–37. The author was identified as from the Jiangsu Provincial Communist Party School.

175. The provincial dispatches indicate a strong emphasis on attaining targets and quotas, strengthening leadership and management, mobilizing activists, and punishing violators severely. For example, see Yu Changhong and Du Xin, "Local Broadcast News Service"; "Hebei Secretary Speaks on Family Planning Work," *HBRB*, August 17, 1989, FBIS, No. 172, September 7, 1989, p. 49; Wang Weicheng, "Ningxia renkou qiwu kongzhi jihua chengwei paoying" ("The Seventh Five-Year Population Plan for Ningxia Has Become a Bubble"), *JKB*, August 27, 1989, p. 1; Changsha radio, Hunan Provincial Service, September 7, 1989, FBIS, No. 173, September 8, 1989, p. 46; and Guangzhou radio, Guangdong Provincial Service, September 7, 1989, FBIS, No., 175, September 12, 1989, pp. 52–53.

176. See "Fifth Interpretation" in chapter 3.

177. Marlowe Hood, "Birth Control Program 'Ineffective' in Provinces," *SoCMP*, November 2, 1988, FBIS, No. 212, November 2, 1988, p. 40.

178. Jiang Zhenghua et al., "Zhongguo shengyulu ji renkou fazhan fenxi" ("Changes in China's Fertility Rate and an Analysis of Population Growth"), *RKYJ*, No. 5, September 29, 1988, pp. 2–8.

179. XINHUA-English, Beijing, May 7, 1988, FBIS, No. 90, May 10, 1988, p. 45.

180. See above, "Implementing the Guidelines."

181. "Pondering the Population Issue in China's Economic Operations," *GMRB*, July 18, 1987, JPRS, No. 87–045, September 9, 1987, p. 81.

182. "Why Must [We] Be Firm . . ."

183. Marlow Hood, "Birth Control Program 'Ineffective.' "

184. Li Xiaoming, "Zaohun zaoyu you yousuo taitou ying yinqi gaodu zhongshi" ("Early Marriages and Early Childbirths Are Again on the Upswing; Serious Attention Should Be Paid to Them"), *ZGRKB*, November 11, 1988, p. 1; Commentator, "Shi shi qiu shi gaohao tongji" ("Seek Truth from Facts and Do Well in Statistics"), *ZGRKB*, November 14, 1988, p. 1; and Peng Peiyun, "Quandang ying zhongshi renkou yu jihua shengyu jiaoyu" ("The Whole Party Should Attach Importance to Population and Family Planning Education"), *ZGRKB*, February 3, 1989, p. 1.

185. Su Suining, "There Are Many Causes of Strained Relations Between Cadres and Masses in Rural Areas," *Nongmin ribao* (*Farmers' Daily*), Beijing, September 26, 1988, FBIS, No. 195, October 7, 1988, pp. 12–14.

186. Wang Shoudao and Wu Yiren, "Nongcun jihua shengyu gongzuo zhong cun ganbu de liang nan chujing ji qi duice" ("The Dilemma of the Village Cadres in Rural Family Planning Work and Measures to Deal with

It"), *ZGRKB*, January 20, 1989, p. 3. The article says that clan power has recently been on the rise in rural areas and that cadres fear that the policies will change, leaving them to face the people against whom they enforced what proved to be temporary measures. The article notes, "This greatly affects their activism in doing the work well."

187. Ai Xiao, "Worries About Population."

188. Shijiazhuang radio, Hebei Provincial Service, January 15, 1988, FBIS, No. 22, February 3, 1988, p. 23. Taken literally, the statement contradicted past experience. Great pressure had frequently evoked resentment rather than enthusiasm.

189. Peng Peiyun, "Zuohao jihua shengyu gongzuo tuijin funu jiefang shiye" ("Do Family Planning Work Well to Push Forward the Liberation of Women"), *ZGRKB*, September 12, 1988, p. 1.

190. Beijing Television Service, April 13, 1989, FBIS, No. 71, April 14, 1989, p. 15.

191. Commentator, "1,100,000,000," *CD*, FBIS, No. 71, April 14, 1989, p. 17. The writer said that "apart from moral persuasion, administrative measures are also necessary," adding delicately, "though they cannot always leave observers with good impressions." He apparently was confident that some foreign "observers" would continue to support the Chinese program despite bad "impressions."

192. Gao Anhing, "Family Planning Achievements, Problems Noted," *CD*, October 5, 1989, FBIS, No. 193, October 6, 1989, p. 20.

193. In August 1989, possibly as a result of the negotiations with the UNFPA, the State Family Planning Commission urged that units that had been successful in family planning work use "prepregnancy management . . . to reduce the rate of induced abortion as much as possible." But a few days later Shaanxi complained that 34.17 percent of the babies born in the province in the second half of 1988 were "outside the plan" because "we failed to adopt remedial measures." It called for remedial measures against 20,000 women with unauthorized pregnancies in the last 4 1/2 months of 1989 in order to fulfill the province's 1989 population plan. (Yu Changhong and Du Xin, "The State Family Planning Commission Gives Guidance to the Grassroots According to Their Local Conditions, With the Focus on the Rural Areas," *RMRB*, August 10, 1989, FBIS, No. 162, August 23, 1989, p, 56; and Yan Yongde, "Birth Rate Rises Rapidly in Shaanxi Province; 400,000 Babies Were Born in the First Half of This Year," *SXRB*, Xian, August 14, 1989, FBIS, No. 171, September 6, 1989, p. 51.)

194. In April 1983 an article in the Chinese journal *Beijing Review* cited UNFPA assistance to China as evidence that the Chinese family planning program had "won international recognition as contributing to the world's effort to control population growth." Qian Xinzhong interpreted the UN population award presented to him as further evidence of international approval for the program and "an encouragement to China's population control drive." Later he added that it was "evidence of the UN support for China's population policy" and a "symbol of UN support and encourage-

ment for China's family planning program" and that it "put the imprimatur of the world body on China's family planning efforts." Remarks by UNFPA Executive Director Rafael Salas at the 1984 world population conference praising China's accomplishments in reducing population growth rates were interpreted by a Chinese spokesman in 1987 as "beyond doubt . . . a full affirmation and appreciation of China's planned parenthood work." In 1987 Wang Wei told a press conference that "the achievements of our family planning program have received wide attention and appreciation from the international community." In November 1988 Peng Peiyun said that the program was "known as one of the most effective in the world." In February 1989, speaking to the United Nations Population Commission, the Chinese representative, Chang Chongxuan said that over the previous 10 years China had "enjoyed financial, technical, and moral support from the United Nations, other international organizations, and many relevant countries, to whom the Chinese government and people are most grateful." ("Female Infanticide Punishable by Law," *BR*, Vol. 26, No. 17, April 25, 1983, p. 9; An Zhiguo, "Family Planning," *BR*, Vol. 26, No. 35, August 29, 1983, p. 4; Beijing radio, English to North America, October 1, 1983, FBIS, No. 192, October 3, 1983, p. K15; "Qian Xinzhong Receives UN Award," *BR*, Vol. 26, No. 41, October 10, 1983, p. 9; Pranay Gupte, *The Crowded Earth*, p. 156; Wang Guoqian, "The World Population Problem and China's Family Planning," *LWOE*, July 6, 1987, FBIS, No. 135, July 15, 1987, p. K9; Wang Wei, "China Marks the Day of the Five Billion," *China Population Research*, Beijing, Vol. 2, No. 1, October 1987, p. 5; XINHUA-English, Beijing, November 1, 1988, FBIS, No. 80, December 19, 1988, p. 48; and Chang Chongxuan, "Statement . . . at the 25th Session of the United Nations Population Commission," February 2, 1989, p. 5.)

UNFPA spokesmen have from time to time made statements that encouraged the Chinese leaders to believe that the UNFPA approved of their program as a whole. In April 1985 Mr. Salas was quoted as saying to a Chinese reporter in New York that "China has done an outstanding job on her population problem" and he reportedly told Premier Zhao Ziyang in Beijing that "China's family planning policy is established on the basis of voluntary acceptance by the people and is therefore accepted by the people" and that China should be proud of its achievements in family planning. In July 1987 the UNFPA representative in China said that the Chinese government had "shown its full commitment to a family planning program that has been internationally acknowledged as one of the most successful efforts in the world today." (Zhou Cipo, "Wei wending shijie renkou er nuli" ["Work Hard to Stabilize the World's Population"], *LW*, No. 14, April 1985, p. 33; "Woguo jihua shengyu gongzuo yinian bi yinian hao" ["China's Family Planning Work is Getting Better Every Year"], *RMRB*, April 26, 1985, p. 1; and XINHUA-English, Beijing, July 11, 1987, FBIS, No. 133, July 13, 1987, p. A1.)

195. Linda Feldmann, "China, UN Alter Population Policy," *CSM*, January 3, 1989; and Ann Scott Tyson, "China, UN Join Forces to Reshape Population

Policy," *CSM*, January 27, 1989, pp. 1–2. The titles of both articles are misleading, as is apparent from their texts. What is proposed is not a change in China's family planning policy but a redirection of some of the UNFPA expenditures in China.

196. AID Office of Press Relations news release of June 7, 1989. The release affirmed the Bush Administration's support for voluntary family planning and quoted AID Deputy Administrator Jay F. Morris as saying that "the door is left open for a new Chinese program which is rooted in voluntarism."

197. Letter to Rep. Mickey Edwards, October 6, 1989.

198. "Transcript of President Bush's News Conference," *WP*, November 8, 1989, p. A18.

199. Yu Changhong and Du Xin, "Local Broadcast News Service."

Appendix A: Family Planning Infanticide

1. Michael Vink, "Abortion and Birth Control in Canton, China," *WSJ*, November 30, 1981, p. 26. Vink attributed his story to "a Chinese source."

2. Rob Stepney, "How China's Doctors Kill Babies," *World Medicine*, London, Vol. 18, No. 19, July 9, 1983, p. 23. The information in this case was attributed to a fifth-year medical student in the obstetrics department of the Guangzhou hospital.

3. Michael Weisskopf, "Abortion Tears at Fabric of Chinese Society," *WP*, January 7, 1985, p. A20. The informant in this case was a Hohhot surgeon who asked that his name not be used for fear of reprisals. He claimed to have destroyed infants himself under the regulation.

4. Bao Fu, "Massacre of the Innocents in China," *China Spring*, Vol. 1, No. 1, January-February 1987, p. 45. This source quoted directly an obstetrician friend who said he had carried out "hundreds of these procedures." The source also claimed that family planning cadres sometimes came to the homes of couples who had had unauthorized births outside of the regular medical facilities to kill the babies "on the spot." He said he had witnessed one such attempt which ended, instead, in the death of the cadres and the baby's father.

5. Blake Kerr, "Witness to China's Shame," *WP*, February 26, 1989, pp. C1 and C4. Kerr seems to have been under the mistaken impression that such treatment was reserved for Tibetans.

6. Ge Hua, "Zhongyang yitai zhengce xia chusi huoyin" ("Live Babies Are Put to Death Under the Communist Chinese One-Child Policy"), *Huayu youbao* (*Washington China Post*), Washington, January 27, 1989, p. 11. The author did not indicate the source of his information.

7. Female infanticide, a not uncommon practice in China before 1949, had apparently been in abeyance until the adoption of the one-child per family limit in 1979. Because daughters join the families of their husbands and are no longer considered part of their parental families, there is no assurance that they will be able to help their parents when the latter become aged. This concern combined with traditional son-preference to make many

rural families feel that if they must stop at one child, the child had better be a boy. The upsurge of female infanticide led to warnings in the Chinese media that if the practice were not curbed the sex imbalance would become so severe that in the future some young men might be unable to find wives. There are some indications that the problem has recently gotten more severe. (Terence H. Hull, "Recent Trends in Sex Ratios in China," International Population Dynamics Program, Research Note No. 96 [Canberra: The Australian National University, November 17, 1988].)

8. See chapter 2.

APPENDIX B: POLICY TRENDS—LOOSENING OR TIGHTENING?

1. Susan Greenhalgh, "The Evolution of the One-Child Policy in Shaanxi, 1979–1988," Working Papers, No. 5 (New York: The Population Council, 1989). This was originally a paper presented at the annual meeting of the Association for Asian Studies and of the Population Association of America in March 1989, but it was subsequently revised as of August 1, 1989. The section of the article that takes issue with this volume was not included in the paper as presented in March. In that month I submitted an early and less complete version of the text of this book to the American Enterprise Institute and suggested that comments be invited from Greenhalgh, since this book criticizes her thesis that the Chinese program has become steadily less coercive, a view she had already advanced in a short piece for the *Wall Street Journal* in July 1986 and in an article in *Population and Development Review* in September 1986. (See note 5 below.) The August 1989 version of Greenhalgh's article begins with a 10–page introduction consisting largely of an attack on the methods and conclusions of this book.

2. Zeng Yi, "Is the Chinese Family Planning Program Tightening Up?" *PDR*, Vol. 15, No. 2, June 1989, pp. 333–337. The Hardee-Cleaveland and Banister article is "Fertility Policy and Implementation in China, 1986–88," *PDR*, Vol. 14, No. 2, June 1988, pp. 245–286.

3. "The Evolution of the One-Child Policy..," p. 45.

4. Ibid., p. 6.

5. Susan Greenhalgh, "Chinese Abortions: Point's Been Made So Now Ease Off," *WSJ*, July 3, 1986; and Greenhalgh, "Shifts in China's Population Policy, 1984–86: Views from the Central, Provincial, and Local Levels," *PDR*, Vol. 12, No. 3, September 1986, pp. 491–515.

6. This position was first advanced in John Aird, "Coercion in Family Planning: Causes, Methods, and Consequences," May 1986.

7. "The Evolution of the One-Child Policy . . .," pp. 11–12.

8. The Chinese authorities sometimes hesitate to give wide publicity to moderate measures allowed experimentally in selected localities because they have learned from experience that people in other places seize eagerly on such changes and carry them far beyond their original intent. Even without publicity, policy relaxations are so popular that the word spreads rapidly as soon as they are implemented. However, the central authorities gave a great

deal of publicity to the additional categories of couples allowed a second child under Party Document No. 7, a policy moderation that was not limited to particular areas.

9. The example she cites in a footnote does not quote from either newspaper but instead contrasts the reports of a State Planning Commission survey contained in a Beijing radio broadcast and a Xinhua English language dispatch, both, incidentally, sourced to a U.S. government translation service. ("The Evolution of the One-Child Policy..," p. 2 and note 12.) On examination, it turns out that in this instance both sources convey essentially the same message: population growth is threatening to exceed the target and therefore it is necessary to strengthen control. Neither says the policy is being relaxed; in fact, while the broadcast warns of what will happen "if no effective measures are taken," it is the Xinhua dispatch that mentions the call to strengthen control. The Xinhua dispatch is shorter—seven sentences compared with fourteen in the Beijing broadcast. The Xinhua dispatch lists four causes for the "rapid increase": the baby boom, failure to implement the one-child policy, failure to control births among the floating population, and an increase in rural early marriages. The broadcast adds two others—allowing people in some localities to have two or more children and a lax policy toward minorities—and omits one—the baby boom. The broadcast begins by asserting that China faces a "grim situation" in population growth and that "if no effective measures are taken it will be difficult to realize the population control target set for this century." The Xinhua dispatch begins: "The State Planning Commission here today urged Party organizations and governments at all levels to strengthen their efforts in family planning work." A later sentence says that at the present rate, "about 200 million people will be born before the end of the year 2000, shattering the country's target." Aside from inaccurate documentation, Greenhalgh's argument is curious in that by implication it contradicts her thesis. She implies that in telling foreigners the program is relaxing while telling domestic audiences it is tightening, the Chinese authorities are withholding information from the foreigners. But this implies that the "tightening" message is true and the "relaxing" message is false. Greenhalgh seems momentarily to have forgotten which side she was on!

10. "The Evolution of the One-Child Policy..," p. 7.

11. For the Population Council's fiscal connection with the UNFPA, see chapter 1. In 1985, the Jiaotong Population Research Institute received $400,000 from the UNFPA for population research. ("Xian jiaoda renkou yanjiusuo yanzhi de renkou yuce moxing ji ruanjian yi xiang quanguo tuiguang" ["The Population Model and Software Designed by Xian's Jiaotong University Population Research Institute Have Been Distributed Throughout the Country"], *JKBJHSYB*, July 12, 1985, p. 1.)

12. Official family planning statistics for the 1980s (not cited by Greenhalgh) indicate that Shaanxi ranked 13th among the provinces in family planning compliance in 1981, 12th in 1982, and 13th in 1983, but had dropped to 19th in 1984 and 21st in 1985. It was still in 21st place in 1988. The ranks in

1981–85 are based on the provincial "birth control rates" given in the tables of family planning statistics by province in *Zhongguo jihua shengyu nianjian, 1986 (Yearbook of Family Planning in China, 1986)* (Beijing: Renmin weisheng chubanshe, December 1987), pp. 384, 394, 408, 417, and 428. The 1988 ranking is based on the provincial "planned birth rates" obtained from the 1988 fertility survey and released by the State Family Planning Commission. The rate for Shaanxi was 46.36 percent and that for the whole country, though not given in the source, can be estimated at about 61 percent. The range among provincial level units was from a low of 14.33 percent for Xinjiang to a high of 97.77 percent for Shanghai. ("1988–nian gediqu zong renkou, zizenglu, jishenglu, duohailu" ["Population Totals, Natural Population Increase Rates, Planned Birth Rates, and Excessive Birth Rates for All Areas"], *ZGRKB*, April 14, 1989, p. 1.)

13. This was revealed in April 1989 by Ma Bin, an advisor in the Research Center for Economic, Technical, and Social Development of the State Council, who has been a frequent commentator on family planning matters at least since 1987. He was quoted in Qu Wei, "China's Population Situation and Measures to Cope with the Problem," *QY*, April 7, 1989, JPRS, No. 89–072, July 10, 1989, p. 35.

14. "The Evolution of the One-Child Policy..," p. 45. Greenhalgh argues that "campaigns are not necessarily equatable with coercion." They are not, but they are certainly not equatable with "steady relaxation" either. Clearly something else is happening, and how can she know whether or not it represents another cycle of coercion if she does not analyze the evidence?

15. In 1983 the national figure for tubal ligations among women of childbearing age rose by 53 percent over that for 1982, but in Shaanxi the figure rose by 127 percent. The figures are given in *Yearbook of Family Planning in China, 1986.*

16. Xian radio, Shaanxi Provincial Service, February 25, 1982, FBIS, No. 39, February 26, 1982, p. T5.

17. "The Evolution of the One-Child Policy..," p. 27.

18. With only two time segments, the most she could find was a steady trend toward tightening, a steady trend toward loosening, a cycle of loosening-tightening, or a cycle of tightening-loosening. The latter is what she finds.

19. "The Evolution of the One-Child Policy..," p. 44.

20. The line would have been bent into an S-curve if Greenhalgh had also taken cognizance of the relaxation of 1984–85 and the tightening of 1986. A September 1989 source says that by then 17 provinces (presumably including Shaanxi) had passed new family planning regulations and that they had helped in "tightening family planning work," which was obviously their purpose. (Commentator, "Zouxiang fazhi de lianghao kaiduan" ["Heading Toward a Good Beginning for a Legal System"], *ZGRKB*, September 4, 1989, p. 1.)

21. In her note 77, p. 65.

22. Xian radio, November 11, 1977, FBIS, No. 226, November 23, 1977, p.

M4; and Xian radio, November 23, 1977, FBIS, No. 228, November 28, 1977, p. M4.

23. XINHUA-English, Beijing, August 2, 1978, FBIS, No. 151, August 4, 1978, p. M5.

24. Xian radio, June 25, 1978, FBIS, No. 124, June 27, 1978, pp. K1–2.

25. Xian radio, September 11, 1979, JPRS, No. 74,396, October 17, 1979, p. 142; and Xian radio, September 23, 1979, FBIS, No. 187, September 25, 1979, p. T4.

26. Xian radio, May 3, 1981, FBIS, No. 85, May 4, 1981, pp. T2–5. By 1981 Shaanxi was apparently behind other provinces in drafting regulations. The source says: "Over 20 provinces, municipalities, and autonomous regions have formulated planned parenthood regulations or rules. At present our province urgently needs a unified set of regulations applicable to the whole province."

27. Xian radio, March 1, 1981, FBIS, No. 51, March 17, 1981, p. T2.

28. XINHUA, Beijing, May 31, 1981, FBIS, No. 105, June 2, 1981, P. K4.

29. The expression "gang of four" is used in China to designate the group of leaders headed by Jiang Qing, Mao's third wife, who ran the country with disastrous effects during the middle 1970s when Mao was largely incapacitated.

30. Xian radio, May 1, 1981, FBIS, No. 85, May 4, 1981, p. T2.

31. Xian radio, February 25, 1982, FBIS, No. 39, February 26, 1982, p. T4.

32. "Conscientiously Do a Good Job in Firmly Grasping Planned Parenthood," SXRB, Xian, September 25, 1981, FBIS, No. 195, October 8, 1981, p. T1.

33. Xian radio, February 22, 1982, JPRS, No. 80,293, March 10, 1982, p. 68.

34. Xian radio, February 25, 1982, FBIS, No. 39, February 26, 1982, pp. T4–5.

35. "Shaanxi sheng jihua shengyu zanxing tiaoli 'buchong guiding' " ("Supplement to the 'Provisional Regulations' on Family Planning of Shaanxi Province"), SXRB, Xian, November 1, 1982, p. 2. Greenhalgh says that the supplemental regulations of 1982 do not distinguish between urban and rural areas, but this is incorrect. The awards they specify for one-child families and the penalties for unauthorized births for state cadres, employees, workers, and urban residents are different from those for peasants.

36. "Sheng jihua shengyu xuanchuan gongzuo huiyi bushu xuanchuan yue huodong; zhuyao lingdao yao qingzi zhua jihua shengyu" ("The Provincial Family Planning Propaganda Work Meeting Arranges for Propaganda Month Activities; the Principal Leaders Must Personally Take Charge of Family Planning"), SXRB, Xian, November 20, 1982, p. 1.

37. Xian radio, December 28, 1982, FBIS, No. 4, January 6, 1983, pp. T1–2.

38. Xian radio, January 16, 1983, JPRS, No. 83,105, March 21, 1983, p. 113.

39. Song Qixia and Zhang Zhiqiang, "Shaanxi nongcun pai she siqianduo

jieyu shoushudian" ("More Than Four Thousand Birth Control Surgery Field Stations Established in Rural Areas of Shaanxi Province"), *JKB*, January 27, 1983, p. 1.

40. See note 15.

41. Xian radio, December 24, 1983, JPRS, No. 84–018, February 27, 1984, pp. 66–67; and Xian radio, December 28, 1983, FBIS, No. 252, December 28, 1983, pp. T2–3.

42. Xian radio, January 17, 1984, FBIS, No. 16, January 24, 1984, pp. T2–3.

43. Xian radio, April 4, 1984, JPRS, No. 84–035, May 10, 1984, p. 93.

44. Nan Gu, "Shaanxi Implements Responsibility System in Population Control," *SXRB*, Xian, October 22, 1984, JPRS, No. 85–015, February 15, 1985, p. 107.

45. "Shaanxi sheng jihua shengyu weiyuanhui jiaqiang xinxi guanli" ("Shaanxi Provincial Family Planning Commission Strengthens Information Management"), *JKBJHSYB*, March 1, 1985, p. 1.

46. The provincial newspaper claimed progress in family planning work in comparison with the 1950s (!) but admitted that early marriages and unauthorized births were continuing. (Xian radio, January 5, 1986, FBIS, No. 21, January 31, 1986, pp. T2–3.) The national family planning journal took a much more critical view of Shaanxi's performance, demanding that the province "resolutely and relentlessly" implement family planning policies. (Zhang Zhiqiang, "Guojia tongjiju zai Shaanxi jingxing shengyu qingkuang diaocha" ["The State Statistical Bureau Conducts Fertility Survey in Shaanxi"], *JKBJHSYB*, February 21, 1986, p. 1.)

47. Liang Naizhong, "Shaanxi shengwei shengzhengfu jueding wei jihua shengyu ban shijian shishi" ("Shaanxi Provincial Party Committee and Provincial Government Decide to Carry Out Ten Specific Items of Work for Family Planning"), *JKBJHSYB*, May 2, 1986, p. 1.

48. Xian radio, July 30, 1986, FBIS, No. 147, July 31, 1986, p. T1.

49. Liang Naizhong, "Shaanxi sheng ba zhongyang jingshen he gexiang cuoshi luodao shichu" ("Shaanxi Earnestly Carried Out the Guidelines of the Party Central Committee and Various Measures"), *JKBJHSYB*, August 29, 1986, p. 1.

50. Xian radio, October 13, 1986, FBIS, No. 198, October 14, 1986, p. T3.

51. Yan Yongde, "Stabilize the Birth Policies; Control Population Growth," *SXRB*, Xian, February 25, 1987, FBIS, No. 47, March 11, 1987, p. T4.

52. Xian radio, July 10, 1987, FBIS, No. 135, July 15, 1987, pp. T1–2; and Xian radio, July 31, 1987, JPRS, No. 87–045, September 9, 1987, p. 83.

53. Yang Quanfu and Zhao Xiuzhen, "Shaanxi sheng Lindong xian wei xian zhengfu zai chuli ganbu chaosheng zhong xian shi xian qi su jue su qing" ("The Party Committee and Government of Lindong County, Shaanxi Province, Set Deadlines and Make Quick Decisions and Quick Settlements When Handling Cases of Excessive Births Among Cadres"), *ZGJHSYB*, September 18, 1987, p. 1.

54. Xian radio, March 13, 1988, FBIS, No. 49, March 14, 1988, p. 56.

55. Xian radio, May 9, 1988, FBIS, No. 95, May 17, 1988, p. 72.

56. Yan Zhaoxiang and Wang Guojun, "Shaanxi sheng geji renda quanmian jiancha jisheng gongzuo" ("People's Congresses at All Levels in Shaanxi Province Conduct All-Around Inspections of Family Planning Work"), ZGRKB, September 12, 1988, p. 1.

57. Huang Huiliang and Wang Guojun, "Shaanxi sheng zhengfu yu ge di shi qianding zerenshu" ("Shaanxi Provincial Government Signs Responsibility Pacts with Prefectures and Municipalities"), ZGRKB, October 7, 1988, p. 1.

58. Jing Xianfeng, "Shaanxi zhiding liudong renkou shengyu guanli banfa" ("Shaanxi Formulates Regulations to Control Births Among the Floating Population"), RMRB, October 12, 1988, p. 3.

59. Xian radio, December 8, 1988, FBIS, No. 237, December 9, 1988, p. 54. Local jurisdictions in Shaanxi devised their own measures for cracking down, some of which were featured in the national media. In October the national family planning journal reported that a district of Xianyang Municipality, the city that Greenhalgh investigated, had installed a deputy director for family planning and had put him also in charge of social relief, allocation of lots for housing, "land readjustment," and marriage and household registration. This "forcefully pushed forward family planning work at the grassroots level." (Jing Xianfeng, "Yangling qu zhuangshe cunji jihua shengyu fu zhuren" ["Yangling District Installs a Deputy Director in Charge of Family Planning at the Village Level"], RMRB, October 20, 1988, p. 3.) In November a district of Nanzheng County set a fixed increase in family income as an "economic prerequisite" for only-daughter families seeking permission to have a second child. This limitation discouraged applications among those who would otherwise have qualified and was therefore said to have "great vitality in practice." (Fan Zhigang, "Yu shenqing ertai shengyu zhibiao xian dadao guiding jingji zhibiao" ["To Apply for the Quota for a Second Birth, One Must First Fulfill the Stipulated Economic Target"], ZGRKB, November 14, 1988, p. 1.)

60. Jing Xianfeng, "Shaanxi Provincial Government Issues Warning to Leaders at All Levels on the Partial Loss of Population Control," RMRB, November 20, 1988, FBIS, No. 229, November 29, 1988, p. 64.

61. Xian radio, January 25, 1989, FBIS, No. 18, January 30, 1989, p. 73.

62. Huang Huiliang, "Renkou xingshi yanjun ren wei yingqi zhongshi" ("The Population Situation Is Grim; Serious Attention Has Not Been Paid"), ZGRKB, February 13, 1989, p. 1.

63. Fan You, "Meinian you 900–wan jihua wai yinger chusheng" ("Every Year Nine Million Babies Are Born Outside the Plan"), GMRB, March 16, 1989, p. 1. The "excessive childbirth rate" is the percentage of all births during the year that exceed the two-child limit.

64. Zuo Jiliang and Zhang Naiwei, "Shaanxi sheng gongshang ju zhiding gaijin cuoshi jiaqiang xiezuo" ("Shaanxi Provincial Bureau of Industry and Commerce Formulates and Improves Measures to Strengthen Coordination"), ZGRKB, August 18, 1989, p. 2.

181

65. Yan Yongde, "Birth Rate Rapidly Rises in Shaanxi Province; 400,000 Babies Were Born in the First Half of This Year," SXRB, Xian, August 14, 1989, FBIS, No. 171, September 6, 1989, pp. 50–51..

66. Zeng Yi, "Is the Chinese Family Planning Program..," p. 334.

67. These changes are discussed in some detail in chapter 4.

68. Yin Su and Li Zheng, "Liaoning kaizhan cangjian 'jihua shengyu hege cun' quanmian guanche jihua shengyu xianxing zhengce" ("Liaoning Carries Out Activities for Establishing 'Qualified Family Planning Villages' and Implements the Current Family Planning Policy Fully"), ZGRKB, September 30, 1988, p. 1.

69. See chapter 4.

70. For example, in February 1989 Peng Peiyun, Minister-in-Charge of the SFPC, said "one of the important reasons why some areas do not perform their family planning work well is that the Party members have failed to take the lead." (Peng Peiyun, "Quandang ying zhongshi renkou yu jihua shengyu jiaoyu" ["The Whole Party Should Attach Importance to Population and Family Planning Education"], ZGRKB, February 3, 1989, p. 1.) In April, the People's Daily editorialized that "the key to making a success of family planning lies in the principal leading comrades of the Party committees and government at all levels grasping the work personally, as well as in instituting a responsibility system and regarding family planning work as an important criterion in judging 'achievements.' " ("Curb the Excessively Fast Population Growth," RMRB, April 14, 1989, FBIS, No. 72, April 17, 1989, p. 50.) The same perception is found at the provincial level. In April the governor and Party secretary of Henan Province conducted "self-criticism" because the province had failed to attain its 1988 population target. "They said that the main reason . . . was because the leaders did not pay enough attention to the work and take effective measures." (Beijing radio, Domestic Service, April 12, 1989, FBIS, No. 71, April 14, 1989, p. 45.) In September the governor of Hunan Province said that "the most outstanding problem currently in family planning in Hunan is weak grassroots work." (Changsha radio, Hunan Provincial Service, September 7, 1989, FBIS, No. 173, September 8, 1989, p. 46.)

71. For example, at a four-day provincial family planning conference in Hebei Province in August 1989, with Peng Peiyun in attendance, Xing Chongzhi, secretary of the Hebei Party committee, told the cadres, "You must guard against making great decisions and speaking loudly at a meeting and doing nothing after the meeting as before, because this is a very bad work style. This year you must adopt effective measures and strive to fulfill the population control target[s] of your own prefectures and cities." ("Hebei Secretary Speaks on Family Planning Work," HBRB, August 17, 1989, FBIS, No. 172, September 7, 1989, p. 49.)

Glossary

Above-quota births. Births not included in the local population plans and hence not approved by the local authorities.

Age composition. The distribution of the population by age.

Birth control. An inclusive expression for IUD insertions, both kinds of sterilization (vasectomies and tubal ligations), and abortions as well as nonsurgical methods.

Birth rate. The total number of births during the year divided by the average population for the year; usually expressed as a rate per thousand population.

Bourgeois class. A Marxist expression for people whose families were neither landless peasants nor ordinary workers.

Broad masses. An expression used in generalizations about what the Chinese people think, want, say, or do to imply that there are exceptions but that they are few; sometimes used where the exceptions are in the majority.

Cadres. Persons occupying positions as officials or technical specialists in government, Party, and other organizations in the People's Republic of China.

Chen Muhua. Vice-premier and former head of the Birth Planning Office under the State Council, predecessor of the State Family Planning Commission, who was appointed as the first Minister-in-Charge of the SFPC when it was established in 1981.

Class struggle. The idea of an epic "struggle" between the "bourgeois" class and the "proletariat," adapted from Marxism, used to explain any popular opposition to the objectives and programs of the Chinese Communist Party.

Commandism. The use of administrative commands rather than propaganda, reason, or other methods of persuasion to induce people to comply with government directives.

Communist Youth League. A Party organization for youth designed to provide political training and indoctrination to prepare them for Party membership when they reach adulthood. Youth League members are sometimes mobilized to help carry out Party policies and programs.

Contradiction. A Chinese Communist expression usually referring to conflicts between social programs or political objectives; also applied to conflicts between official policies and the popular will.

Death rate. The total number of deaths during the year divided by the average population for the year; usually expressed as a rate per thousand population.

Deng Xiaoping. Long-time Party leader and associate of Mao Zedong, discredited during the Cultural Revolution but rehabilitated in 1973, who by 1978 had emerged as supreme leader within the top echelon of the Party and directed the economic and political reforms of the 1980s from his position as the chairman of the Central Military Commission.

Excessive births. Births of the third or higher parity order.

Five-Year Plan(s). National economic and social plans which are drafted for five-year periods by the Party leaders and the planning agencies of the central government and adopted by the National People's Congress.

Floating population. Rural migrants to urban areas who are licensed to carry on trade and other nonagricultural activities but arrange for their own food and lodging and are not entirely under the control of the urban authorities.

Great Leap Forward. Domestic policy devised by Mao Zedong in 1958 on the theory that worker and peasant masses in China, inspired by political enthusiasm, could manifest unlimited creativity and productivity, overcome all economic restraints, and transform China into a modern, prosperous, thriving society within a few years.

Great Proletarian Cultural Revolution. Political mass movement initiated by Mao in 1966 to punish former colleagues within the Chinese Communist Party who had attempted to limit his powers after the fiasco of the Great Leap Forward; the movement resulted in domestic chaos and had to be terminated, for all practical purposes, in 1969.

Han Chinese. The majority ethnic group within the Chinese population (as opposed to the "minority nationalities"); the Hans account for 96 percent of the total population of China.

Hua Guofeng. Successor to Mao Zedong as supreme leader after the overthrow of the so-called gang of four, the group that ruled China during Mao's waning years; Hua sought to establish himself as a leader on the Maoist pattern until he was outmaneuvered and shoved aside by Deng Xiaoping in 1980.

Hundred flowers. Part of a classical Chinese slogan ("Let a hundred flowers bloom and a hundred schools of thought contend"); names a policy initiated in 1956 to permit expression of dissenting views on the assumption that letting Chinese intellectuals and scholars "bloom and contend" would lead to improved Party policies. But in 1957 the resulting criticism surprised the Party leaders and they severely punished those who had dared to speak out.

Large gap. A Chinese metaphor for the large proportion of births that are unauthorized, or "outside the plan," that is, the gap between authorized and actual births.

Li Peng. Associate of Deng Xiaoping who became premier in 1988; had a major role in the supression of the student democracy movement in June 1989.

Mao Zedong. Chairman of the Chinese Communist Party, leader of the Chinese revolution and chief mentor, theoretician, and decision-maker from the founding of the People's Republic in 1949 until 1959, following the failure of the Great Leap Forward; regained control of the Party by 1965 and initiated the Great Proletarian Cultural Revolution the following year; died in September 1976.

Masses. Ordinary citizens in China who have no technical or administrative position in the government, in enterprises or organizations, or in the Chinese Communist Party; also excludes rank and file Party members.

National People's Congress. The national government body consisting of representatives from lower level political units. This body, like the corresponding bodies at provincial and lower levels, sometimes debates but always approves policies proposed by the Party leadership and exercises no real power.

Natural increase rate. Births minus deaths divided by the average population for the year; usually expressed as a rate per thousand population.

Party Central Committee. The ruling group within the Chinese Communist Party.

Peng Peiyun. Fourth Minister-in-Charge of the State Family Planning Commission, 1988 to the present, who directed the tightening of family planning controls in 1988–1989.

Political Bureau. The policy-making group of the Party Central Committee consisting of several dozen Party leaders.

Propaganda. A term normally applied to programs for public education and indoctrination to promote "socialist awareness" and acceptance of the policies and programs adopted by the Party leaders; sometimes includes measures to induce the people to comply with policies they do not accept.

Qian Xinzhong. Second Minister-in-Charge of the State Family Planning Commission, who succeeded Chen Muhua in August 1982 and was removed in December 1983, reportedly because of his identification with the extremely coercive birth control surgery drive of 1983.

Quota. Official permission to have a birth; sometimes the specific pink authorization slip issued to women whose pregnancies have been approved.

Remedial measures. The standard Chinese euphemism for abortions.

Rightists. A term of reproach used mainly in the 1950s in China to designate and denounce those who opposed some of the more radical Party policies.

Sex ratio. The number of males divided by the number of females (usually multiplied by 100).

Small gap. Chinese metaphor for the few categories of Chinese couples in special circumstances allowed to have a second child; sometimes refers only to the slight enlargement of the list of eligible categories introduced in 1984.

Standing Committee of the Political Bureau. The top echelon of power within the Party, consisting of a very few senior Party leaders.

State Council. The supreme executive body of the State, consisting of the premier, vice-premiers, ministers, and heads of central commissions.

State Statistical Bureau. The central statistical organ of the People's Republic of China, responsible for establishing national statistical policy, conducting censuses, compiling and publishing national statistics, and maintaining statistical standards at lower levels.

Technical measures. An expression used in family planning contexts to refer obliquely to the four "birth control surgeries": IUD insertions, vasectomies, tubal ligations, and abortions.

Total fertility rate. The average number of children who would be born per woman living through the childbearing years at the age-specific birth rates for a given year.

Unplanned pregnancies. Pregnancies not authorized under the government's birth plans, which may, however, have been both planned and wanted by the couples involved.

Wang Wei. Third Minister-in-Charge of the State Family Planning Commission, from January 1984 to January 1988, reportedly removed because of his failure to control rising birth rates after 1984.

Work style. The manner in which cadres carry out the work required by their assignments; specifically how the cadres treat ordinary Chinese citizens when executing official policies.

Yuan. Basic Chinese monetary unit, officially valued at around 2.5 to the U.S. dollar.

Zhao Ziyang. Associate of Deng Xiaoping and advocate of political and economic reform who was premier of China during the middle 1980s until purged by Deng for his support of a moderate response to the student democracy movement in the spring of 1989.

Zhou Enlai. Premier of the PRC from its founding in October 1949 until his death in January 1976; one of the more moderate and humane Party leaders of his time, widely respected among the Chinese people.

Abbreviations

AID	U.S. Agency for International Development
BR	*Beijing Review*, Beijing
BYT	*Banyue tan (Semi-monthly Forum)*, Beijing
CB	*Current Background*, American Consulate General, Hong Kong
CCP	Chinese Communist Party
CD	*China Daily*, Beijing
CFPA	Chinese Family Planning Association
CSD	*China Spring Digest*, New York
CSM	*Christian Science Monitor*, Boston
DZRB	*Dazhong ribao (Mass Daily)*, Jinan
ECMM	*Extracts from China Mainland Magazines*, American Consulate General, Hong Kong
FBIS	Foreign Broadcast Information Service, *Daily Report: China*, Washington
FJRB	*Fujian ribao (Fujian Daily)*, Fuzhou
GMRB	*Guangming ribao (Bright Daily)*, Beijing
GRRB	*Gongren ribao (Daily Worker)*, Beijing
HBRB	*Hebei ribao (Hebei Daily)*, Shijiazhuang
HLJRB	*Heilongjiang ribao (Heilongjiang Daily)*, Haerbin
IPPF	International Planned Parenthood Federation
IUDs	Intrauterine devices
JFRB	*Jiefang ribao (Liberation Daily)*, Shanghai
JJRB	*Jingji ribao (Economic Daily)*, Beijing
JJYJ	*Jingji yanjiu (Economic Research)*, Beijing
JKB	*Jiankang bao (Health Gazette)*, Beijing
JKBJHSYB	*Jiankang bao jihua shengyu ban (Health Gazette Family Planning Edition)*, Beijing
JPRS	Joint Publications Research Service, Washington
LNRB	*Liaoning ribao (Liaoning Daily)*, Shenyang
LW	*Liaowang (Outlook)*, Beijing
LWOE	*Liaowang Overseas Edition*, Hong Kong

NCGZTX	*Nongcun gongzuo tongxun* (*Rural Work Bulletin*), Beijing
NFRB	*Nanfang ribao* (*Southern Daily*), Guangzhou
NXRB	*Ningxia ribao* (*Ningxia Daily*), Yinchuan
NYT	*The New York Times*
PDR	*Population and Development Review*, New York
PRC	People's Republic of China
QY	*Qunyan* (*Popular Tribune*), Beijing
RKYJ	*Renkou yanjiu* (*Population Research*), Beijing
RKYJJ	*Renkou yu jingji* (*Population and Economy*), Beijing
RMRB	*Renmin ribao* (*People's Daily*), Beijing
SCMM	*Survey of China Mainland Magazines*, American Consulate General, Hong Kong
SCMP	*Survey of China Mainland Press*, American Consulate General, Hong Kong
SCRB	*Sichuan ribao* (*Sichuan Daily*), Chengdu
SFPC	State Family Planning Commission
SoCMP	*South China Morning Post*, Hong Kong
SXRB, Xian	*Shaanxi ribao* (*Shaanxi Daily*), Xian
SXRB, Taiyuan	*Shanxi ribao* (*Shanxi Daily*), Taiyuan
UN	United Nations
UNFPA	United Nations Fund for Population Activities (now called United Nations Population Fund)
WHB	*Wenhui bao* (*Wenhui Daily*), Shanghai
WP	*The Washington Post*
WSJ	*The Wall Street Journal*
XHNB	*Xin Hunan Bao* (*New Hunan Daily*)
XHRB	*Xinhua ribao* (*New China Daily*), Nanjing
ZGJHSYB	*Zhongguo jihua shengyu bao* (*China Population*), Beijing
ZGQN	*Zhongguo qingnian* (*Youth of China*), Beijing
ZGQNB	*Zhongguo qingnian bao* (*China Youth Gazette*), Beijing
ZGRKB	*Zhongguo renkou bao* (*China Population*), Beijing
ZJRB	*Zhejiang ribao* (*Zhejiang Daily*), Hangzhou
ZMRB	*Zhengming ribao* (*Contention Daily*), Hong Kong

Index

195

A NOTE ON THE BOOK

This book was edited by the
publications staff of the American Enterprise Institute.
The index was prepared by Evanthia Speliotis.
The text was set in Palatino, a typeface designed by Hermann Zapf.
Coghill Composition Company, of Richmond, Virginia,
set the type, and Edwards Brothers Incorporated,
of Ann Arbor, Michigan, printed and bound the book,
using permanent, acid-free paper.

The AEI PRESS is the publisher for the American Enterprise Institute for Public Policy Research, 1150 17th Street, N.W., Washington, D.C. 20036: *Christopher C. DeMuth,* publisher; *Edward Styles,* director; *Dana Lane,* editor; *Ann Petty,* editor; *Andrea Posner,* editor; *Teresa Fung,* editorial assistant (rights and permissions). Books published by the AEI PRESS are distributed by arrangement with the University Press of America, 4720 Boston Way, Lanham, Md. 20706.